# Defusing Censorship:
## The Librarian's Guide to Handling Censorship Conflicts

by Frances M. Jones

ORYX PRESS
1983

The rare Arabian Oryx is believed to have inspired the myth of the unicorn. This desert antelope became virtually extinct in the early 1960s. At that time several groups of international conservationists arranged to have 9 animals sent to the Phoenix Zoo to be the nucleus of a captive breeding herd. Today the Oryx population is over 400 and herds have been returned to reserves in Israel, Jordan, and Oman.

Copyright © 1983 by The Oryx Press
2214 North Central at Encanto
Phoenix, AZ 85004

Published simultaneously in Canada

Printed and Bound in the United States of America

Library of Congress Cataloging in Publication Data

Jones, Frances M. (Frances Mary)
    Defusing censorship.

    Bibliography: p.
    Includes index.
    1. School libraries—United States—
Censorship.    2. Public libraries—United States
—Censorship.    I. Title.
Z675.S3J727       1983              025.2′13′0973              82-73734
    ISBN 0-89774-027-0
    ISBN 0-89774-022-X (pbk.)

*For my parents, Ruth and Henry Nachtsheim, with love*

*And to the Hennepin County Library staff, especially its directors*
*Lora Landers, Robert Rohlf, and David Smith,*
*with affection and gratitude for their teaching*


*"How many other things might be tolerated in peace*
*and left to conscience, had we but charity, and were it*
*not the chief stronghold of our hyprocrisy to be ever*
*judging one another."*

*John Milton,* Areopagitica

# Contents

## Appendixes    139

# Foreword

At some time in his or her professional life, every librarian, teacher, board member, or administrator will inevitably have to face a concerned patron or parent who objects to an "item" found on the library's shelf. If these would-be censors' complaints are to be handled effectively, all librarians (as well as others involved) must be prepared for the challenge.

Using her experience as a censorship workshop planner/presenter, and as a public librarian, Frances M. Jones in *Defusing Censorship: The Librarian's Guide to Handling Censorship Conflicts* gives practical advice, guidelines, and tools for managing censorship conflicts. She also provides librarians and teachers with a firm background in library censorship cases in both school and public libraries, skillfully covering issues ranging from the *Pico v. Board of Education, Island Trees* school library case (upon which the Supreme Court recently ruled) to such problems faced by public library staffs as those involving the uses of library meeting rooms. The too-often unexamined issue of internal censorship is also explored in this book. Many librarians are often tempted to avoid selecting certain titles in an attempt to prevent controversy or as a conscious or unconscious reflection of their own beliefs. And some librarians find it safer and easier to restrict access to certain items, to literally lock them away. It is, however, the librarian's duty to select and provide library materials in the widest range of subject and viewpoints possible within budget and, in the case of school libraries, age-level constraints. Moreover the act of precensoring does not necessarily prevent conflict: because of the diversity of people's beliefs and values, any seemingly innocuous item may be challenged at any time by an offended citizen. This book offers guidelines for creating a professional environment where censorship initiated by the librarians themselves will be less likely, if not unlikely, to happen.

School and public librarians must be able to capably *manage* the challenge of censorship rather than merely react to it in a defensive and ineffective manner. And effectively managing the challenge takes planning, which involves these steps:

- Having a written policy,
- Supporting the policy with appropriate selection procedures,

- Establishing a process for citizen complaints and dealing with those complaints,
- Providing the library staff with training in selection procedures and in handling citizen complaints,
- Becoming informed of organizations that can help in resisting censorship, and
- Informing and educating school and library boards in the principles of intellectual freedom.

When the appropriate policies and procedures have been adopted and are thoroughly understood by all library staff members, effective handling of censorship conflicts becomes, finally, a matter of communication. First, it is essential to understand what censorship is and what it is not. By distinguishing between questions, complaints, and objections, the librarian is more able to prevent a situation from worsening. Often the alleged censor merely wishes to air an opinion and does not intend to remove material from the library's collection. Second, librarians and library employees need to know how to firmly and tactfully handle the initial meeting with the protesting individual or group. A communication process which includes active listening (but not arguing or apologizing), assuring the citizen that his/her concern will be acted upon, and formally responding to any questions, objections, or complaints provides the librarian with a firm foundation upon which to meet the challenge.

Censorship, unfortunately, is not the type of problem that can be eradicated simply by preventive planning. As long as schools and public libraries serve to educate and inform citizens through the provision of information and ideas, some ideas, or the language used to present them, will at some time offend or alarm some people. But it is the librarian's responsibility to understand the principles of intellectual freedom, to realize what a loss it is to our collective freedom when even one book or one film or one idea is censored from public access. We hope this book will help you, the librarian, understand and accept this responsibility and meet the challenge of censorship.

*The Publisher*

# Preface

One day early in 1979 three new books appeared on the shelves of the library I was then supervising. They were *The Joy of Gay Sex, The Joy of Lesbian Sex,* and *The Sex Atlas.* The staff came to refer to them—albeit incorrectly—as "the trilogy." Although they occasioned some public comment and complaint, they remained in the collection.

But they also caused concern and puzzlement for the library staff, some of whom wanted to know why the books had been selected for the collection. A response was in order. At my supervisor's recommendation, I designed a training workshop for staff members who were not library school graduates in order to explore with them the Library Bill of Rights and its relation to the Hennepin County (Minnesota) Library "Materials Selection Policy." Staff evaluations of the workshop indicated that it had allayed their concerns and fulfilled its teaching objectives. In the course of the next two years, the workshop was given more than 20 times for professional and nonprofessional staff in the Hennepin County Library and elsewhere in Minnesota.

In the fall of 1981, at Sanford Berman's recommendation, Susan Slesinger of The Oryx Press suggested that I prepare a manuscript on recent censorship cases in school and public libraries. The experience of presenting the workshop had persuaded me that a book describing recent censorship developments in libraries could be useful to library employees facing difficult times.

The cases described in the pages that follow were selected because they were timely, and because they illustrate the difficulties faced by school and public libraries when they adhere to the principles expressed in the Library Bill of Rights in the face of censorship attempts. A word of caution is in order, however: although censorship is successfully resisted in most of the cases included in this book, it does not follow that all or even the majority of censorship attempts are resolved so successfully. The cases here have something to teach by way of example or analogy, but they by no means represent all attempts at library censorship.

Many helped with the manuscript. Terry Anderson and Mike Bernauer of the Forest Lake (Minnesota) schools briefed me on the attempts in Forest

Lake to censor the film version of "The Lottery." Terry also provided valuable information from files she kept on that case.

Ronald Coles, plaintiffs' attorney in *Sheck v. Baileyville School Committee,* supplied valuable information and a priceless example of concern for First Amendment values. I am also grateful to him for the model challenged materials policy for school libraries which appears in Appendix 1.

To my colleague Jeanne Gelinas I am indebted from the first for the suggestion that the workshop be designed and offered.

Attorney Patrick Jarvis's offer to review and make recommendations for the chapters on school library censorship cases was eagerly and gratefully accepted.

Library directors Michael O'Brien (Oak Lawn [Illinois] Public Library) and Marcy Sims (Virginia Beach [Virginia] Public Library) gave their time generously to answer my questions and make helpful recommendations for improvements in the manuscript.

William H. Roberts, director of the Forsyth County (North Carolina) Public Library, provided helpful insights into the controversy surrounding Ku Klux Klan exhibits there, as well as documents relating to the controversy.

Judith F. Krug, director, Office for Intellectual Freedom (American Library Association), generously supplied permission to reprint the Library Bill of Rights and its related documents as appended matter.

The staffs of the library of the William Mitchell College of Law (St. Paul, Minnesota) and the Hennepin County Law Library were patient, kind, and helpful. They serve their patrons with grace and competence.

My colleague Sanford Berman helped immensely. He consistently supplied me with the appropriate resource or just the right word of encouragement when it was most needed. For such help, but more importantly for his confidence in me, I am forever grateful.

Anne Thompson edited the manuscript. Among Anne's gifts are a huge kindness and apparently infinite patience. For her thorough and painstaking efforts with the manuscript I am grateful, of course. But I thank her most of all for her steady belief that it could and should be completed.

# Chapter 1
# A Brief History of Censorship in Libraries

Censors exercise power over the freedom of others to choose among intellectual options. Their beliefs and motivation are of interest, but their actions compel attention because they challenge intellectual freedom in American society. In the 1970s and 1980s reports of such challenges have greatly disturbed contemporary intellectual life. America's school and public libraries are no less threatened by censorship than its press, theater, cinema, or fine arts. In common with them, libraries must resist censorship in order to fulfill their missions and to retain their identities in the marketplace of ideas.

The censor has been defined as "an authorized examiner of literature, plays, or other material, who may prohibit what he considers morally or otherwise objectionable."[1] For self-appointed censors, a more apt definition may be "any person who condemns or censures."[2]

Censorship can be official or unofficial. Official censorship results from the implementation of recognized legal or administrative procedures, whereas unofficial censorship most frequently involves pressure or persuasion brought to bear on those with the authority or power to censor or prohibit the dissemination of disapproved works, without regard for legitimate procedures. Censorship can occur either before or after publication or dissemination of a work. Censorship prior to publication or dissemination is termed prior restraint. Occuring afterwards, it can be termed subsequent punishment.[3]

## A HISTORY OF CENSORSHIP

The word censor has roots in the Greek and Latin languages. It is derived from the Latin *censere,* whose meanings are to appraise or estimate, and to express an opinion.[4] The role of the censor, a magistrate in

Roman times, was well-regarded. Roman censors were inspectors of morals and conduct, census takers, and assessors; thus, great responsibility for the welfare of the state was vested in them.

The Christian era produced its censors. As early as 95 A.D., the Apostolic Constitution prohibited the reading of gentile works by Christians. In the fourth century the death penalty was ordered to punish heretical writings, and in 499 the first papal Index of proscribed works appeared. The submission of manuscripts prior to publication to monastic or other religious superiors was a form of prior restraint common in the Middle Ages.[5]

The familiar contemporary debate on the issue of censorship of the printed word has its origins with the advent of books printed from movable type. In 1502 Pope Alexander VI issued a bull, intended to forestall heresy, against the printing of books. By 1586 books printed in England required approval by the Archbishop of Canterbury or the Bishop of London. Effective political control of publishing was maintained by Henry VIII through the Court of Star Chamber, which licensed the publication of printed books. Elizabeth I continued that control by granting a monopoly on printing to the Stationers' Company.

In 1649 England's Long Parliament abolished the Court of Star Chamber and provided a three-year respite from the necessity of licensing books. But in 1643 Parliament again introduced licensing.

John Milton's outraged response to this parliamentary act has been conveyed down the centuries in his *Areopagitica,* written in 1644 "to deliver the press from the restraints with which it was encumbered."[6] This seminal work is a tapestry of seventeenth century thought, enduring in both its beauty and its usefulness. In it the writer-poet addressed Parliament concerning the history of censorship and demonstrated its unending folly. He acknowledged that books were powerful and allowed that as "books are not absolutely dead things" they may require "sharpest justice on them as malefactors." Yet he cautioned that "unless wariness be used, as good almost kill a man as kill a good book: who kills a man kills a reasonable creature, God's image; but he who destroys a good book kills reason itself, kills the image of God, as it were, . . . "[7]

Milton held that books should not be seen as temptations to evil, but as useful remedies against error. Even books containing error should be allowed to exist, in order that they might serve as stepping stones on the way to truth. If books were prohibited because of some error in them, the truth in them would also be lost.

He addressed the issue of appointing censors, asking how many and how wise the censors would need to be in order to do justice to the need to examine each and every work proposed for publication; and he speculated upon the difficulty of finding so many persons, learned and wise enough to perform all the censor's tasks effectively.

Milton was confident that truth would emerge from discussion and debate, and that it appeared in many forms, growing and changing, as it emerged. The *Areopagitica* was a statement of belief in the underlying rightness of human intellectual endeavor, and in human pursuit of truth. It remains among the most persuasive documents available to those who seek to counter arguments advanced by censors.

Although its publication did not produce immediate change, a new law was passed in 1693. It substituted punitive censorship for the form of prior restraint which licensing represented. Then in 1695, the law was not reenacted, and licensing was removed altogether.

The seventeenth and eighteenth centuries saw great strides in the development of ideas and laws that reflected emerging social confidence in the concept of the value and dignity of each human individual. This enlightened precondition was necessary for the formation and adoption of the U.S. Constitution and its first 10 amendments, the Bill of Rights. It is to the First Amendment that the nation is indebted for the concept of lawful freedom of expression, which is now firmly held in case and statutory law despite many attempts to diminish or infringe it. It reads:

> Congress shall make no law respecting an establishment of religion, or prohibiting the free exercise thereof; or abridging the freedom of speech, or of the press; or the right of the people peaceably to assemble, and to petition the Government for a redress of grievances.

In the eighteenth century this nation's founders expressed their collective belief in the dignity of each human and in the right of each citizen to pursue truth unaided and unimpeded by the state. It reflects on the times that some twentieth century observers have expressed doubt that the Bill of Rights could be passed into law today, if passage depended on a popular vote. But nineteenth century censorship had far-reaching consequences, and its effects are still palpable.

Censorship in the last century concerned itself less with religious and political matters and more with personal morals and obscenity. Perhaps, after constitutional guarantees of religious freedom and democratic elections were established, the one remaining area for controversy and control was that of personal morality.

Among the important laws of the nineteenth century were England's Obscene Publications Act of 1857 and the United States' Comstock Act of 1873. Both laws governed morality in print, with the Comstock Act specifically governing publications sent through the mails. Products of the

Victorian era, they attempted to regulate what was good for common reading consumption, thus departing from the beliefs of Milton and of the framers of the Constitution in the importance of the individual and the individual's right to choose freely among available ideas. Even today obscenity has no protection under the First Amendment.

## CENSORSHIP AND LIBRARIES

Given the tenor of the times which permitted passage of these early obscenity laws, there is little wonder that public librarianship, just emerging in the United States, should see itself in the role of the guardian of public morality.

> From its very beginnings, the concept of the public library involved an education function that may have entailed ''elitism'' or ''profession-alism'' depending on how you look at it but also more than that. As William Fletcher wrote, the librarian was accountable ''to accept and exercise full responsibility for the moral character and influence of the library.''[8]

Libraries and librarians reflect their times, and the current position of the library profession, expressed in the Library Bill of Rights, has changed markedly from the one described by Fletcher.

> The most telling indicator of the difference between 19th and 20th Century views of censorship is the changing meaning of the word. It is only recently that the word ''censor'' became a term of opprobrium. In the time span covered here, censorship could be invidious or not—one could exercise a legitimate or an arbitrary censorship.[9]

The 1939 adoption of the Library's Bill of Rights by the Council of the American Library Association signaled the change. Today's Library Bill of Rights is the association's basic policy on intellectual freedom and can serve as such for the library profession in the United States. Like the Bill of Rights, it is a slender but powerful document; and it provides a firm foundation for the profession's efforts to support and defend intellectual freedom. It is impossible to stand for intellectual freedom without grappling with censorship.

Censorship in schools and libraries has been described as attempting ''to suppress materials presenting certain viewpoints, or to exclude those viewpoints from library and classroom materials.''[10] It can also be done ''intentionally to prevent someone from viewing and/or hearing meaning-ful verbal, graphic, dramatic or sonic materials for the purpose of protecting a preferred belief or attitude.''[11] Analysis of the process of censorship discloses that:

- It includes partial or complete examination of works that are expressions of ideas or intellectual entities, such as books, films, speeches, paintings, or songs.
- The intent of the examiner is to discover something in the works that may be disapproved.
- The examination is undertaken with a view to preventing the dissemination of works of which the censor disapproves.
- The censor either has or intends to have the authority or the power to prevent dissemination of the work through the school or library.

Censorship restricts intellectual choices. Censors use their power to select those works and thus those ideas which are sufficiently palatable or acceptable to them to see the clear light of day in schools and libraries.

Censorship is frequently a manifestation of elitism, that is, the belief by individuals or groups that their moral or intellectual superiority makes it possible, even desirable, for them to determine which beliefs, ideas, opinions, or information should be available to others.

The origins of censorship may be ''tribal'' and have been described by one author as being ''at least as old as authority itself,''[12] a sensible conclusion considering that controlling or attempting to control human intellectual choices is an effective and deceptively benign method of controlling human behavior.

Conflict results from these attempts at control, as the cases discussed in the following chapters illustrate. The sources of conflict and school and public library censorship confrontations are discussed in Chapters 2–9; internal censorship is discussed in Chapter 10; and suggestions for dealing with censorship are provided in the concluding chapter. The Appendixes provide tools for the librarian to use in handling censorship conflicts. Most of the cases found in the following pages are stories of hard-won victories against censorship. A word of caution is in order: for every decisive victory, there are many other skirmishes whose outcomes are not so decisive or victorious.

## REFERENCES

1. *American Heritage Dictionary of the English Language* (Boston: American Heritage Publishing Co. and Houghton Mifflin, 1976), s.v. ''censor.''

2. Ibid.

3. William O. Douglas, "Censorship and Prior Restraint," in *The First Freedom*, ed. by Robert B. Downs (Chicago: American Library Association, 1960), p. 42.

4. D.F. Simpson, *Cassell's New Latin Dictionary* (New York: Funk and Wagnall, 1959), s.v. "censeo."

5. David L. Sills, ed., *International Encyclopedia of the Social Sciences* (New York: Macmillan, 1968), s.v. "Censorship."

6. John Milton, "Second Defense of the English People," in *Complete Poems and Major Prose*, ed. by Merritt Y. Hughes (Indianapolis, IN: The Odyssey Press, 1957), p. 831.

7. ———, "Areopagitica," in *Complete Poems and Major Prose*, p. 720.

8. Evelyn Geller, "The Librarian as Censor," *Library Journal* 101 (11) (June 1, 1976): p. 1255.

9. Ibid.

10. L.B. Woods, "Censorship in the Schools," *Phi Delta Kappan* 61 (October 1979): 104–06. Condensed in *Education Digest* (January 1980): 10.

11. C. Benjamin Cox, "The Varieties of Censorial Experience: Toward a Definition of Censorship," *High School Journal* (May 1979): 313.

12. John McCormick and Mairi MacInnes, eds., *Versions of Censorship* (Chicago: Aldine Publishing Company, 1962), p. xii.

# Censorship in School Libraries

# Chapter 2
# Sources of Conflict: Rights of School Boards, Teachers, Parents, and Students

School library censorship is distinguished from public library censorship by the number and importance of school library censorship cases decided by the courts in recent years and the comparative absence of court action in public library censorship to date. Court decisions appear to be part of a national balancing act that seeks to find a firm middle ground in the conflict among the traditional, statutory rights of school boards and the constitutional rights of teachers, parents, and students. To understand how censorship may infringe these rights, some understanding of what they are and how they have been derived is useful.

## RIGHTS OF SCHOOL BOARDS

School boards are creatures of the state, responsible for the education of the nation's youth. They have the power to control the formal educational process and the responsibility to consider the welfare of the students under their care. In most states school boards are granted authority over book selection.[1]

The state has at least two interests in creating and maintaining school boards. Its interest in the welfare of its minor citizens results in the need to provide for their education. It also has an interest in assisting and supporting parents in the fulfillment of their child-rearing responsibilities.[2] Public school education is intended to satisfy the needs created by these interests.

School board authority in educational matters is granted by the state legislatures, and it is derived from the common law doctrine *in loco parentis,* whereby some portion of parental authority may be assumed by the school in order that it may carry out its educative function and teach the child effectively. This doctrine has served as the ''conventional basis for respecting the discretion exercised by local boards of education and school officials in determining how to manage public schools.''[3]

A more recent view holds that ''public schools serve an indoctrinative function: they instill in students basic concepts, skills, knowledge, and values which the community considers important.''[4] This indoctrinative function fits the model of prescriptive education in which ''information and accepted truths are furnished to a theoretically passive, absorbent student.''[5]

The prescriptive model can be contrasted with two other theoretical models: the analytical and the open models. In general, the analytical and/or open models call for ''the examination of data and values in a way that involves the student and teacher as active participants in a search for truth.''[6] High school graduation has provided a traditional dividing line between the application of the prescriptive and analytical theoretical models, prescriptive education taking place in the elementary and secondary school, and analytical education occurring at the undergraduate and graduate levels of education. An open model may require a larger measure of academic freedom for teachers and students than the traditional prescriptive or indoctrinative approach and may restrict the school board's traditional control.

The nation's courts have not been anxious to intervene in matters relating to school board decisions because of the authority vested in the boards, and because it has seemed desirable to leave the education of the nation's youth under the control of local authorities who are subject to the direct influence of those who elect them. The tension between the court's responsibility to uphold the constitution and other statutes and its desire not to interfere in matters under the control of the school boards is apparent in its decisions in school cases.

Among them is *Epperson v. Arkansas* (1968). In this case an Arkansas teacher, Susan Epperson, sued for a declaration that an Arkansas statute which prohibited the teaching of evolution was void and to enjoin school district officials from dismissing her, should she teach the theory of evolution in biology classes. Her dilemma was caused by the school district's selection of a biology textbook for the 1965–66 school year which included a section on evolution theory (despite the statute). The provisions of the statute were such that if she taught the material in the book's evolution section, she could be dismissed and charged with a criminal offense.

The Arkansas Chancery court found the statute unconstitutional, but the supreme court of Arkansas reversed that decision. The United States Supreme Court in turn reversed the Arkansas high court's decision and found that the statute violated the freedom of religion mandate of the First

Amendment and the Fourteenth Amendment. Although freedom of religion, not freedom of expression, was crucial in the Supreme Court ruling, Justice Fortas's opinion has often been cited for its interpretation of the relationships between the courts and the school and between school boards and First Amendment rights. In it he states:

> By and large, public education in our Nation is committed to the control of state and local authorities. Courts do not and cannot intervene in the resolution of conflicts which arise in the daily operation of school systems and which do not directly and sharply implicate basic constitutional values.[7]

He noted an earlier case, *Keyishian v. Board of Regents* (1967), in which college faculty members' refusal to sign certificates stating they were not Communists resulted in their dismissals. The Court found the regulation requiring the certificates to be unconstitutionally overbroad and in its decision noted that the First Amendment "does not tolerate laws that cast a pall or orthodoxy over the classroom."[8]

In *Epperson,* the Court noted that while courts have not failed to "safeguard the fundamental values of freedom of speech and inquiry and of belief,"[9] care and restraint have nevertheless governed when court intevention has been necessary to secure those values.

These court-produced definitions of roles and responsibilities have been of major recurring importance in cases over the last decade or so. They have defined the importance of the local school board and its near sovereignty in the day-to-day management of school operations. But they have also set forth the courts' necessary role as intervenor when constitutional rights, especially First Amendment rights, are jeopardized by school board or school officials' decision making.

## RIGHTS OF TEACHERS AND ACADEMIC FREEDOM

Academic freedom is a vital doctrine in the school censorship controversy, and the courts have recognized its constitutional significance.

In its 1923 decision in *Meyer v. Nebraska,* a decision which laid the foundation for secondary school academic freedom, the Supreme Court held that a statute prohibiting the teaching of a subject in a language other than English and the teaching of a foreign language to students not yet in eighth grade was unconstitutional. In the decision, the Supreme Court observed that "the statute violated the due process clause of the Fourteenth Amendment since it arbitrarily and impermissibly interfered with the calling of language teachers."[10]

Later, in *Keyishian v. Board of Regents,* the Court noted the nation's "deep commitment" to academic freedom and that academic freedom is a "special concern" of the First Amendment. Some hold to the view that academic freedom in the secondary school should be more limited than that required for colleges and universities. But in *Tinker v. Des Moines Independent Community School District* (1969), a case which involved high school students, the Court made it clear that "First Amendment rights, applied in light of the special character of the school environment, are available to teachers and students."[11]

## RIGHTS OF PARENTS

Parents' rights in the educational process have been seen to be derived from their right to privacy. This right "prevents governmental interference in intimate personal relationship or activities, [or in the] freedom of individuals to make fundamental choices involving themselves or their families."[12] Parents are compelled by law to educate their children. They may also be compelled to send their children to public school for financial reasons or for lack of a workable alternative. Thus the state through its school boards may be required to recognize parental rights in the public school setting. Such rights derive from a privacy right inherent in the child rearing process.[13]

Courts have recognized parents' rights in school-related matters. In *Meyer v. Nebraska,* (1923) the Supreme Court viewed the statute prohibiting foreign language teaching to students below eighth grade as depriving parents of a "liberty interest in raising their children and directing their education."[14]

A 1925 Oregon case, *Pierce v. Society of Sisters,* upheld parents' "liberty interest" again. The Supreme Court found that a law which forbade children between the ages of eight and 16 to attend private schools was unconstitutional.[15]

Amish parents in Wisconsin prevailed in the case of *Wisconsin v. Yoder* (1972). Wisconsin law compelled school attendance by all children until they reached the age of 16. Amish parents desired to send their children to school only through the eighth grade. Because the state law threatened their First Amendment right of free exercise of religion, the Supreme Court ruled that enforcement of the law was unconstitutional.[16]

Parental challenges to school board decisions concerning book removal have not always been successful in the courts, and school board decisions have been permitted to prevail. But school boards themselves have been responsive to parental objections to school library materials in a number of recent court cases and in many reported incidents. These will be explored more thoroughly in Chapters 3–5.

## RIGHTS OF STUDENTS

Students' First Amendment rights have been called the right to read, the right to know, the right to receive information, or the right to have access to information. Courts have determined that these rights are of fundamental importance to American education.

The right to receive information was established in the case *Virginia State Board of Pharmacy v. Virginia Citizens Consumer Council, Inc.* (1976). The controversy in the case concerned the advertisement of prescription drug prices, a practice challenged by the state board of pharmacy. The Supreme Court held that consumers had a right to receive price information, and that this right to receive was a reciprocal right of the advertisers' right to express it. It held that the communication was protected, as were both the sender and the receiver, and that consumers had a right to the information provided by the advertisers.

But in a case concerning the sale of "harmful material" to minors (*Ginsberg v. New York,* 1968), the Court "held that the state had the power to regulate for the well-being of children and could constitutionally prescribe different standards of obscenity . . ." for minors from those established for adults.[17] This case also established a "variable obscenity" standard by upholding more restricted access to pornography for minors than for adults.[18]

A further indication that minors' rights may not be as broad as those accorded to adults is found in the Supreme Court's decision in *FCC v. Pacifica Foundation* (1978). It upheld the authority of the Federal Communications Commission to "impose sanctions on broadcasting stations airing broadcasts, which although not obscene, contained 'indecent' language." The decision "apparently authorized the withholding of some forms of offensive expression from children."[19]

The Supreme Court's celebrated decision in *Tinker v. Des Moines Independent Community School District* (1969) provided a significant advance in the cause of student rights. The Court clearly stated that students' exercising of the right of free expression was valid in the nation's schools. *Tinker* was concerned not with books but with peaceful protest. In December 1965 a group of adults and students decided to protest against the war in Vietnam by wearing black armbands during the holiday season and by fasting on two days in December. Des Moines school officials, upon becoming aware of the plan, adopted a policy requiring that any student wearing an armband to school be asked to remove it. Refusal would result in suspension. Mary Beth Tinker, a junior high school student, and Christopher Eckhardt and John Tinker, senior high school students, wore their armbands to school. All were suspended. They filed a complaint in federal district court, asking for an injunction restraining school officials from disciplinary action and for nominal damages. The district court dismissed the complaint, upholding the school's action on the grounds that it was reasonable to prevent disturbance of school discipline. The case was appealed. The Court of Appeals for the Eighth Circuit was equally divided and the district court's judgment was affirmed. The Supreme Court granted certiorari, and its decision followed.

The Supreme Court decision read, in part: "It can hardly be argued that either students or teachers shed their constitutional rights to freedom of speech or expression at the schoolhouse gate."[20] The Court found that the wearing of armbands as a symbol of protest involved "direct, primary First Amendment rights akin to 'pure speech'."[21] It also determined that the expression sought by the protesting students would not interfere with school activities and did not threaten the rights of other students in any way. The fact that school officials feared that a disturbance might result from the wearing of armbands was not sufficient to justify forbidding them. The decision also noted that the prohibition against armbands did not apply to the wearing of similar symbols. Students were permitted to wear political campaign buttons, and some had worn the Iron Cross, the traditional symbol of Nazism.[22] The prohibition affected only the wearing of black armbands in protest of the country's involvement in Vietnam. The Court found that the prohibition of one expression of opinion was not constitutionally permissible in the absence of evidence that it was necessary "to avoid material and substantial interference with schoolwork or discipline."[23]

Thus a "Tinker test" was formulated, under which student expression enjoys protection unless it "materially disrupts classwork or involves substantial disorder or invasion of the rights of others."[24]

Although not concerned with books and other media, the decision has had value for subsequent book censorship cases. It recognized that students' First Amendment rights cannot be infringed merely because school officials find it desirable to do so. Nor can their desire to avoid unpleasantness and conflict be sufficient reason for curtailing students' First Amendment rights. In this landmark decision, the Court determined that students may not be regarded as "closed-circuit recipients of only that which the State chooses to communicate."[25]

Censorship in public schools may infringe on teachers', parents', or students' rights. When book removal results in students being deprived of access to information that parents want them to have, both parents' and students' rights may have been violated. When a book is removed to satisfy parental objections, it is possible that students' or teachers' rights may be infringed. And book removal that results in unnecessary restrictions upon the capacity of teachers or librarians to fulfill their professional responsibilities in the classroom or library may encroach upon their constitutional rights.

## CONSTITUTIONALLY ACCEPTABLE BOOK REMOVAL

It should be noted, however, that not all instances of book removal violate the First Amendment. The removal may have no constitutional implications and be neutral in First Amendment terms. For example, a book may be removed for such practical reasons as worn or defaced physical condition, obsolete content, or lack of shelf space for it. And a work judged obscene* by the courts has no constitutional protection: a judgment of obscenity could be sufficient reason for removal. Books may also be removed when their presence threatens school discipline or "an interest comparable to school discipline," such as psychological or emotional damage to students.[26] When books are removed for such reasons, the authority that removed them is required to prove that actual harm took place, or that it had good cause to believe that the book would interfere materially and substantially with the educational process.[27]

Simply stated, school library censorship cases occur when the rights of school boards, teachers, parents or students are in conflict. But such cases are never simple, nor are they easy experiences for the participants. The following chapters discuss eight cases of school library book removal and one case involving the removal of a film from a school's curriculum. Far from simple, the conflict in these cases was so complex that it required resolution by the courts.

---

*Black's Law Dictionary* (5th edition, 1979) defines *obscene:* Objectionable or offensive to accepted standards of decency. Basic guidelines for trier of fact in determining whether a work which depicts or describes sexual conduct is obscene is whether the average person, applying contemporary community standards would find that the work, taken as a whole, appeals to the prurient interest, whether the work depicts or describes, in a patently offensive way, sexual conduct specifically defined by the applicable state law, and whether the work, taken as a whole, lacks serious literary, artistic, political, or scientific value.

## REFERENCES

1. Arlen W. Langvardt, "Not on Our Shelves: A First Amendment Analysis of Library Censorship in the Public Schools," *Nebraska Law Review* 61 (1982): 101.
2. Louise E. Tudzarov, "Comment: Censorship in the Public School Library-State, Parent and Child in the Constitutional Arena," *Wayne Law Review* 27 (1980): 170.
3. Langvardt, p. 100.
4. Langvardt, pp. 100–01.
5. "Reflections on Developing Trends in the Law of Student Rights," *University of Pennsylvania Law Review* 118 (1970): 614.
6. Ibid.
7. 393 U.S. 97, 104 (1968).
8. 385 U.S. 589, 603 (1967).
9. 393 U.S. 97, 104 (1968).
10. Frances R. Niccolai, "The Right to Read and School Library Censorship," *Journal of Law and Education* 10 (1) (January 1981): 26.
11. 393 U.S. 503, 506 (1969).
12. *Black's Law Dictionary,* 5th ed. (St. Paul, MN: West Pub. Co., 1979), p. 1075.
13. Tudzarov, p. 174.
14. Langvardt, p. 103.
15. Ibid.
16. Langvardt, p. 104.
17. Langvardt, p. 112.
18. Niccolai, p. 29.
19. Langvardt, p. 112.
20. 393 U.S. 503, 506 (1969).
21. 393 U.S. 503, 507 (1969).
22. 393 U.S. 503, 510 (1969).
23. 393 U.S. 503, 513 (1969).
24. Ibid.
25. Ibid.
26. Niccolai, p. 30.
27. Ibid.

# Chapter 3
# Conflict in the Courts: Public School Library Book Removal Cases, 1972–1980

School library book removal cases in the 1970s met with two distinct and differing responses in the courts. This decade was marked by the contrast between the opinions of the Second Circuit Court of Appeals and those of the Sixth Circuit Court of Appeals. They differed in their views of the authority of local school boards and of the constitutional rights of students, faculty, and parents to challenge that authority in library book removal cases. The Second Circuit Court's decision in *Presidents' Council, District 25 v. Community School Board No. 25* (1972) upheld the school board's authority to remove library books. The Sixth Circuit Court of Appeals, in *Minarcini v. Strongsville City School District* (1976), held that the school board could not remove books from the school library without regard for students' First Amendment rights. Two subsequent federal district court decisions also reflected that view: *Right to Read Defense Committee of Chelsea v. School Committee of the City of Chelsea* (1978) and *Salvail v. Nashua Board of Education* (1979).

## Presidents' Council, District 25 v. Community School Board No. 25 (1972)

The first major decision concerning school library book removal was reached in this case. The case was one of first impression, i.e., it presented ''an entirely novel question of law for the decision of the court'' and was not governed by any existing precedent.[1] At issue was the school board's decision to restrict the circulation of Piri Thomas's *Down These Mean Streets*, a novel which describes life in Spanish Harlem, and includes such aspects of the life there as drug use, sexual acts, and criminal activities. The language in the book is the language of the barrio—street language.

The case resulted from conflict over the board's decision to remove all copies of the book from junior high school libraries in the Queens, New York school district, after some parents complained that it would have an ''adverse moral and psychological affect on eleven to fifteen year-old children.''[2] The board voted five to three in executive session to remove the book and cast a similar vote again at a public meeting in the spring of 1971. In June 1971, at another public meeting, the board passed a resolution to return the books to those school libraries that had owned copies and to make the book available to be loaned to parents of children in those schools.

The plaintiffs in the case were presidents and past presidents of various parent and parent-teacher organizations, junior high school students, parents and guardians of minors, teachers, a librarian, and a principal who together formed an organization called the Presidents' Council. In court, they sought to have the board's resolution declared unconstitutional and to have the court order the books restored to their former circulating status. It was clear in the case that the authority to select instructional material was delegated by the state legislature to the school boards and that administrative procedures to review the actions of school boards were available. The United States District Court for the Eastern District of New York dismissed the plaintiffs' complaint. Upon appeal, the Second Circuit Court of Appeals held that the school board had not violated the First Amendment.

The appellate court determined that constitutional rights had not been infringed because the book could still be discussed by teachers in class, be assigned as outside reading, and be borrowed by parents for their children's use. It found no problem of freedom of expression in the case.

Acknowledging the authority of school boards over school libraries, it stated:

> The public school library obviously does not have to become the repository, at public expense, for books which are deemed by the proper authorities to be without merit either as works of art or science, simply because they are not obscene within the statute.[3]

Although the plaintiffs had acknowledged the board's authority to select school library material, they had challenged its right to remove it. The court, however, found it clear that ''books which become obsolete or irrelevant or were improperly selected initially, for whatever reason, can be removed by the same authority which was empowered to make the selection in the first place.''[4]

The plaintiffs then petitioned the Supreme Court, but the Court declined to hear the case. Justice William O. Douglas disagreed with this decision. In his dissent he asserted that the "First Amendment is a preferred right and is of great importance in the schools."[5] He noted that the actions of school boards are not immune from constitutional scrutiny and that the courts have upheld academic freedom against attack. *Down These Mean Streets* was not alleged to be obscene and expert witnesses had testified both for and against it. Despite the restriction placed on circulating the book to students, they could obtain it with help from their parents, and teachers could discuss it in class, thus weakening "the contention that the subject matter of the book was not proper."[6] To Justice Douglas it appeared that students could do everything but borrow the book from the junior high school library and read it. He concluded, "Because the issues raised here are crucial to our national life, I would hear argument in this case."[7] The Second Circuit Court, however, had the last word in *Presidents' Council* and established a difficult precedent for later cases on that circuit.

## Minarcini v. Strongsville City School District (1976)

The first decision that found that removing school library material was contrary to students' First Amendment rights was written by the Sixth Circuit Court of appeals in 1976. Plaintiffs in the case were Susan Lee Minarcini and four other public high school students who, through their parents, brought a class action against the school district of Strongsville, Ohio. Their action was precipitated by the school board's 1972 decisions to:

- Refuse to approve Joseph Heller's *Catch 22* and Kurt Vonnegut's *God Bless You, Mr. Rosewater* as texts or library books despite faculty recommendations.
- Order Vonnegut's *Cat's Cradle* and Heller's *Catch 22* to be removed from the library.
- Issue resolutions prohibiting classroom discussion of these works and their use as supplemental reading.

The federal district court dismissed the students' case for failure to state a claim, and they appealed.

The appeals court held that the board's decisions with respect to the selection of *Catch 22* and *God Bless You, Mr. Rosewater* were not unconstitutional. It affirmed the school board's prerogative to make decisions about textbook selection, even when such decisions might run contrary to faculty recommendations. Under state law the school board was the appropriate decision maker for textbook selection. The court further determined that the board's decisions were not arbitrary and capricious and that they did not violate procedural due process. Three groups—board, faculty, and citizens' committees—had participated in the book recommendation process.

With respect to the removal of books from the school library, however, the finding of the court was different. Both parties to the case agreed that the books had literary value, and obscenity was not an issue. Noting that the district judge had relied upon the Second Circuit court's opinion in *Presidents' Council,* the appellate judge stated that that opinion did not give the school board "an absolute right . . . to remove from the library and presumably to destroy any books it regarded unfavorably without concern for the First Amendment."[8] He wrote:

> A library is a storehouse of knowledge. When created for a public school it is an important privilege created by the state for the benefit of the students in the school. . . . Of course, a copy of a book may wear out. Some books may become obsolete. Shelf space alone may at some point require some selection of books to be retained and books to be disposed of. No such rationale is involved in this case, however.[9]

The school board's record offered only one explanation for its action, and it was contained in minutes of a school board meeting of July 17, 1972:

> Mrs. Wong reviewed the Citizens Committee report regarding adoption of *God Bless You, Mr. Rosewater.*
>
> Dr. Caine presented the following minority report:
>
> 1. It is recommended that *God Bless You, Mr. Rosewater* not be purchased, either as a textbook, supplemental reading book or library book. The book is completely sick. One secretary read it for one-half hour and handed it back to the reviewer with the written comment, "Garbage."
>
> 2. Instead, it is recommended that the autobiography of Captain Eddie Rickenbacker be purchased for use in the English course. It is modern and it fills the need of providing material which will inspire and educate the students as well as teach them high moral values and provide the opportunity to learn from a man of exceptional ability and understanding.
>
> For the same reason, it is recommended that the following books be purchased for immediate use as required supplemental reading in the high school social studies program: *Herbert Hoover,* a biography by Eugene Lyons, and *Reminiscences of Douglas MacArthur.*
>
> 4. It is also recommended in the interest of a balanced program that *One Day in the Life of Ivan Denisovich* by A. I. Solzhenitsyn be purchased as a supplemental reader for the high school social studies program.
>
> It is also recommended that copies of all of the above books be placed in the library of each secondary school.

6. It is also recommended that *Cat's Cradle,* which was written by the same character (Vennegutter) who wrote, using the term loosely, *God Bless You, Mr. Rosewater,* and which has been used as a textbook, although never legally adopted by the Board, be withdrawn immediately and all copies disposed of in accordance with statutory procedure.

7. Finally, it is recommended that the McGuffy Readers be bought as supplemental readers for enrichment program purposes for the elementary schools, since they seem to offer so many advantages in vocabulary, content, and sentence structure over the drivel being pushed today.[10]

Because there was no explanation that was ''neutral'' in First Amendment terms (worn condition, shelf space needed, etc.) the court concluded that the books were removed because the school board found their content objectionable and because it believed it had the power to do so.

The court wrote that neither the state nor the board was required by the constitution to provide a library for Strongsville students. But, having done so, the board could not constrain the use of the library for reasons arising from the members' social or political tastes. Although the board made no attempt to prohibit classroom discussion of the books, the fact that they were not available in the library would hamper the students' ability to discuss them. The court noted that ''the removal of books from a school library is a much more serious burden upon freedom of classroom discussion than the action found unconstitutional in *Tinker.*''[11] And that ''a library is a mighty resource in the market place of ideas. It is specially dedicated to broad dissemination of ideas. It is a forum for silent speech.''[12] Even though the books could be obtained from other sources—the public library or bookstores—removing them from the school library could not be justified.

The court recognized that the issue was not only one of freedom of speech for the students but also one of the students' rights to receive information that they wanted and that their teachers wanted them to have. Citing the Supreme Court decision in *Virginia State Board of Pharmacy v. Virginia Citizens Consumers Council, Inc.,* the court recognized the First Amendment's protection of the student's right to read or to have access to information. It said that this decision and several others served ''to establish firmly both the First Amendment right to know which is involved in our instant case and the standing of the student plaintiffs to raise the issue.''[13]

Thus the Sixth Circuit court arrived at a different decision and established a different precedent from those of the Second Circuit in *Presidents' Council.* Two cases heard in the federal district courts of the First Circuit followed this new precedent.

## Right to Read Defense Committee of Chelsea v. School Committee of the City of Chelsea (1978)

Two years later, in 1978, a controversy erupted in Chelsea, Massachusetts, over a 17-line poem written by a 15-year-old girl from Brooklyn: "The City to a Young Girl."[14] The poem was contained in an anthology of student writings, *Male and Female under Eighteen,* which was purchased for the high school library. The high school had 1200 students; the library contained 7400 volumes. The English curriculum included courses in adolescent literature, Hispano-American literature, poetry, creative writing, and women in literature.

Librarian Sonja Coleman purchased 1,000 books on a special purchase plan offered by Prentice-Hall. *Male and Female under Eighteen* came as part of the plan, and Coleman examined it, as she had examined other titles when they were received. She had the option to return any unwanted books to the publisher. *Male and Female under Eighteen* was regarded as useful for student writers in the school and was retained.

In May 1977, School Committee Chairman Andrew P. Quigley received a complaining telephone call from a student's parent about the language in "The City to a Young Girl." He obtained the book from the parent and later read the poem. He found it "filthy" and its language "offensive." He did not read the entire book. He scheduled an emergency meeting of the school committee immediately, to discuss the objectionable school library material.

Chairman Quigley was publisher of the community's daily newspaper, the *Chelsea Record,* and that same evening he wrote an article about the matter for publication in the newspaper the next day. In it he wrote, "I want to make certain that no such filth will be distributed in our schools."[15]

At the May 23 emergency meeting, Quigley provided copies of the poem to the men of the school committee. Women members did not receive copies because of the poem's language. He voiced his objections to the poem and moved that the school superintendent be requested to provide a report on how books were selected, with special reference to *Male and Female under Eighteen.*

The *Chelsea Record* of May 25 contained a Quigley editorial describing "The City to a Young Girl" as obscene and offensive. At another special meeting of the committee on May 26, School Superintendent Vincent McGee made a report on the book. He identified "City" and one other poem as its objectionable portions. He noted that the book was educationally sound but that the book would be removed from the library until there could be a final decision to remove the whole book or its objectionable parts. At that meeting, Sonja Coleman explained the library's selection process and noted recommended American Library Association procedures for dealing with challenged material. But Quigley asked the superintendent to determine whether the library had put "trash" in the library knowingly and said that the committee could determine whether librarian Coleman was "the type of person we want to continue in that position."[16]

Coleman published a statement in the June 14 *Chelsea Record*. In her opinion the poem was not obscene; the anthology should not have been removed without a proper hearing; and students and faculty should have access to it. Quigley responded in the newspaper, indicating his shock and disappointment at her opinion.[17]

Another special committee meeting on July 20 dealt with the issue of how such a book could have been placed in the library, and again, Coleman defended the work.

On July 28, at a special meeting called by Quigley, his motion that the removal of the book from the library be affirmed by the school committee was adopted 6–0, with one abstention. A regular meeting followed the special meeting. There Quigley urged consideration of transferring Coleman to a classroom because of her selection "mistake." Another motion to transfer her because she was "out of the mainstream of contact with the youngsters in a classroom situation" was also proposed. However, a motion to table the discussion of her transfer so that she could "think things over" prevailed.[18]

The school committee also directed Superintendent McGee to study the feasibility of forming a selection committee for the school system's libraries. Later McGee directed the high school principal to remove the page containing "The City to a Young Girl" from the anthology. The principal did so and kept the book in his office.

A lawsuit was filed on August 3. Plaintiffs in the suit were the Right to Read Defense Committee of Chelsea, the Massachusetts Library Association, Sonja Coleman, and several teachers, parents and students.

Quigley learned of the suit, and he was quoted as follows in the *Chelsea Record:*

> Who needs employees like that? Who needs employees that will fight to keep the kind of tasteless, filthy trash that is contained in the poem we voted to remove? I may even call a special meeting to discuss what we'll do with these insubordinate teachers.[19]

He observed in an August 4 editorial that he might "seek the resignations of those teachers who have taken the legal action to restore the poem to the High School Library" and that it might be necessary "to institute a petition to let the people know just that the 'community standards' do NOT include accepting the 'filth' of that poem.''[20]

Petitions were circulated. In addition, the school committee's attorney recommended a newspaper survey be conducted and a citizens' conference be organized, both to determine what Chelsea community standards were. Thirty letters were sent to local clergy to solicit their evaluation of the poem, but only two responded. They supported the school committee.

At an August 17 special meeting, two resolutions, prepared for the school committee by its attorney, were passed. One established grounds for removal of *Male and Female under Eighteen,* including that:

1. Sex education was part of the book's subject matter, but it was not a school subject.
2. It could have a harmful effect on some students.
3. School committee preference was for sex education books that did not employ vocabulary that was "filthy" or that would shock a large portion of the community.[21]

The second resolution protected the librarian, the faculty, and the students from sanctions.

After a hearing on August 18, the district court issued a temporary restraining order giving protection to the teacher and librarian plaintiffs from transfer or removal and requiring that the book be returned to the librarian. The librarian was ordered not to permit students to use the book without written parental permission.

In its decision on July 5, 1978, the district court disagreed with the determinations of the school committee and found that its action had violated student and faculty First Amendment rights. The court noted that there is tension between the administrative powers of school boards and the constitutional rights of teachers and students. While in agreement that the board had the authority to determine what materials could be selected for a school library, and even to determine whether there would be a library at all, it treated the question of *book removal* from libraries as a separate issue.

The court noted that not every book removal "implicated First Amendment values," but that in this case it was clear the school committee had found the contents of the book offensive and removed it for that reason. This type of removal—as opposed to removals which occur when a book becomes obsolete or when shelf space is a problem—had definite constitutional implications. Because this was true, the standard established in *Tinker* was applied: that when First Amendment values are implicated, some "substantial and legitimate government interest" must be demonstrated to justify the action of book removal. The district court found no such interest, and determined that the school committee's objection to the contents of the book (its theme and language) and its concern that they might do damage to students were the foundations for its decision. Expert testimony at the trial did not support the board's concern.

Nor did the court find that the objections of some parents were sufficient to justify the school committee's action. It quoted an earlier decision in a similar case: "With the greatest of respect to such parents, their sensibilities are not the full measure of what is proper education."[22]

In denying the school committee the absolute right to remove books from the library's shelves, the court said, "what is at stake here is the right to read and be exposed to controversial thoughts and language—a valuable right subject to First Amendment protection.[23]

In its conclusion the court noted that the library is a place where:

> a student can literally explore the unknown, and discover areas of interest and thought not covered by the prescribed curriculum . . . a place to test or expand upon ideas presented to him, in or out of the classroom. . . .
> The most effective antidote to the poison of mindless orthodoxy is ready access to a broad sweep of ideas and philosophies. There is no danger in such exposure. The danger is in mind control. The Committee's ban of the anthology *Male & Female* is enjoined.[24]

The court ordered that the ban on *Male and Female under Eighteen* be lifted. Sonja Coleman received the 1978 John Phillip Immroth Memorial Award given by the Intellectual Freedom Round Table of the American Library Association for her work in the case.

A 1979 case involving the removal of *Ms.* magazine from a high school library in Nashua, New Hampshire had a similar judicial result.

## Salvail v. Nashua Board of Education (1979)

On March 27, 1978 the board of education of Nashua, New Hampshire voted to remove all copies of *Ms.* magazine from its school library and to cancel its subscription. The decision was based upon the objection of one board member to:

> advertisements for "vibrators," contraceptives, materials dealing with lesbianism and witchcraft, and gay material. He also objected to advertisements for what he described as a pro-communist newspaper ("The Guardian") and advertisements suggesting trips to Cuba. In addition he felt that the magazine encouraged students and teachers to send away for records made by known communist folk singers.[25]

Another board member, who supported the objections, suggested that an appropriate test for material for high school students was "whether it could be read aloud to his daughter in a classroom."[26]

At the time, the New Hampshire State Department of Education had provided guidelines for the selection of instructional materials and for review of challenges to its school districts. The guidelines were intended to be advisory. The Nashua board had appointed a committee charged with the responsibility of drafting guidelines for selecting instructional materials, and interim guidelines were effective at the time of the challenge to *Ms*. The interim guidelines required that:

1. Materials be consistent with the general educational goals of the school district.
2. Materials meet high standards of quality in factual content and presentation.
3. Materials be appropriate for the subject area and for the age, maturation, ability level, and social development of the students.
4. Materials have aesthetic, literary, or social value.
5. Materials be designed to help the students gain an awareness and understanding of the contributions made by both sexes, and by religious, ethnic, and cultural groups to American heritage.
6. A selection of materials on controversial issues be directed toward maintaining a balanced collection representing various views.[27]

The interim guidelines also provided for a reconsideration committee to be appointed in the event of a public question or complaint. Library staff, the principal or his/her representative, an assistant superintendent, the original selectors, and the users of the materials in the individual school would be represented on the reconsideration committee.

At its meeting on April 10, the board heard comments concerning its failure to follow the guidelines and comments for and against its decision to remove *Ms*.

In March of the next year (1979), after the plaintiffs in this case had filed suit, the board modified its original decision and voted to restore two issues of the magazine to the library, with advertisements removed. It also approved the final instructional material selection guidelines.

The lawsuit was brought by a high school student, Rhonda Salvail, individually and collectively representing the class of all students at the high school; and by others, including a teacher representing other teachers as a class; a graduate individually and collectively representing the class of all 1978 graduates of the high school; and parents individually and collectively representing concerned teacher/parents, parents, and citizens.

Salvail's testimony asserted that *Ms.* was valuable in carrying out her high school assignments, "as it discussed important social issues from a feminist viewpoint." She testified further that sexual matters were openly discussed at the Nashua senior high school and that she worked afternoons in a store where vibrators were sold.[28]

Teachers testified that they had made assignments for which *Ms.* was a valuable resource. Other expert testimony held that the magazine was not obscene or patently offensive, nor did it violate community standards.

The court, after reviewing issues of the magazine, found that it was not obscene and that it did contain material that would satisfy the research needs of those inquiring for the feminist viewpoint in matters. It also determined that the board had been required to follow its own interim guidelines for selection and challenged materials, and that its failure to do so was impermissible.

Agreeing with the *Minarcini* and *Right to Read* courts, the district court stated that, to justify the removal of *Ms.* because of its political content, substantial and legitimate government interest would need to be satisfied by the removal. No such interest was demonstrated. It also determined that the availability of *Ms.* from other sources, such as the public library, did not justify its removal from the high school library.

The district court recognized that "students have a right to receive information which would be infringed by a publication's removal based on the board members' personal objections to its political content."[29]

In the cases heard in the courts between 1972 and 1979, all of the challenged materials were new or of recent publication. Objections that they were vulgar, obscene or contained sexually offensive material were made of all of them, and some social or political objections were also lodged against them. All four cases were concerned with the removal of materials from school libraries. *Presidents' Council* was also concerned with restricting the circulation of *Down These Mean Streets* to only those students with parental permission to borrow it. In two of the cases—*Right to Read Defense Committee* and *Salvail*—portions of the contents were excised from the challenged materials: the poem "The City to a Young Girl" was removed from the anthology *Male and Female under Eighteen*; and advertisements were removed from issues of *Ms.*

In all four cases the defendants were local school boards, and in all of them, students were plaintiffs. In three of the four, teachers, parents and/or other citizens joined with the students as plaintiffs in the lawsuits. In none of them were librarians forced to stand alone.

Despite differences between the courts' decisions in *Presidents' Council* and the three later cases:

*President's Council, Minarcini, Right to Read* and *Salvail* present a consistent and coherent body of law concerning the removal of books from public school libraries. Although the result in *President's Council* differed from the results in the latter three cases, the courts' analytical approaches were similar. *Epperson* stated that only actions which directly and sharply implicated constitutional values warranted judicial intervention. The Second Circuit in *President's Council* indicated that only library book removals which curtailed free speech or thought directly and sharply implicated constitutional values. The Sixth Circuit in *Minarcini* extended the *Epperson* standard by reasoning that removal of library materials, based solely on the social or political tastes of individual board members, also directly and sharply implicated a constitutional value, the first amendment right to receive information. The district courts in *Right to Read* and *Salvail* almost mechanically applied the Minarcini standard to find first amendment violations.[30]

The Seventh Circuit Court of Appeals, however, "introduced inconsistency and confusion to the law concerning book removals"[31] in its decision in the following case.

## Zykan v. Warsaw Community School Corporation (1980)

In *Zykan* the Seventh Circuit court veered away from the direction provided by earlier courts in *Presidents' Council, Minarcini, Right to Read,* and *Salvail.* Relying instead upon *Cary v. Board of Education* (1979), an action by teachers to enjoin a school board from prohibiting the use of various textbooks, it concluded that a school board may base decisions concerning textbooks, library books, and curriculum upon the personal social, political, and moral views of its members.

This lawsuit was one of several brought to challenge censorship in the Warsaw, Indiana schools. They followed a period during which books were banned; teachers were fired; the student newspaper was shut down because it supported the teachers; the school board ordered most elective literature courses removed from the curriculum; and the town's Senior Citizens Club burned 40 copies of *Values Clarification* in a parking lot while its president "defended himself against charges of evoking images of Nazism by claiming that he was only carrying out his obligation to the club."[32]

In July, 1977 the school board banned the textbook *Values Clarification,* in a manner that violated its written policy "which required a review committee and the superintendent's recommendation for removal of library or instructional materials."[33] In August, courses in Black literature, science fiction, and folklore were discontinued, effectively eliminating the elective literature program. Because the books criticized traditional roles for women, English teacher Teresa Burnau was forbidden to use *The Stepford Wives, Growing Up Female in America, The Bell Jar,* and *Go Ask Alice* in her course on women in literature. *Go Ask Alice* was also removed from the school library.

The lawsuit was brought by a high school student and a former high school student, Brooke and Blair Zykan, as a class action suit. The students alleged that the removals of text and library books, when viewed together, violated their First and Fourteenth Amendment rights. In December 1979 the federal district court dismissed the suit for lack of subject matter jurisdiction. On appeal, the Seventh Circuit Court of Appeals found that there was no cause for action for violation of constitutional rights, but because the case was "sufficiently novel" the court granted the plaintiffs leave to amend their complaint.[34]

The appellate court's August 1980 decision was significant for its discussion of academic freedom at the secondary school level. It found that the right to academic freedom could be limited by students' intellectual development, and thus that the extent of academic freedom in secondary schools may be less than that accorded to students in colleges and universities.[35]

The decision also noted that intellectual development is only one aspect of the educational process, which includes "nurturing of those fundamental social, political, and moral values that will permit a student to take his place in the community."[36] In this court's view, school boards had almost complete power over curriculum, textbooks, and other eduational matters. It said: "The breadth of these powers in part reflects the perception that at the secondary school level the need for educational guidance predominates over many of the rights and interests comprised by 'academic freedom'."[37] Thus it was seen as not only permissible but appropriate that school boards should make decisions based upon members' personal social, political, and moral views. This decision-making power ceased only when school board members began "to substitute rigid and exclusive indoctrination for the mere exercise of their prerogative to make pedagogic choices regarding matters of legitimate dispute."[38] The appellate court affirmed the district court's dismissal of the students' complaint.

The court's views on academic freedom in the secondary schools and of the school board's authority over curriculum were troubling. As one observer noted:

> Somehow, the indoctrinative function of the secondary school has become the judicial rationale for Constitutionally protected "educational elitism." This rationale is clearly articulated by the Court in its assertion that academic freedom has limited "relevance" at the secon-

dary school level and that those limits are defined in the following terms:

First, "the high school students lack of the intellectual skills necessary for taking full advantage of the marketplace of ideas . . ." and Second, the student's need for academic freedom "is bounded by the level of his of her intellectual development."

The theory that access to the marketplace of ideas is reserved to those who have the financial, physical or mental capacity to enter, in the words of the Court, "the rarified atmosphere of the college or university . . ." seems fundamentally at variance with the tradition of American education. But, perhaps of greatest concern, is the idea that the "need" for academic freedom is a function of intellectual development when most educators recognize academic freedom as indispensable to intellectual development.[39]

Also troubling was the fact that four of the five forbidden books dealt with women's roles or feminism, thus lending substance to the complaint that the board had in fact acted to censor the ideas in the books. The Seventh Circuit Court established a stricter standard than the *Minarcini* court, a standard which appeared to require that, in order to establish that book removal violated constitutional freedoms, it must be part of an attempt to "purge all materials offensive to a single, exclusive perception of the way of the world."[40] It was a disconcerting decision and, unfortunately, although the next two school library cases were heard on the Second Circuit, that court's decisions did not succeed in resolving the inconsistencies or remedying the confusion in the law governing public school library book removal.

## REFERENCES

1. *Black's Law Dictionary,* 5th ed. (St. Paul, MN: West Pub. Co., 1979), p. 572.
2. 457 F. 2d. 289, 291 (1972).
3. 457 F. 2d. 289, 292–93 (1972).
4. 457 F. 2d. 289, 293 (1972).
5. 93 S. Ct. 308, 309 (1972).
6. Ibid.
7. 93 S. Ct. 308, 310 (1972).
8. 541 F. 2d. 577, 581 (1976).
9. Ibid.
10. Ibid.

11. 541 F. 2d. 577, 582 (1976).

12. Ibid.

13. 541 F. 2d. 577, 583 (1976).

14. Nancy Larrick and Eve Merriam, eds., *Male and Female under Eighteen* (New York: Avon, 1973). The text of the poem is supplied at 454 F Supp. 703, 705 (1978), as follows:*

   "The City to a Young Girl"

   The city is
   One million horney lip-smacking men
   Screaming for my body.
   The streets are long conveyor belts
   Loaded with these suckling pigs.
   All begging for
   a lay
   a little pussy
   a bit of tit
   a leg to rub against
   a handful of ass
   the connoisseurs of cunt
   Every day, every night
   Pressing in on me closer and closer.
   I swat them off like flies
   but they keep coming back.
   I'm a good piece of meat.

   *Jody Caravaglia, 15, F.*
   *Brooklyn, New York*

15. 454 F. Supp. 703, 707 (1978).

16. 454 F. Supp. 703, 708 (1978).

17. Ibid.

18. Ibid.

19. 454 F. Supp. 703, 709 (1978).

20. Ibid.

21. Ibid.

22. *Keefe v. Geanakos,* 418 F. 2d. 359, 361–62, cited at 454 F. Supp. 703, 713 (1978).

23. 454 F. Supp. 703, 714 (1978).

24. 454 F. Supp. 703, 715 (1978).

25. 469 F. Supp. 1269, 1272 (1979).

---

*Reprinted from *Male and Female under Eighteen,* edited by Nancy Larrick and Eve Merriam, by permission of Nancy Larrick.

26. Ibid.

27. 469 F. Supp. 1269, 1271 (1979).

28. 469 F. Supp. 1269, 1272 (1979).

29. Arlen W. Langvardt, "Not on Our Shelves: A First Amendment Analysis of Library Censorship in the Public Schools," *Nebraska Law Review* 61 (1982): 109.

30. Richard Ricci, "Public School Library Book Removals: Community Values v. First Amendment Freedoms," *Notre Dame Lawyer* 57 (1981): 173.

31. Ibid.

32. Stephen Arons, "Book Burning in the Heartland." *Education Digest* (December 1979): 12.

33. Ibid.

34. 631 F. 2d. 1300, 1309 (1980).

35. 631 F. 2d. 1300, 1304 (1980).

36. Ibid.

37. 631 F. 2d. 1300, 1305 (1980).

38. 631 F. 2d. 1300, 1306 (1980).

39. William D. North, "Zykan v. Warsaw; The Non-decision Decision," *Newsletter on Intellectual Freedom,* 29 (6) (November 1980): 141.

40. 631 F. 2d. 1300, 1308 (1980).

# Chapter 4
# Conflict in the Courts,
# 1980–1982


On October 2, 1980 the Second Circuit Court of Appeals decided two cases: *Bicknell v. Vergennes Union High School Board of Directors* and *Pico v. Board of Education, Island Trees Union Free School District*. The judgments were rendered by Circuit Judges Mansfield and Newman, with District Judge Sifton sitting by designation. Judges Newman and Sifton were the majority in *Pico* with Judge Mansfield dissenting. Judges Mansfield and Newman were the majority in *Bicknell*, with Judge Sifton dissenting. Although the same judicial standards were applied to the facts of the two cases, the outcomes were not the same.

## Bicknell v. Vergennes Union High School Board of Directors (1980)

The plaintiffs in the case alleged that this Vergennes, Vermont school board violated the constitutional rights of high school students and of the school librarian when it removed Richard Price's *The Wanderers* from the library, placed Patrick Mann's *Dog Day Afternoon* on a restricted shelf, and prohibited the librarian from purchasing additional major works of fiction. The board's decisions were prompted by complaints from parents about vulgarity and indecency of language in both books.[1] The board also voted "that any book purchases other than those in the category 'Dorothy Canfield Fisher, science fiction and high interest-low vocabulary' must be reviewed by the school administration in consultation with the Board."[2]

Earlier, the board had adopted a book selection and removal policy for the high school library; it specified the rights and responsibilities of parents, students, staff and the board, as follows:

> Rights of the board: "to adopt policy and procedures, consistent with statute and regulation that they feel is in the best interests of students,

parents, teachers and community.''

Rights of the staff: ''to freely select, in accordance with Board policy, organize and administer the media collection to best serve teachers and students.''

Rights of students: ''to freely exercise the right to read and to free access to library materials.''[3]

Under the policy, parents were permitted to request reconsideration of the selection of books that they found objectionable. When requests for reconsideration were received, the policy directed that the librarian would discuss them with the parents. If no resolution were possible by this means, the matter would then be referred to the school board for a vote to determine the outcome. The librarian, however, was not consulted about *The Wanderers* and *Dog Day Afternoon*. The prescribed sequence of steps was not followed; instead the board voted its decision upon receiving the complaints.

The plaintiffs in the case were students, parents, library employees, and an organization called the Right to Read Defense Fund. Together they claimed violation of their constitutional rights, alleging that the books were removed or restricted because they offended board members' personal tastes and values, and that they were denied due process of the law when the board did not follow established book selection policy and procedures. They sought injunctions to prevent both removal of the books and change in the school board's library policies.[4] The plaintiffs acknowledged that the board had the power to remove the books, but they argued that the board's personal tastes and values should not have been the only standards used to determine vulgarity and indecency.

The two concurring opinions in the case found no cause for legal complaint. Judge Newman's opinion stated: ''But so long as the materials removed are permissibly considered to be vulgar or indecent, it is no cause for legal complaint that the Board members applied their own standards of taste about vulgarity.''[5] With respect to the students' right to receive or have access to the books he said: ''. . . young students have no constitutionally protected right of access on school property to material that, whatever its literary merits, is fairly characterized as vulgar and indecent in the school context.''[6] And with respect to the plaintiffs' allegation of denial of due process he found that ''the removal of books from a school library . . . is not the sort of deprivation that entitles a student or librarian to a hearing before that removal takes place.''[7]

The school librarian's particular claim regarding the restrictions placed upon her job responsibilities was likewise rejected by Judge

Newman, who said: "In general, an employee of a government agency has no constitutionally protected interest in the particular duties of a job assignment."[8]

Judge Sifton dissented, asserting that the plaintiffs ought to have been provided the opportunity, through a trial, to demonstrate whether the school board had used its power incorrectly by removing and restricting the two books because of ideas in them, and whether the reasons for the procedural irregularities involved in the removal process were that the board objected in fact to the views expressed in the books, and not simply to their language.[9]

Despite conflicting opinions in *Bicknell,* Judges Newman and Sifton concurred in the result in *Pico*, decided that same day.

## Pico v. Board of Education, Island Trees Union Free School District (1979) (1980) and Board of Education, Island Trees Union Free School District v. Pico (1982)

This landmark case has been heard in three courts as of this writing: the United States District Court for the Eastern District of New York, which decided for the defendants in 1979; the United States Court of Appeals, Second Circuit, which reversed the district court decision and remanded the case for trial; and the United States Supreme Court, which affirmed the appellate court decision in 1982.

It was the first school library censorship case to reach the Supreme Court, and it occasioned considerable comment and controversy during the six years prior to the Supreme Court's decision. It seems reasonable to predict that discussion of the case will continue for years to come.

The courts' decisions record the facts of the case. In the fall of 1975, three members of the Island Trees Union Free School District school board attended a conference in Watkins Glen, New York. The conference was sponsored by an organization called Parents of New York United. Richard Ahrens, who was then president of the school board, described some of the other conference participants:

> an attorney from Washington, D.C., who represented the Heritage Foundation, a conservatively oriented organization, George Archibald, a legislative assistant to Rep. John Conlon of Arizona, and other speakers with reputations in education circles who spoke about current topics about which the conservative community was concerned including litigation involving the control of textbooks and library books in the schools. The speaker on this topic was a Mr. Fike from Kanawa County, West Virginia, which had undergone such litigation.[10]

Board members obtained lists of books considered objectionable in high school libraries elsewhere in the country. The lists contained authors, titles, and quotations for which page references were supplied. Comments accompanied quotations, and the appeals court decisions records excerpts from them:

> Title: *Soul on Ice* by Eldridge Cleaver (Leader of Black panther [sic] and not allowed to live in America)
> THIS BOOK WAS RETAINED FOR SENIORS ONLY IN RANDOLPH. THE BOOK IS FULL OF ANTI-AMERICAN MATERIAL AND HATE FOR WHITE WOMEN. WHY WOULD TEACHERS WANT HIGH SCHOOL STUDENTS TO READ THIS???? OUR GROUP IS GOING TO FILE A COMPLAINT AGAINST THIS BOOK ON SEDITIOUS AND DISLOYAL MATTER.
>
> Title: *Go Ask Alice* by Anonymous (*Suppose* to be diary of 15-year old girl)
> Note: This book, after being reviewed by three teachers, was retained. Parents, do not be fooled by the movie version of this book. It reads a lot different. If teachers cannot find a better book than this to illustrate drugs are bad then what are we paying them for. They justify their viewpoint because the girl dies in the end. A lot of teachers think this is a great book??????
> [Handwritten] LEGISLATORS: KEEP MORATORIUM ON SEX ED! PROVIDE CRIMINAL PENALITIES SO D.A.'S CAN PROSECUTE VIOLATORS! PROTECT THE CHILDREN.[11]

The appeals court decision described the lists as:

> devoted principally to quotations of vulgar and indecent language referring to sexual and other bodily functions and crude descriptions of sexual behavior, although the manner of excerpting, including the use of underlining, elision, apparent errors, and interspersed editorial comment leaves no great sense of confidence in the literal accuracy of the quotations.[12]

On November 7, 1975 Ahrens attended "Winter School Night" at the Island Trees senior high school with another board member, Frank Martin, who had also attended the Watkins Glen conference. That night they asked a school custodian to let them into the library. There they compared the lists with the library's holdings. They found nine of the listed books on file in the library.

The next action was not taken until February 1976. Two high school principals were asked to remain after a regular school board meeting to discuss the books. Ahrens described the meeting as:

> a lengthy discussion with them . . . during which there was much concern and wringing of hands over the potential of the situation. One principal, after reading the excerpts said, "If this stuff is in the books they don't belong in the school."[13]

The principals were directed to remove the books from the libraries immediately, as a result of this informal meeting. The books in question were:

*Best Short Stories by Negro Writers*, Langston Hughes, editor
*Black Boy*, Richard Wright
*Down These Mean Streets*, Piri Thomas
*The Fixer*, Bernard Malamud
*Go Ask Alice*, Anonymous
*A Hero Ain't Nothing but a Sandwich*, Alice Childress
*Laughing Boy*, Oliver La Farge
*The Naked Ape*, Desmond Morris
*A Reader for Writers*, Jerome Archer, editor
*Slaughterhouse Five*, Kurt Vonnegut
*Soul on Ice*, Eldridge Cleaver

Nine were found in the senior high school library, and two were in the junior high school library. Malamud's *The Fixer* had been approved by the board in 1972 for use in a senior literature course.

On February 27, Richard Morrow, superintendent of schools, sent a memorandum to the school board. Its subject: "Lists of Books to Be Banned." In part it said:

> My objection to direct action banning all the books on the list . . . is that we don't know who developed the list, nor the criteria they used. I don't believe we should accept and act on someone else's list, unless we first study the books ourselves . . . we already have a policy . . . designed expressly to handle such problems. It calls for the Superintendent, upon receiving an objection to a book or books, to appoint a committee to study them and make recommendations. I feel it is a good policy—and it is Board policy—and that it should be followed in this instance. . . .
> . . . I have no doubt (but of course no proof) that such a committee would end up agreeing about most of the books on the list. The Board's feelings on them are not so different from the staff's and parents'—after all, that is shown by the fact that the large majority of the books listed are not and apparently never have been recommended and used by the staff.[14]

But on March 3, despite Morrow's objections to the use of "someone else's" lists and his reminder to the board of the requirements of its policy, Board President Ahrens directed in a memo that "*all copies* of the library books in question" be removed from the libraries.[15]

Word of the board's action reached the local press. The school board held a press conference to respond to published articles. A press release was issued. It read, in part:

The Board of Education finds it necessary to call this press conference because of distortions, misinformation, and the obvious attempt by the New York Daily News in a cartoon published this morning, to characterize two members of the Board as a pair of shady hoods who surreptitiously sneak into school buildings under cover of darkness to snatch library books.

It comes as no surprise to this Board of Education that it is once again the subject of attack by Teacher Union leaders, headed by Walter Compare. With the election of school board candidates just two months away, the Teachers' Union is once again attempting to discredit the Board and win the seats for two union-backed lackeys.

While at the conference, we learned of books found in schools throughout the country which were anti-American, anti-Christian, anti-Semetic [sic], and just plain filthy. Upon their return, Ahrens & Martin in early November went to the Senior High School to check the card catalog to see if any of these objectionable books were in our library. We discovered nine such books. We neither removed books, nor cards from the card file.

At the next meeting of the Board, the entire Board discussed how to handle this situation, realizing that to make the titles of the books public might cause a sudden run on the library by the students.

The Board decided that the Principals of the Senior and Junior High Schools would be called in and be directed to gather up the books in question and bring them to the entire Board, for review. This order was carried out earlier this month. The Board is presently reviewing the contents of the books.

To date, what we have found is that the books do, in fact, contain material which is offensive to Christians, Jews, Blacks, and Americans in general. In addition, these books contain obscenities, blasphemies, brutality, and perversion beyond description.

This Board of Education wants to make it clear that we in no way are BOOK BANNERS or BOOK BURNERS. While most of us agree that these books have a place on the shelves of the public library, we all agree that these books simply DO NOT belong in school libraries, where they are so easily accessible to children whose minds are still in the formulative stage, and where their presence actually entices children to read and savor them. . . .

. . . . We have some books which have been reviewed, marked, and underlined. However, if they are read in front of a television camera, the FCC would never permit it to be aired. This stuff is too strong for adult viewers, but some of our educators feel it is appropriate for child consumption.

We are sure that when most of our teachers are given the opportunity to review the material, they will side with the Board, and against the Executive Committee of their own union. When most of the parents review these books, we are confident they will back us to the hilt, grateful that we have done our job and remained as they elected us . . . their faithful Watchdogs.

Finally, we have the books here for your inspection. We will gladly make copies of individual pages to [sic] the UNbelievers.

BOARD OF EDUCATION
Island Trees Union Free School District
March 19, 1976[16]

During the same month, an entire issue of the board's *Newsletter* was devoted to the library book controversy. Here again the board attributed published news stories to ''lies and misinformation which had been spread by the teachers' union.'' It accused union leader Walter Compare of fighting to keep offensive books in the libraries and available to the students. It read, in part: ''One such book refers to Jesus Christ as a 'man with no connections.' One must ask oneself what motivates this man? . . . Why . . . does Mr. Compare insist that these books remain in the hands of our children?''[17] The *Newsletter* asked school district residents to attend the March 30 board meeting in order to have the opportunity of examining the banned books.

The March 30 meeting was concerned with the objectionable books. Superintendent Morrow, in a prepared statement, said that it was ''wrong for the Board—or any other single group—to act to remove books without prolonged prior consideration of the views of both the parents whose children read these books, and the teachers who use these books to instruct.'' He stated further that it was wrong ''to judge any book on the basis of brief excerpts from it'' and ''to take action based on a list prepared by someone outside the Island Trees community.'' He asserted that it was wrong ''to by-pass the established procedure for reviewing the challenged books'' and recommended that they be returned to the shelves until they could be reviewed according to procedures. He noted his understanding that ''every parent has the right and the responsibility to supervise the materials his child reads.''[18]

But, despite Morrow's advice and recommendation, the board ratified its removal of the books. It also decided to appoint a book review committee, consisting of four parents and four staff members (none of them a librarian) to ''read . . . and make recommendations to the board'' concerning ''the educational suitability of these books and whether they are in good taste, appropriate and relevant.''[19]

In other action the board selected May 26 as the date for the election of new board members. The banned books were to become a major issue in the school board election campaign. As Board President Ahrens later stated: ''Nevertheless (or more probably because of this) the incumbent members were re-elected.''[20]

In another memo, dated April 2, Superintendent Morrow urged the board to restore the books to the library until the book review committee's recommendations could be available, but the books were not restored.

On April 6 Morrow, together with the board, selected the book review committee. On April 30 it met, and at the meeting after discussion regarding *The Fixer,* it decided by a vote of 6 to 2 to return the book to the libraries and the curriculum, subject to parental approval of its use by students.

At its second meeting on May 12, the committee voted unanimously to return *Laughing Boy* to the library. In a 5 to 3 vote, *Slaughterhouse Five* was also approved for return, but to a restricted shelf. *Black Boy, Go Ask Alice,* and *Best Short Stories by Negro Writers* were approved for return by votes taken at meetings in May and June. *The Naked Ape, Down These Mean Streets* and *Soul On Ice* were not approved.* The committee could not agree about *A Hero Ain't Nothing but a Sandwich.* No decision was reached about *A Reader for Writers,* because it was not available for examination.

The committee reported its recommendations to the board on July 1. At an open meeting on July 28, the board voted on each challenged book. Despite the book review committee's decision, the board voted to return only *Laughing Boy* to the library without restrictions. *Black Boy* was returned for use by students having parental approval. The remaining nine books were "removed [sic] from elementary and secondary libraries, and for use in the curriculum."[21] Board President Ahrens explained that this meant that the nine books should not be assigned as required, optional, or even suggested reading, although the books might still be discussed in class.[22]

On January 4, 1977 a lawsuit was filed in New York State Supreme Court. The plaintiffs were Stephen Pico and other junior and senior high school students, represented by the New York Civil Liberties Union. Defendants were the Island Trees Union Free School District Board of Education. The suit alleged that the plaintiffs' rights, under state and federal constitutions, had been violated by the board's removal of the books from the libraries and the curriculum.

In late January, in response to the defendants' petition, the case was moved from the state court to federal district court. There both sides moved for summary judgment.

---

*The records provided by the district and appellate courts' decisions differ somewhat on this point. The appellate court's decision indicates that *Soul on Ice* was not returned, while the district court's indicates that the book review committee could not reach agreement about recommending it.

## Federal District Court Decisions

The student plaintiffs alleged five causes for legal action. They cited violation of the guarantees of freedom of speech or expression and of academic freedom for librarians provided by the New York State and United States Constitutions, as well as violation of the Civil Rights Act. The district court determined that the question of academic freedom for librarians could not be raised by the students but must be raised by librarians, and that the five causes for action reduced to a single cause under the Civil Rights Act: "that the school board's removal of the library books violates the first amendment rights of the student plaintiffs."[23]

The students lost the case. The court decided in favor of the school board. Relying on the decision in *Presidents' Council* it said:

> Here, the issue is whether the first amendment requires a federal court to forbid a school board from removing library books which its members find to be inconsistent with the basic values of the community that elected them. *Presidents' Council* resolved that issue by holding that a book that was improperly selected "for whatever reason" could be removed "by the same authority which was empowered to make the selection in the first place." *Presidents' Council* is controlling here.
>
> Even if this court were not bound by the Second Circuit's holding, it would reach the same result.[24]

The court found that the board had removed the books because of their content, which it had viewed as vulgar and in bad taste. District Judge Pratt noted that:

> Whether they were correct in their evaluation of the books is not the issue. Nor is the issue whether, assuming the books to be vulgar and in bad taste, it is a wise or even desirable educational decision to sanitize the library by removing them, thereby sheltering the students from their influence. Such issues should be decided and remedied either by the school district's voters, or by the State Commissioner of Education on an appropriate administrative appeal.[25]

Judge Pratt's decision also discussed the Sixth Circuit Court's holdings in *Minarcini* and those in *Right to Read* and *Salvail*, stating that the distinction made by those courts between book selection and book removal was "not grounded in any sound constitutional principle."[26] The decision questioned how a court could avoid hearing and judging a school board's refusal to acquire a book because of content if it were willing to judge its removal for content-based reasons and stated that such judgments would be beyond the court's competence. School boards, it held, were the proper agency for making decisions about both acquisition and removal of library books. Judge Pratt observed that the board action did not involve a religious question, nor did it ban the teaching of any theory or doctrine. It did not restrict classroom discussion or punish any teacher or librarian. The board had simply restricted access to certain books which it believed to be "vulgar;" and Judge Pratt noted that, "While removal of such books from a school library may, indeed in this court's view does, reflect a misguided educational philosophy, it does not constitute a sharp and direct infringement of any first amendment right."[27]

## Second Circuit Court of Appeals Decisions

The district court decision was appealed, and on February 6, 1980 a hearing was held in the Second Circuit Court of Appeals. The court's October 1980 decision reversed the district court's decision and remanded the case for trial.

In the appeals court decision Judge Sifton contrasted *Pico* with *Presidents' Council:*

> Were it the case here, as in *President's Council,* that nothing more was at issue than the conflicting inferences to be drawn from the act of removal of a controversial text from the shelf of a high school library, we would affirm the decision of the district court because no *prima facie* case was established.[28]

By contrast, however, Judge Sifton noted that school library operations in the Island Trees school district had been subject to "an unusual and irregular intervention"[29] by members of the school board. Unlike *Presidents' Council,* there was more at stake than a difference of opinion between plaintiffs and defendants about the constitutional significance of a decision to withdraw a book. He observed that the circumstances surrounding the book removal and the explanations that board members gave for their actions raised serious questions. Rather than focusing on the reasons for book removal, Judge Sifton emphasized the board's methods, and said: "In circumstances of such irregularity and ambiguity, a *prima facie* case is made out . . . because of the . . . real threat that the school officials' irregular and ambiguous handling of the issue will . . . serve to suppress freedom of expression."[30]

The decision acknowledged that some latitude should be granted to school officials in order that they may carry out their duties. Referring to *Tinker,* it recalled that speech that "materially disrupts classwork or involves substantial disorder or invasion of the rights of others is, of course, not immunized by the constitutional guarantee of freedom of speech."[31] But limits that officials might impose upon students' constitutional rights would be permissible only if a sound basis existed for determining that education or discipline might be threatened if the limits were not established.[32] And any limitations would have to be carefully drawn and applied only as absolutely needed to assure an appropriate educational environment.

School board members had acted without sufficient "sensitivity or precision."[33] The general criticism that the books were "filthy" was definite, but complaints that the books were anti-Christian or anti-American were not sufficiently precise and did not "provide the kind of reasonably clear guidance necessary for free and open debate."[34] Although the complaints furnished definite opinions, they did not provide a clear basis for discussion of the problem presented in the book controversy. In addition, the board did not adhere to its own established policy for dealing with controversial books, nor did it replace that policy with any other set of criteria or procedures.

The "erratic, arbitrary and free-wheeling manner in which the defendant school officials proceeded"[35] was also criticized by the court. Specifically it criticized the removal of the books before the officials had read them, and the use of the critiques obtained at the Watkins Glen conference, because it "revealed political concerns reaching far beyond the education and well-being of the children of the Island Trees Union Free School District."[36] Judge Sifton observed that the board's actions had been "calculated to create public uproar"[37] by drawing the controversy into the board election, a labor dispute, and public meetings.

The court required more of the board: more specificity in the criteria it used for book removal and more sensitivity in applying those criteria. It further required that the student plaintiffs should have been granted the opportunity of a trial in order to establish, if possible, that the board's objections to the language or grammar of the controversial books masked its real objections to the ideas they contained.[38] Citing *FCC v. Pacifica Foundation,* it noted that government may not "seize upon the censorship of particular words as a convenient guise for banning the expression of unpopular views."[39]

The appeals court would have permitted the use of board members' personal tastes or ideas of morality as standards in the performance of their duties to administer the school library. But when the court noted, as it did in the case at bar, that personal standards were used and that there was also a failure to follow established procedures, then another question arose: did the school board act in the students' interests only, or did it seek to establish its own views as "the correct and orthodox ones for all purposes in the particular community?"[40] Evidence that suggested to the court that concerns other than the welfare of students might have motivated the board included:

- The lapse of three months from the date of discovery of the books in the libraries to the date of the board's first official action concerning them.
- The appointment of the book review committee after the books were removed, not before.
- The failure to follow the committee's recommendations.
- The lack of support for the board's decision from school professional personnel, including Superintendent Morrow.
- The removal of works by recognized authors.[41]

Thus the court concluded that a *prima facie* case of First Amendment violation existed because of the book removal, the irregular intervention by the board, and the questionable explanations given by the board for its actions. The district court decision was reversed and the case was remanded for trial.

In a lengthy dissent from the majority's decision, Judge Mansfield asserted that the Second Circuit court's decision in *Presidents' Council* could and should have been applied as precedent for a decision in *Pico*. The court's holding in *Bicknell* that school officials might remove a library book because of vulgarities or indecencies in it without infringing students' First Amendment rights was also, in Judge Mansfield's view, an appropriate holding for *Pico*.[42]

## The Supreme Court's Decision

The case *Pico v. Island Trees* did not go to trial. Instead the school board petitioned the Supreme Court to hear the case, and the Court granted certiorari. The case was heard in March 1982 and the decision, the first for a case concerning school libraries, was published on June 25, 1982. The principal question presented in the case was ''whether the First Amendment imposes limitations upon the exercise by a local school board of its discretion to remove library books from high school and junior high school libraries.''[43] Although the Court was divided on the issue, a majority affirmed the appellate court's decision in favor of the student defendants and remanded the case for further trial proceedings. But the majority, although concurring in the judgment, could not concur in an opinion. Justice Brennan delivered the judgment and filed an opinion in which Justices Marshall and Stevens joined and in which Justice Blackmun joined in all but one part. Justice Blackmun also filed an opinion concurring in the judgment and concurring in part of the opinion. Justice White filed an opinion concurring only in the judgment. Chief Justice Burger and Justices O'Connor, Powell, and Rehnquist dissented. The chief justice filed an opinion in which the others concurred, and each of the others also filed dissenting opinions.

In his opinion Justice Brennan described library books as "books that by their nature are optional rather than required reading."[44] The case, therefore, contained no issues relating to the classroom or to courses offered there. Early in his discussion he acknowledged that courts have granted school boards broad discretion and that courts do not ordinarily intervene in the day-to-day management of the nation's schools. But he also acknowledged that courts may act out of concern for the First Amendment rights of those affected by school officials' action. In this case he found that "the First Amendment rights of students may be directly and sharply implicated by the removal of books from the shelves of a school library."[45] Noting the constitutional protection given to the right to receive information and ideas, he also noted that this right, "an inherent corollary of the rights of free speech and press that are explicitly guaranteed by the Constitution,"[46] follows from the sender's right to convey ideas and information and is "a necessary predicate to the *recipient's* meaningful exercise of his own rights of speech, press, and political freedom."[47] *Tinker* had recognized that students have First Amendment rights available to them in the school environment. Justice Brennan observed that "the special characteristics of the school *library* make that environment especially appropriate for the recognition of the First Amendment rights of students."[48]

The arguments advanced by the school board in favor of its "unfettered discretion"[49] to inculcate and transmit community values overlooked the role of the school library, as viewed by Justice Brennan. Students use the library voluntarily. They can choose books there freely. When the school board argued that its discretion extended "beyond the compulsory environment of the classroom, into the school library and the regime of voluntary inquiry that there holds sway," it was in error.[50]

Although school boards may usually determine what is added to libraries under their jurisdiction, they may not do so, in Justice Brennan's opinion, in a "narrowly partisan or political manner."[51] They may not suppress ideas without violating the Constitution. Thus the school board's motivation came under consideration. If their intent in removing the books was to suppress the ideas in them, then they did so wrongly under the Constitution.

The Court concluded that the available evidence raised a question as to whether the school board had exceeded constitutional limitations. The record showed that, in addition to the claims that the books were vulgar and indecent, there were other claims made by the board that the books were "anti-American" and "offensive to Americans in general."[52] And, although it did not contain objectionable language, *A Reader for Writers* was also removed. The board had also rejected the book review committee's recommendations without giving explicit reasons for doing so.

Justice Brennan wrote: "This would be a very different case if the record demonstrated the petitioners had employed established, regular, and facially unbiased procedures for the review of controversial materials."[53] Thus the evidence did not preclude the possibility that the board had acted to censor the ideas in the books and had, therefore, acted wrongly. On this basis, the Supreme Court upheld the appeals court decision and ordered a trial to be held.

Justice Blackmun's concurring opinion disagreed in part with Justice Brennan's. With respect to the *right to receive* doctrine he stated: "I do not suggest that the State has any affirmative obligation to provide students with information of ideas, something that may well be associated with a 'right to receive.' "[54] And concerning school libraries, he said: "And I do not believe, as the plurality suggests, that the right at issue here is somehow associated with the peculiar nature of the school library; . . . if schools may be used to inculcate ideas, surely libraries play a role in that process."[55]

He observed that the state may not indulge in certain forms of discrimination between ideas, and that it may not "act to deny access to an idea simply because state officials disapprove of that idea for partisan or political reasons."[56] However, he also expressed the view that criteria such as relevance to the curriculum, the quality of the writing, or offensive language in the book could be used by school officials in selection and removal of books.[57] But they may not, intentionally, "shield students from certain ideas that officials find politically distasteful;"[58] and the argument that a majority in the community are in agreement with the board in rejecting the ideas involved is not a good one. The Constitution protects even unpopular ideas.

Chief Justice Burger was joined by Justice O'Connor, Powell and Rehnquist in the dissent. The Chief Justice's opinion noted two issues:

> *First,* whether local schools are to be administered by elected school boards, or by federal judges and teenage pupils; and *second*, whether the values of morality, good taste, and relevance to education are valid reasons for school board decisions concerning the contents of a school library.[59]

He rejected the plurality's assertion of a right to receive information and ideas, saying that there is no basis in the First Amendment or in any decisions of the Court for such a right.[60] He noted further; "It does not follow that the decision to *remove* a book is less 'official suppression' than the decision not to acquire a book desired by someone.' '[61] He categorically rejected "this notion that the Constitution dictates that judges, rather than parents, teachers, and local school boards must determine how the standards of morality and vulgarity are to be treated in the classroom.' '[62]

Justice Powell, in a separate opinion, also rejected the idea of a right to receive and expressed his concern that the plurality's opinion would erode the authority and effectiveness of local school boards.

Justice Rehnquist viewed school libraries as having a share in the inculcative role of the schools[63] and asserted that the right to receive doctrine is misplaced in the elementary and secondary school setting.[64] In his view, the most obvious reason that the board did not violate the students' rights was the availability of the books in other locations.[65]

Seven separate opinions were written by Supreme Court justices. The majority were not in complete agreement among themselves, and the dissent was vigorous. The decision raised, or failed to settle, some crucial issues. It did not address school library acquisitions. Justice Brennan observed that "nothing in our decision today affects in any way the discretion of a local school board to choose books to *add* to the libraries of their schools.' '[66] Nor did the decision seem to address the potential issue of censorship of library books which might be required, rather than optional, reading.

The decision also attached great importance to the following of established procedures but "left unclear . . . the extent to which procedures must be adopted and adhered to in connection with book removals.' '[67]

It was clear, however, that the Court viewed the school board's motivation or intentions as important in determining the constitutional propriety of school library book removal, and that it viewed the intentional suppression of ideas as improper. And it was overwhelmingly clear that school library book removals have potential constitutional implications, and that school authorities do not have an unfettered right to remove books and other materials "because they dislike the ideas" contained in them.[68]

Two months after the Supreme Court's decision the school board voted 6–1 to restore the books. (It also voted to require librarians to send notes to the parents of any students who borrow books identified as objectionable by the school board.)[69]

Future court decisions may and probably will clarify remaining issues. Until the time that the courts again speak on school library book removal, "librarians, publishers and others committed to the First Amendment principles at stake in this area can be pleased that the Supreme Court—even if in less than compelling fashion—has recognized and preserved those principles."[70]

## REFERENCES

1. 638 F. 2d. 438, 441 (1980).
2. Ibid.
3. 638 F. 2d. 438, 440 (1980).
4. 638 F. 2d. 438, 441 (1980).
5. Ibid.
6. Ibid., at Note 2.
7. 638 F. 2d. 438, 442 (1980).
8. Ibid.
9. 638 F. 2d. 438, 443 (1980).
10. 638 F. 2d. 404, 407 (1980).
11. 638 F. 2d. 404, 407, 408 (1980).
12. 638 F. 2d. 404, 408 (1980).
13. Ibid.
14. 638 F. 2d. 404, 409 (1980).
15. Ibid.
16. 474 F. Supp. 387, 390, 391 (1979).
17. 638 F. 2d. 404, 410 (1980).
18. Ibid.
19. Ibid.
20. 638 F. 2d. 404, 411 (1980).
21. Ibid.
22. 474 F. Supp. 387, 391 (1979).
23. 474 F. Supp. 387, 394 (1979).
24. 474 F. Supp. 387, 396, 397 (1979).
25. 474 F. Supp. 387, 396 (1979).
26. 474 F. Supp. 387, 397 (1979).
27. Ibid.
28. 638 F. 2d. 404, 414 (1980).
29. Ibid.
30. 638 F. 2d. 404, 414–15 (1980).
31. 89 S. Ct. 741 (1969).

32. 638 F. 2d. 404, 415 (1980).
33. 638 F. 2d. 404, 416 (1980).
34. Ibid.
35. Ibid.
36. Ibid.
37. Ibid.
38. 638 F. 2d. 404, 417 (1980).
39. 98 S. Ct. 3038 (1978).
40. 638 F. 2d. 404, 417 (1980).
41. 638 F. 2d. 404, 418 (1980).
42. 638 F. 2d. 404, 419 (1980).
43. 102 S. Ct. 2799, 2806 (1982).
44. 102 S. Ct. 2799, 2805 (1982).
45. 102 S. Ct. 2799, 2807–08 (1982).
46. 102 S. Ct. 2799, 2808 (1982).
47. Ibid.
48. 102 S. Ct. 2799, 2809 (1982).
49. Ibid.
50. Ibid.
51. 102 S. Ct. 2799, 2810 (1982).
52. Ibid.
53. 102 S. Ct. 2799, 2811 (1982).
54. 102 S. Ct. 2799, 2814 (1982).
55. Ibid.
56. Ibid.
57. 102 S. Ct. 2799, 2815 (1982).
58. 102 S. Ct. 2799, 2816 (1982).
59. 102 S. Ct. 2799, 2817 (1982).
60. 102 S. Ct. 2799, 2819 (1982).
61. 102 S. Ct. 2799, 2821 (1982).
62. Ibid.
63. 102 S. Ct. 2799, 2830 (1982).
64. 102 S. Ct. 2799, 2831 (1982).
65. 102 S. Ct. 2799, 2832 (1982).
66. 102 S. Ct. 2799, 2805 (1982).

67. R. Bruce Rich, "The Supreme Court's Decision in Island Trees," *Newsletter on Intellectual Freedom* 31 (5) (September 1982): 175.
68.   102 S. Ct. 2799, 2810 (1982).
69. "Island Trees School Board Lifts Seven Year Book Ban," *Library Journal* 107 (16) (September 15, 1982): 1694.
70. Rich, p. 175.

# Chapter 5
# The Conflict Continues: Other Recent Issues in School Censorship

The Supreme Court's landmark decision in *Pico* was not the only decision affecting school libraries or curriculum in 1982. The federal district court in Maine and the Eighth Circuit Court of Appeals also decided suits brought as a result of censorship in the schools.

## HARMFUL LANGUAGE: THE STUDENTS DISAGREE

On January 22 a preliminary injunction against the banning of Ronald Glasser's *365 Days* from the Woodland High School Library was granted in Maine federal district court. *365 Days*, a nonfiction account of the experiences of American soldiers in combat in Vietnam, is by a physician whose tour of duty in an Army hospital put him in contact with soldiers who had been severely wounded in action. Glasser's book is a compilation of factual accounts of their experiences. The soldiers' dialogue uses four-letter words, according to Dr. Glasser, "because those were the words that were portrayed to me by the patients that I was talking to."[1]

The Woodland High School Library served 300 junior and senior high school students; elementary school students and adult residents of the community could also borrow books there. *365 Days* had been in the library since 1971 and had circulated 32 times during the 10-year period. In early 1981, a high school student, Betsy Davenport, checked it out of the library. Her stepmother objected to the book. At the hearing in federal district court on December 21, 1981, Mrs. Davenport testified as follows:[2]

The following is taken from direct examination by plaintiffs' attorney Ronald Coles (Q) of Mrs. Davenport (A) at the December 1981 hearing.

*Q*. Now, Betsy Davenport is your stepdaughter, is that correct?

*A*. Yes, she is.

*Q.* Now there came a time in April of this year that you first became aware that Betsy had brought home a book entitled *365 Days?*

*A.* Yes, she did.

*Q.* And how did you become aware that your stepdaughter had that book?

*A.* My girlfriend called me and told me.

*Q.* Had you seen your daughter with the book at home before your girlfriend had called you?

*A.* No. She hid it so I wouldn't see it.

*Q.* Do you know if your stepdaughter read the book?

*A.* No. She started it, and when she saw what was in it, she decided to take it back to the school before I found it.

*Q.* All right. Did she take the book back to the school?

*A.* No, she didn't.

*Q.* What did she do with the book?

*A.* She showed it to her girlfriend on the school bus, and her girlfriend showed it to her mother, in turn. Then her mother called me.

*Q.* Oh, her girlfriend's mother then called you?

*A.* Yes.

*Q.* Was that mother in possession of the book at that time?

*A.* Yes, she was.

*Q.* Okay. And did that mother then bring the book back to your home?

*A.* No. She called me and my husband, and I went out to her house and looked at it.

*Q.* Okay. Do you remember when in April that was, approximately?

*A.* I think it was the 14th.

*Q.* Okay. And you went out to your friend's home and the book was there?

*A.* Right.

*Q.* I would now show you a paperback edition marked as Plaintiffs' Exhibit 1 and ask you if this is the book referred to (indicating)?

*A.* Yes, it is.

*Q.* Now, when you drove out, you and your husband drove out to your friend's home, did you then take the book back with you to your home?

*A.* Not—well, we did later on in that day.

*Q.* Did you—what, if anything, did you do at your friend's home, in terms of that book? Did you start reading it?

*A.* I read through it. I didn't read the whole book, word-for-word. I glanced through it and seen what was in the book, and then we went to the school.

*Q*. Okay. Would it be fair to say that you thumbed through the book?

*A*. Yes, but I read paragraphs through it.

*Q*. Okay. Let me rephrase it. You're aware that there are some 16 or 17 separate vignettes in that book?

*A*. Yes.

*Q*.Did you read any vignette in its entirety?

*A*. Chapter 8.

*Q*. Chapter 8. And that is the chapter that is entitled ''No,'' the word, ''Cornflakes,'' is that correct?

*A*. Right.

*Q*. And after reading—did you read the entire chapter?

*A*. Yes.

*Q*. Did you take note of the number of times the word appeared in that chapter?

*A*. I took note of the number of times all questionable words were in the whole book, not just that chapter.

After obtaining the book, Mr. and Mrs. Davenport registered a complaint about it with the librarian and the school superintendent and showed it to Baileyville School Committee Chairman, Thomas Golden. At the committee's meeting on April 28, 1982, the Davenports' complaint was considered. (However, only their names appeared on the meeting agenda, and there was no evidence to show that three of the five members had been informed about the substance of their complaint prior to the meeting.)

At the meeting the Davenports urged that *365 Days* be banned. School Superintendent Raymond Freve presented a photocopy of Chapter 8, entitled ''No Fucken Cornflakes.'' He also presented reviews of the book. All were favorable, and one recommended it as ''a book for all libraries.''[3] The committee discussed the book and the reviews, then voted 5 to 0 to remove it from the school library.[4]

At the Committee's May 5 meeting, two high school students, Michael Sheck and Heather Beebe, spoke on behalf of the book, urging that the ban be lifted. In his testimony at the hearing, Sheck described the meeting: ''What it was was a public meeting, and there were probably 50 people or so in the audience, and I suppose around six or seven stood up after my presentation, spoke to the board, all of them favoring the book.''[5]

In mid-May Sheck brought a copy of *365 Days*, obtained on interlibrary loan, to school. His testimony also described what occurred then:

And Mr. Morrison, the principal, saw it and said to me that I was unable—I was not allowed to have that book in the school, that it had been banned, and that he would treat it as if it were a Playboy or

Hustler magazine, and that I was to put it in my car or leave it in the office or risk confiscation. . . .

It was my form of silent protest, à la the black armbands worn by the students in *Tinker vs. Des Moines Independent Community School District*.[6]

On May 14, the high school student council also requested that the committee return the book to the library. At the school committee meeting on May 19, a motion to place it on a restricted shelf was defeated on a three to two vote. Later, on June 17, another committee vote did place the book on restricted loan, enabling students to obtain it with parental approval, a practice intended to remain in effect until a challenged materials policy could be developed. A form called "Citizen's Request for Reconsideration of a Book" existed and was kept in the English department files, but it had not been used to request reconsideration of *365 Days*.

The "Baileyville School Department Challenged Material Policy" was adopted on August 17 and became effective immediately. A motion to submit *365 Days* to consideration under the policy failed to carry, and the book was banned from the library again. Superintendent Freve's testimony described his recommendation to the Committee: "There was discussion, pre-empted by myself, because they had asked me my recommendation, and I told them I recommended they not go through the process, because it would be too much pressure on those people that were on that committee."[7] When asked at the hearing what the function of the policy was if it were not to be used to consider *365 Days*, Freve responded that it was for "future books."[8] School Committee Chairman Golden also testified that no purpose would be served in submitting the book to the Challenged Materials Policy:

Because we had made our decision earlier based on the information and the knowledge that we had at that time. If you would, after something has happened, you can't adopt a law to put it back through. We'd already made our determination.[9]

In response to the school committee's action, Michael Sheck and other students and their parents brought suit challenging the constitutionality of the book ban and asking that the book be restored to the library. The court determined that preliminary injunctive relief was warranted. It was clear to the court that the irreparable injury that loss of First Amendment freedoms causes would be likely to result if relief were not granted. The court stated that, with the exception of the threatened confiscation of Michael Sheck's borrowed copy of the book, the banning did not "deprive these plaintiffs of their right to initiate expression. Book bans do not directly restrict the readers' right to initiate expression but rather their right to receive information and ideas. . . ."[10]

The decision continued:

> Public schools are major market places of ideas, and first amendment rights must be accorded all "persons" in the market for ideas, including secondary school students. . . .[11]

> The way would be open to pare the protections of the first amendment to constitutional insignificance in our public schools were courts to accede to suggestions . . . that the banning of library books, *the least obtrusive conventional communication resources available,* does not at least presumptively implicate the reciprocal first amendment right of secondary students to receive the information and ideas there written. . . .[12]

> As long as words convey ideas, federal courts must remain on first-amendment alert in book-banning cases, even those ostensibly based strictly on vocabular considerations. A less vigilant rule would leave the care of the flock to the fox that is only after their feathers.[13]

With respect to Fourteenth Amendment due process considerations, the decision stated:

> There is no more appropriate context than the present for the careful delineation and observance of "due process" standards and procedures . . . The fourteenth amendment has been held to mandate that governmental units adhere to their own rules and regulations. . . .[14]
> Nothing that has as yet been brought to the attention of the court would warrant relaxation of these procedural standards in library book-removal cases.[15]

The court found no indication in the records of the case that students would be harmed by the language in *365 Days*, or that the Committee believed that harm would result. The language was considered objectionable, but not necessarily harmful. Even if it had been shown that harm might result to some young or immature students, the assumption that harm would result to all students and adults in the community would have been unwarranted. Neither was there evidence that the book was removed because of "its conceptual or emotive content,"[16] or because it was obscene. In sum, the ban was imposed "because three Committee members considered some of its language, although not obscene, inappropriate for use in a library book available to students."[17]

In the court's view:

> The criteria to be considered in advance of state action restricting student access to "objectionable" language include "the age and sophistication of the students, the closeness of the relation between the

specific technique used and some concededly valid educational objective, and the content and manner of presentation.[18]

It found no evidence that these or any other specific criteria had been used. Indeed, it found that ''it is difficult to understand how at least two members of the Committee, who have not read the book, could have given fair consideration to its content.''[19]

Preliminary injunctive relief was granted, and the book was restored to the Woodland high school library pending a final decision. Before a final decision was reached, however, a school committee election was held, the membership of the Committee changed, and it voted to restore *365 Days* to the library. Thus, in one sense, the citizens, not the courts, had the final word. In November 1982 an agreement, signed by attorneys for both parties, also stipulated that *365 Days* would remain in the library.

Ronald R. Coles, attorney for the plaintiffs, made the following statement in his closing argument at the December hearing:

> I would submit that the world is full of people who feel like Carol Davenport, Tom Golden, Mr. Morrison, and Mr. McPhee. I think that they are essentially decent people, well-intentioned, but, I believe, misguided. They're applying their moral principles. They don't like the book, so no one else should read the book. That's the real First Amendment problem.[20]

Through his efforts and those of Michael Sheck and others, the problem in Woodland, Maine was, for the moment, solved.

## WHEN "FAMILY VALUES" CLASH WITH SCHOOL FILMS

A Minnesota dispute concerning a film version of Shirley Jackson's short story, ''The Lottery,'' and a trailer film used with it in the Forest Lake schools was ultimately resolved in the Eighth Circuit Court of Appeals.

In the case, students in the junior and senior high school, through their parents, asked the court to require that the Forest Lake school district return the films to use in the curriculum.

Although the school district did not own copies and was accustomed to renting them as needed, the films had been in use in the secondary school since 1972. During the 1977–78 school year, a group of parents and other citizens expressed concern about the films and asked that they be removed from the curriculum. They objected to the violence in the film's story and to thematic material that might have a damaging effect upon students' religious and family values.

The English department of the high school responded by scheduling a meeting on February 21, 1978 to inform concerned members of the community about *The Lottery*. At the meeting, the short story was read and the film was shown. Faculty members explained the educational rationale for their use.

A short time after this meeting, "Citizens Request for Reconsideration of Instructional Materials" forms were filed, requesting removal of the films. (This form was routinely attached to the school district's selection policy, and when completed, was forwarded to the director of curriculum.) The request for removal was denied, and both films were retained in the curriculum; but a challenge committee composed of three teachers, two administrators, one student, and one citizen was then assigned to review them.

The challenge committee held an open meeting on March 28 and, after hearing public comment and deliberating on the matter, recommended that the films continue in use in the senior high school but be discontinued in the junior high school. Another recommendation was that parents be advised in writing when the films were scheduled to be shown, in order that their children might not see them if their parents objected.[21]

On April 17 the school board overturned the challenge committee's recommendation to retain the films, on a four to three vote, giving no reasons for its decision.[22] The board's action prompted a response from Forest Lake Education Association President Terry Anderson, who wrote in a letter dated April 27:

> Members of the Forest Lake Education Association and the teaching staff of District 831 are disappointed in the April 17 actions of the Board, which resulted in the exclusion of the film "The Lottery" from the Senior High curriculum. This action is depriving the eleventh and twelfth grade students from an educational opportunity. . . .
>
> Since teachers are constantly held accountable for their actions, we would ask the Board to also be accountable for their actions. We would be interested in receiving rationale from the board members for making this decision. The most important question we would like answered is how this action was made in the best interests of the majority of students in Forest Lake. . . .
>
> As educators who were hired by the School Board we are confused by the Board's action and how it will affect the job we were hired to perform. We sincerely hope that this kind of action does not become a trend. There is more at stake here than one film. . . .[23]

On May 16 Ms. Anderson reported to the board the results of a survey of teachers "on materials, concepts, books, other printed material, and class activities that have been questioned or challenged. . . ."[24] She wrote:

> The number of occurrences and the widespread effect they have confirm the concerns I have expressed in the name of the Education Association in response to the question of academic freedom. . . .

As you read on, I hope you will understand why the teachers have voiced our concerns this year and why we feel "The Lottery" issue may not be just one isolated issue.[25]

A partial listing of the challenged items or events reported to Ms. Anderson in her survey follows:[26]

From elementary teachers:

- Yoga exercises were questioned, even though they were conducted without reference to any religious meaning or significance.
- The Holt Data Bank social studies materials were questioned by parents.
- The previous summer some people had entered the schools when staff was not present in order to obtain school books for examination. The school was not in their "attendance area."
- Some teachers avoided portions of curriculum or other activities from fear of possible challenges.
- Some teachers had been discouraged from using materials of their choice that deal with a child's self-esteem, e.g., values clarification.

- In the library:
  —One book was removed from a library shelf and the catalog cards removed from the catalog by someone who was not a staff member.
  —Another book was checked out by a citizen. When it was returned several months later it had been defaced.

From junior high school teachers:

- Questioning the teaching of the Holocaust and instances of anti-Semitism were of concern to the teachers.

From senior high teachers:

- A social studies field trip to a conference on global priorities was questioned.
- The teaching of logic in geometry was questioned.
- A citizen borrowed library books in June, 1977 for a possible challenge and did not return them until January, 1978. No challenge was issued, but the staff had to make several special requests to get the books returned.
- Thirty-five copies of *The Feminine Image in Literature* were discovered to be missing after a school open house in November 1977 and had not yet been returned in May 1978.

- The teaching of human sexuality and death education had been questioned/challenged.

Ms. Anderson's report closed with some comments that had been expressed to her while conducting the survey:

> The issue of censorship through community pressure does not always take the form of deleting specific materials already in the curriculum. Instead, a feeling of paranoia develops—teachers feel they do not have community support so creative projects and ideas are never tried, simply because a community member may become forceful in opposing an idea and the teacher will have to defend himself before a committee, board, etc.[27]

That the teachers had reason to be concerned was at least partially confirmed by an advertisement which appeared in the *Forest Lake Times*, November 23, 1977. Paid for by Parents Who Care About Education in District No. 831, it read in part:

> Sex Ed is an intrusion into the privacy and rights of children and parents. Noted psychiatrists across the country have said that Sex Ed, giving adult facts to children, causes harm to their mental development because they cannot understand it in an adult way. It encourages children to try out what was taught. . . .
> SEX ED WITHOUT MORALS IS HUMANISTIC!
> Humanism is a religion, and has been so declared even by the U.S. Supreme Court. It is a way of life, a philosophy, and all-encompassing ideology. The Humanist Manifesto states that there is no God, every man is his own creator, there is no right or wrong, ethics are situational, there are no absolutes, there must be no feeling of individuality, the individual must be trained to think of himself as part of a group willing to be manipulated for the good of society rather than for individual gain or achievement. . . .
> WHO WANTS SEX ED?
> People who make money producing books! People who make money producing films! People who make money producing contraceptives! People who make money performing abortions. Pornographers who want to become "Honest" without changing their ways!. . . .[28]

In this atmosphere of conflict and concern, the plaintiffs filed suit in federal district court. The court concluded that the plaintiffs had established a *prima facie* case that the board's action was unconstitutional because the objections of the board's majority had "religious overtones" and because the films had been removed because of their "ideological content."[29] The court ordered the films returned.

The decision was appealed. The Eighth Circuit Court of Appeals affirmed the lower court's decision in January 1982. It found that, while there was no question that the school board was the appropriate local policymaker for the schools, it did not have an unfettered right to remove materials from use in the curriculum.[30]

Opponents of the films concentrated on ideological and religious concerns, contending that "the movies must be removed from the curriculum because they posed a threat to the students' religious beliefs and family values." Teachers, however, testified that both the film and the short story had legitimate places in the curriculum. And a study conducted by the education faculty at the University of Maryland had concluded that the film version produced "no negative effects on students in terms of violence and attitudes toward family or religious values."[31]

To act in accordance with constitutional requirements, the board would have needed to establish "that a substantial and reasonable governmental interest existed for interfering with the students' right to receive information."[32] In the views of both courts, the board did not establish such an interest. Another requirement of the First Amendment not met by the board was that it should act "so that the reasons for its decision are apparent to those affected."[33] The board's failure to respond to the opportunity to provide a rationale for banning the film until requested to do so by the district court was also a failure to meet this requirement.

In its conclusion, the court stated that it had a responsibility to uphold the constitution and to protect the fundamental rights of all citizens, and it noted that "the vigilant protection of constitutional freedoms is nowhere move vital than in the community of American schools."[34]

## CREATIONISM, SECULAR HUMANISM, AND OTHER CONCERNS

Despite these legal victories, the vitality of constitutional freedoms in schools and school libraries continues to be under attack. Censorship advocates claim a variety of justifications for their attempts to challenge school library materials, but the majority share the common purpose of placing limits upon students' learning experiences in classrooms and libraries. Censors continue to challenge a wide range of materials. Not all share the viewpoints of those involved in the court cases discussed in previous chapters, nor do all affiliate with New Right or conservative groups. Indeed, many conservatives assert that they act out of concern for a preexisting censorship of their viewpoints and an apparent abundance of materials which conflict with them. Nevertheless, although school library materials have been challenged for other reasons (e.g., racism and sexism), many of the more recent challenges appear to have originated from New

Right or conservative individuals and groups. Of these challenges, a significant number are related to two current *-isms*: scientific creationism and secular humanism.

Scientific creationism is more limited in focus than secular humanism. Its advocates oppose the teaching of evolution theory as the only theory of human origins. A key tenet of creation science is:

> The first human beings did not evolve from an animal ancestry, but were specially created in fully human form from the start. Furthermore, the "spiritual" nature of man (self-image, moral consciousness, abstract reasoning, language, will, religious nature, etc.) is itself a supernaturally created entity distinct from mere biological life.[35]

Bills that would require equal treatment of creation science and evolution theory in the classroom have been introduced into at least 15 state legislatures.[36] In 1981 Arkansas and Louisiana enacted legislation that required the public schools to provide instruction in scientific creationism as well as evolution theory no later than the 1982–83 school year. The Arkansas federal district court found that state's "balanced treatment" act to be unconstitutional because it violated the establishment clause of the First Amendment.[37] And a federal district judge, citing the Louisiana State Constitution which gives control over public schools to the state board of education, not the legislature, struck down the Louisiana law in late 1982[38] There are, nevertheless, more than 50 antievolution organizations nationwide and their influence on state legislatures and statewide adoptions of textbooks and other instructional materials is spreading. Among the leaders are the Creation Research Society of Ann Arbor, the Institute for Creation Research of the Christian Heritage College in San Diego, and the Creation Science Research Center, also of San Diego.[39]

Secular humanism is wider-ranging than scientific creationism in its potential for engendering a diversity of objections to school library materials, and because of their diversity, the objections raised may be more difficult to comprehend and confront.

What is secular humanism? It is important to note that there is confusion between secular humanism and humanistic education. Furthermore, the apparent confusion between the humanism expressed in educator John Dewey's *Humanist Manifesto I* and B.F. Skinner's *Humanist Manifesto II* and a religion, secular humanism, which was noted by the Supreme Court in *Torcaso v. Watkins* (1960)[40], also tends to confound the definition.

> There is indeed a church of secular humanists, and one congregation was involved in litigation in California. This church is rather Unitarian in outlook and does not deal with God in an overt way. Rather, the church focuses on human life at the present moment.

To say that all, or nearly all, teachers are members of this church is to say that teachers are not Protestants, Catholics, Jews, or members of any of the large number of religions that are allowed freedom to worship in this country by virtue of the Bill of Rights. Clearly, the definition of secular humanism, a specific religion, is not the definition that critics of public education are using. These groups have seized upon a term that sounds like ''humanities'' and ''humanistic education,'' and they are bent upon labeling teachers across the country with a term defined by their own standards.[41]

Secular humanism, then, is a label that has been applied to much of what had been and is being taught in public schools and could as readily be applied to school library materials. Secular humanists have been described by their critics as:

Anti-God. The secular humanist wants to tear God down from His Throne and make Man the sovereign of the universe.

Anti-democracy. The secular humanist hopes to do away with present governments and make the world one huge, totalitarian state.

Anti-family. The secular humanist undermines the family concept, denies Christian values that are taught in the home, and preaches to the youth of America that there are no absolute morals.

Anti-Christian. The secular humanist preaches the religion of Secular Humanism through textbooks and by means of the following teaching techniques: values clarification, moral education, human development, family life and human relations, affective education, and psychological learning, to name a few.[42]

Thus those who label instructors or instructional material as promoting secular humanism can and do challenge a wide range of school library materials and textbooks, teaching topics, and techniques.

Perhaps the most famous of these critics are Mel and Norma Gabler, whose Longview, Texas organization, Educational Research Analysts, has ''become a clearinghouse for critiques written by almost anyone of textbooks, dictionaries and library books.''[43] The Gablers, along with others, have provided thousands of textbook reviews since they began their work in 1961.

Reviewers use 10 categories to summarize their objections to contents: ''attacks on values; distorted contents; negative thinking; violence; academic unexcellence; isms fostered (Communism, socialism, internationalism); invasions of privacy; behavioral modification; humanism, occult, and other religions encouraged; and other important educational aspects.''[44]

An example of a Gabler objection to textbook content is shown in the following comments concerning *Magruder's American Government:*

> The book says: "year after year, the Defense Department takes a very substantial slice of the federal budget." The Gablers call that a "subtle bias" in favor of the view that America should disarm. The book also quotes a statement by President Eisenhower in which he voices the historic concern that money for weapons is money not spent to feed the hungry or clothe the cold. Again the Gablers object because they think that the statement shows excessive "stress on the opinion that money spent to defend the *whole* country should be used to help the poor." They also see bias in the book's standard claim that the Constitution has endured since 1787 through continual interpretation. The fault they find here is "emphasis on the changing nature of our Constitution. The amazing fact about our constitution is its stability," they observe.[45]

Despite the startling nature of such claims, the Gablers have obviously touched a nerve, and their influence has been perceived in challenges to schoolbooks all across the country. Educator Edward B. Jenkinson summarized their effect in this way:

> There is little question that the Gablers and their followers have put public education on trial. The question facing public education now is this: Can teachers and administrators throughout the country unite long enough to put the Gabler thinking on trial?[46]

Librarians, too, must join with other educators in confronting any and all such attacks upon academic freedom in the schools.

A decade has elapsed since the first appellate court decision in a school library censorship case: a decade of rapid and, to many, shattering changes in American society. Changes in personal and societal values have been welcomed by some, met with pained surprise by others, and with genuine outrage by many. That Americans should express a longing for familiar values, for a return to old remembered ways, is not surprising. And so long as that expression does not conflict with the even older values expressed by the First Amendment, there is little to fear from this longing. But when conflict occurs, the loss of precious freedoms is greatly to be feared and must be fiercely resisted.

Societal changes have also led to censorship attempts by those who are concerned with reinforcing what many people would agree are beneficial changes in our culture. Most notably, some people, concerned about the images of minority groups and women presented in some library materials, have attempted to remove and censor certain titles from school (and public) libraries. This is often a very difficult situation for a librarian, administrator, or board member to handle. An often appropriate and useful method to defuse attempted censorship of racist or sexist material is for a librarian or teacher to use the objected-to material in a learning session. For example, the school librarian or a teacher could involve students in a discussion of why people object to a book such as *Little Black Sambo*. Most parents and others who object to racist or sexist material can be persuaded that it is better to discuss and expose the possibly harmful social attitudes found in some material than it is to censor and remove the item altogether.

No matter how much the librarian may agree with a concerned parent who objects to a, say, racist portrayal in a book, the librarian must not bend to any attempts at censorship. It must be remembered that censorship is not an issue that can be graded; there is no such thing as acceptable or "good" censorship and unacceptable or "bad" censorship. All resistance to censorship must be equitably applied in order for the resistance to be effective and fair.

## REFERENCES

1. *Sheck v. Baileyville School Committee*, United States District Court, District of Maine, Civil No. 81-0153 B., "Transcript of Hearing on Plaintiffs' Motion for Preliminary Injunction," p. 131.
2. *Sheck v. Baileyville School Committee*, pp. 9–11.
3. *Sheck v. Baileyville School Committee*, p. 240.
4. 530 F. Supp. 679, 681 (1982).
5. *Sheck v. Baileyville School Committee*, p. 356.
6. *Sheck v. Baileyville School Committee*, p. 359.
7. *Sheck v. Baileyville School Committee*, p. 256.
8. Ibid.
9. *Sheck v. Baileyville School Committee*, p. 102.
10. 530 F. Supp. 679, 685 (1982).
11. 530 F. Supp. 679, 687 (1982).
12. Ibid.
13. 530 F. Supp. 679, 688 (1982).
14. 530 F. Supp. 679, 690 (1982).
15. 530 F. Supp. 679, 691 (1982).
16. 530 F. Supp. 679, 692 (1982).
17. Ibid.
18. Ibid.
19. Ibid.
20. *Sheck v. Baileyville School Committee*, p. 397.

21. 670 F. 2d. 771, 774 (1982).
22. Ibid.
23. Terry Anderson, President of Forest Lake Education Association to District 831 School Board, April 27, 1978.
24. Terry Anderson, President of Forest Lake Education Association to District 831 School Board, "Report on Censorship," p. 1.
25. Ibid.
26. Anderson, pp. 1–3.
27. Anderson, p. 30.
28. Advertisement in *Forest Lake Times* (November 23, 1977): p. 11.
29. 670 F. 2d. 771, 776 (1982).
30. Ibid.
31. 670 F. 2d. 771, 776, 777 (1982).
32. 670 F. 2d. 771, 777 (1982).
33. 670 F. 2d. 771, 778 (1982).
34. 364 U.S. 479, 487 (1960).
35. Institute for Creation Research, *Impact* 85 (July 1982): ii–iii.
36. Delos McKown, " 'Scientific' Creationism: Axioms and Exegesis," *Free Inquiry* (Summer 1981): 23.
37. Andrew D. Bing, "Evolution, Creationism and the Religion Clauses," *Albany Law Review* 46 (Spring 1980): 924.
38. Alex Heard, "U.S. Judge Overturns Louisiana Creationism Law," *Education Week* 2 (3) (December 8, 1982): 4.
39. McKown, p. 23.
40. 367 U.S. 488, 491 (1960).
41. Robert T. Rhode, "Secular Humanism," in *Dealing with Censorship,* ed. by James E. Davis (Urbana, IL: National Council of Teachers of English, 1979), p. 122.
42. Rhode, p. 120.
43. "Was Robin Just a Hood; a Team of Texas Critics Take Textbooks to Task," *Time* (December 31, 1979): 76.
44. Edward B. Jenkinson, "How the Mel Gablers Have Put Textbooks on Trial," in *Dealing with Censorship*, p. 108.
45. "Was Robin Just a Hood," p. 76.
46. Jenkinson, p. 115.

# Censorship in Public
# Libraries

# Chapter 6
# Intellectual Freedom and Censorship in Public Libraries: The Rights of Library Users and Library Employees

The nation's courts have not dealt with public library censorship as often as school library censorship. The lack of legal decision making might suggest to some that public libraries experience censorship only rarely. Such a belief would be in error, however, and the explanation for the lack must lie elsewhere.

## REASONS FOR LACK OF COURT DECISIONS

One obvious explanation is that public libraries serve all age groups, including adults, and thus may provide materials that might be considered objectionable in school libraries. But this is only a partial explanation: because children also use public libraries, objections are often raised concerning public library materials for many of the same reasons advanced against school library materials. Many censorship attempts involving public libraries have been the direct result of adult fears that "objectionable" materials might fall into the hands of children.

Yet, because of the diversity in the population served by public libraries, the governance of public libraries, whether it is provided indirectly by advisory boards, or directly by elected officials, may be more supportive of a broad range of library materials than school boards are. In fact, many library boards have taken firm stands against censors.

Other reasons have been offered for the relatively few court cases:

1. If or when book bans do occur in public libraries, there is little economic incentive to challenge them. No great financial hardship is caused to authors and publishers by the failure of a few libraries to purchase their works. In fact, such a ban may increase interest

and sales. Several years ago when a small public library in Iowa banned a sensational novel, the librarian received a thank you note from the publisher, who reported that many orders for the book had been received as a direct result of the censorship action.

2. Potential censors may be discouraged from challenging public libraries in court because library or local government administrative procedures operate to make court challenges unnecessary, or because an open challenge to a public library may receive little popular support or even be criticized.[1]

3. As several studies have indicated, censorship may take place before materials are acquired. Librarians may seek to avoid public censorship controversy by avoiding the purchase of potentially controversial materials. (See Chapter 10 for more discussion of "precensorship" or "internal censorship.")

Finally, use of the public library is voluntary, and as public librarians are only too well aware, many citizens are not regular library users. Public library users as a group may not be inclined to find library materials objectionable, or to object formally if they do.

## CONSTITUTIONAL ISSUES RELATING TO PUBLIC LIBRARY MATERIALS

The absence of clearly defined legal precedents need not prevent discussion and consideration of the potential constitutional and professional issues in public library acquisition and circulation activities, nor of raising such questions as: does a public library patron have a constitutional right to obtain materials from the public library? If so, what responsibility does the public library have to make those desired items available?

### The Right of Access to Public Library Materials

The right to read and/or to have access to information and ideas is an available right under the constitution. The higher courts have not yet had the opportunity to determine the extent to which an individual may exercise that right with respect to specific items in a public library. It seems reasonable to assume that fewer judicial restrictions would be placed upon the contents of a public library than upon those of a school library, because of the diverse clientele served by the public library.

The library profession, however, has asserted its commitment to the idea of freedom of access to the information and ideas available in library materials. The American Library Association has taken a firm position in favor of the freedom to read. It has said:

> The freedom to read is essential to our democracy. . . . It is in the public interest for publishers and librarians to make available the widest diversity of views and expressions, including those which are unorthodox or unpopular with the majority. . . . It is the responsibility of publishers and librarians to give full meaning to the freedom to read by providing books that enrich the quality and diversity of thought and expression. By the exercise of this affirmative responsibility, book-men can demonstrate that the answer to a bad book is a good one, and the answer to a bad idea is a good one.[2]

This freedom of access to ideas is not limited to adults and should be freely available to children as well.

> The American Library Association opposes libraries restricting access to library materials and services for minors and holds that it is the parents—and only parents—who may restrict their children—and only their children—from access to library materials and services. Parents who would rather their children did not have access to certain materials should so advise their children. The library and its staff are responsible for providing equal access to library materials and services for all library users.[3]

Censors often argue that materials should be removed or restricted because they are inappropriate or objectionable for use by children. Although their concern may be and frequently is genuine and well-intentioned, it is misguided. Were libraries to carry out the censors' wishes and prevent children from using and/or borrowing materials available in their collections, far greater harm would result. Libraries are not parents, and they undertake parental duties at the risk of usurping parental rights.

Although public libraries derive funding from a variety of sources, most of their support comes from taxes paid in and by the communities they serve. For this reason they have a clear mandate to provide the broad range of materials necessary to serve the needs and interests of citizens in those communities. It has been pointed out that the public library is the only alternative for the majority of citizens to meet their literary, informational, and intellectual needs. They must be met by the public library, or they may not be met at all:

> Private bookstores and libraries do exist, but are accessible only to those who can afford to pay. For those who cannot pay, the public library is the sole channel of access not only to relatively expensive hardcover books but to less costly items like magazines and even daily newspapers.[4]

As a practical matter, however, no public library can afford to purchase, catalog, and house every publication that comes on the market. For this reason, selection and acquisition must be carried out under established policies and guidelines. Selection or acquisition policies may establish purchase priorities and may of necessity exclude certain types of materials. A library may be unable or unwilling to duplicate little-used or expensive materials that are accessible elsewhere in its community or service area. For example, a public library might reasonably decide not to purchase legal reference works when a local law library makes those resources available to the public.

There are other circumstances in which the interests of public libraries may be best served by withholding materials from circulation or by declining to acquire them. In wartime, for example, it may be legitimate to withhold secret or classified materials relating to military operations, should they, by unusual circumstance, be among the library's holdings. Similarly, in times of civil disorder, a public library may have a legitimate interest in not acquiring or in withholding inflammatory materials from circulation. If the circulation of materials might render the library or its staff liable for civil damages because the contents are defamatory, or because they invade privacy, refusing to circulate them would be justified. But such circumstances are all highly unusual, and care and caution must be exercised to avoid overraction to potential hazards. A clear and present danger must exist in order to justify restrictions on materials which, under normal circumstances, would satisfy the library's selection standards.[5]

Obscene or pornographic materials may pose serious questions and difficulties for library policymakers. The laws governing obscenity and pornography vary from state to state,[6] and:

> Until recently, one would have thought that the material itself was dispositive, so that a librarian would enjoy no greater latitude than a bookseller or newsdealer. Since the Supreme Court stressed the motives of the distributor, and linked culpability with "pandering," the position of the librarian is much less clear. Some states have specific statutory exemptions for the "scientific or educational" dissemination of obscene material, a defense presumably available to the librarian if it is available to anyone. At least one court has implied such a defense without explicit legislative authority, recognizing a vital distinction between profit-making and educational or scientific objectives. Thus arguably the library need not suppress allegedly obscene matter even when the bookseller must do so. This is not to say that a library must make such material available, but only that a decision to withhold it may be judged by a different standard than that to which the prudent bookseller or newsdealer adheres.[7]

Even though obscene or pornographic materials are rarely requested by their patrons, public librarians may still occasionally require a rational or philosophical foundation for decisions to acquire or not to acquire them. It is possible that a patron could request obscene or pornographic materials for use in research, to satisfy an interest in obscenity laws or related social issues, or for other purposes. Whereas content in and of itself may not be sufficient reason for not acquiring the materials, cost or infrequency of demand for them may provide sufficient justification for not purchasing them, should that decision be the one taken.

Another difficulty may arise when the means or methods libraries use to achieve their political or financial interests result in restrictions upon the access or availability of materials. For example, libraries have a legitimate interest in maintaining good relations with governing authorities, but failure to acquire controversial material solely in order to avoid conflict with authority is not legitimate.

> The curtailment of first amendment or other civil liberties has never been permitted on fiscal or expediency grounds. Unpopularity or feared loss of legislative support cannot justify denial or abridgment of individual rights. . . . The possible reduction of support for the public library cannot justify the withholding or suppression of controversial works.[8]

An agonizing dilemma is posed for the library caught between the rock of censorship and the hard place of loss of funding. In reality no happy solution may be possible, but the optimistic view is that the education of the governing authority by the library staff in the principles of intellectual freedom, and the unwavering support of those principles by librarians and by other interested groups in the community, may provide substantial help in a present difficulty and prevent a future recurrence.

A public library may also have a legitimate interest in "raising the literary standards of the community by encouraging citizens to read higher quality literature and to eschew the vulgar."[9] But if book purchase funds are used to supply only those authors whose works will meet the standards of "higher quality," censorship results because access to the full range of available authors has been restricted. Appropriate selection decisions result in a balanced collection, with quality literature represented in it along with those works that receive less critical regard but more popular acclaim and demand. Finally, the claim that "the circulation of certain materials would imply approval of the contents, either by the library itself or by the governmental unit that supports the library"[10] is not sufficient to warrant restricting them. "If anything the conclusion is precisely opposite; only the avoidance of censorship will dispel the impression of approval or disapproval of views expressed in particular works."[11]

The American Library Association and the Association of American Publishers have addressed the issue explicitly in "The Freedom to Read" statement:

> Publishers, librarians and booksellers do not need to endorse every idea or presentation contained in the books they make available. It would conflict with the public interest for them to establish their own political, moral or aesthetic views as a standard for determining what books should be published or circulated. Publishers and librarians serve the educational process by helping to make available knowledge and ideas required for the growth of the mind and the increase of learning. They do not foster education by imposing as mentors the patterns of their own thought. The people should have the freedom to read and consider a broader range of ideas than those that may be held by any single librarian or publisher or government or church. It is wrong that what one man can read should be confined to what another thinks proper. [12]

Public libraries are responsible for providing information on a wide variety of topics and interests and for representing in their collections all available points of view in controversial matters in equitable proportions. They have a responsibility to support intellectual freedom both in concept and in practice.

> Because the public library seeks to enlighten rather than indoctrinate, a basic goal of the institution is the preservation of intellectual freedom. The public library offers the whole spectrum of man's knowledge without moralizing as to its use and without fear of its potential impact on users. It attempts to escape the narrow confines of an imposed way of thinking. There is no starting place; there is no end; there is no "graduation." It offers materials at all levels of development on many subjects of interest and in all forms, to be studied as superficially or as deeply as a person wishes, needs, or is capable of doing. [13]

## The Rights of Library Employees

The preservation of intellectual freedom is correctly described as a goal to be achieved. It is no easy matter, and difficulties are bound to occur along the way. But it is a goal worth pursuing, and a worthy mission for an honorable profession. Library policies, procedures, and practices should further its attainment and safeguard those who work towards it. Thus another question arises; what are the constitutional rights of librarians and other library employees?

Library staff members may be able to assert rights in two areas:

1. When it is determined that library patrons have constitutional rights of access to library materials, librarians or other library workers may argue that they may not be compelled to withhold those materials from the patrons. Thus:

> a librarian might argue that he may not constitutionally be compelled to withhold books to which his patrons have a right of access because forcing him to violate the liberties of persons he serves imposes an unconstitutional condition or obligation on his own job. The force of this argument would of course depend upon judicial acceptance of the reader's claim of access to library materials.[14]

2. Drawing on the "well-established body of constitutional protection for academic freedom,"[15] librarians may also be able to claim the intellectual component of their work—reviewing, selection, cataloging, reference and information service—as a constitutionally protected form of expression.

> While the applicability of academic freedom to the community public library is less obvious, society's interests in safeguarding freedom of expression and inquiry do seem comparable. The library shares with the university a prime function of transmitting knowledge and information from one generation to another. Both institutions provide the raw material with which to question, challenge and probe accepted values and entrenched ideas. Censorship and the abridgement of acquisition and circulation policies jeopardize these interests much as oaths, investigations and surveillance endanger academic freedom. If public libraries are to be storehouses of intellectual freedom, performing the function that society expects of them, then like universities they must be freer than other institutions.[16]

## Importance of Library Policy

If public libraries are to fulfill their intellectual missions and thus serve their communities, they *must* adopt policies and procedures that take explicit cognizance of the rights of citizens in those communities and those of their employees as well. By doing so they may reduce the potential for conflict and they will increase their readiness to deal with it. When public libraries operate consistently in accordance with clearly defined and explicitly stated principles derived from legal and professional standards, they have two major points in their favor when controversy arises:

1. They can assert that they have operated consistently with those standards and not from lesser motives.
2. They can assert that they have adhered to their own established procedures.

See Chapter 11 for more discussion on the importance of established policies for libraries. Controversy does arise, as the following chapters show. Censorship challenges may be issued in court or they may be issued in the social or political arenas. They are to be expected in a nation populated by persons of widely differing backgrounds and values, especially when they are connected with an institution, the public library, that is intended to serve as an intellectual forum for them all.

## REFERENCES

1. Robert M. O'Neill, "Libraries, Liberties and the First Amendment," *University of Cincinnati Law Review,* 42 (2) (1973): 212–14.
2. "The Freedom to Read. A Joint Statement by: American Library Association and Association of American Publishers" (Chicago: Office for Intellectual Freedom, American Library Association, 1953). See Appendix 2 for the complete statement of "The Freedom to Read."
3. American Library Association. "Free Access for Minors: An Interpretation of the Library Bill of Rights" (Chicago: Office for Intellectual Freedom, American Library Association, 1981). See Appendix 2 for the complete statement of "Free Access for Minors: An Interpretation of the Library Bill of Rights."
4. O'Neill, p. 240.
5. O'Neill, p. 248.
6. See, for example, Paul S. Wallace, *Regulation of Obscenity: A Compilation of Federal and State Statutes and Analysis of Selected Supreme Court Opinions* (Washington, DC: U.S. Library of Congress, Congressional Research Service, 1976).
7. O'Neill, p. 248.
8. O'Neill, p. 251.
9. O'Neill, p. 249.
10. O'Neill, p. 250.
11. Ibid.
12. "The Freedom to Read. . . ."
13. Gerald M. Born, "Public Libraries and Intellectual Freedom," in *Intellectual Freedom Manual* (Chicago: Office for Intellectual Freedom, American Library Association, 1974) Part 3, p. 4.
14. O'Neill, p. 241.
15. O'Neill, p. 244.
16. O'Neill, p. 246.

# Chapter 7
# Public Library Censorship:
# Legal Issues

Public librarians have suffered the trial of censorship in and out of the courtroom. Library directors' jobs in Alabama, Florida, and Utah have been threatened by censorship controversy, and in Virginia and Washington objections to materials in their collections resulted in lawsuits filed against public libraries. The cases described in this chapter all involved either some form of litigation or some formal change in the governance of the public library by its local governing body.

## DISMISSAL OF LIBRARY DIRECTORS: TWO CASES

### Davis County, Utah

Jeanne Layton, director of the Davis County (Utah) Public Library, was dismissed from her position in 1979 for " 'spending of taxpayer's money for books whose value to the community is not optimum.' "[1] At issue was Don DeLillo's *Americana,* a novel containing passages that were alleged to be obscene. After her dismissal, Layton told reporters: "I'm not a good person to pick on—I fight back when I'm attacked."[2] She had had nine years of service as the library's director and had been employed by the library for 19 years, during which time she had "enjoyed a harmonious, honest and straightforward relationship" with the five-member library board of trustees."[3] The relationship changed with the appointment of Morris Swapp to the board in January 1979. Prior to his appointment, in his role as mayor of one of the communities served by the county library, he had filed a complaint against *Americana.* Although he described the novel as "rot and filth," a library staff review committee disagreed and recommended that it be retained in the collection.[4] Once appointed to the library board, Swapp asked the other trustees to ban the book, and they too refused. Subsequently he borrowed the book, said that he would not return it, and paid for it. Layton, following the board's instructions, replaced the missing copy with one of several gift copies of *Americana* the library had received.

In May 1979, two more new trustees were appointed. One was a "conservative businessman, the other a member of Citizens for True Freedom, an antipornography organization."[5] On August 9, 1979 the county commission, "for reasons known only to its membership," removed the position of director from the county's merit system, thus depriving Layton of the protection of the merit system's normal dismissal and grievance procedures.[6] The following week, Swapp and the two new trustees asked Layton for her resignation in a letter that they signed. The letter contained seven "objections" to her management, including one objection to her selection of library materials.[7]

Calling the objections "trumped up charges," Layton responded to them at a library board meeting on August 21.

> She explained that she followed library policy on four of the issues—selecting books—including *Americana*, choosing book categories, processing materials, and setting up bookmobile stops. On the charge that she had destroyed a set of Hardy Boys books, she pleaded ignorance. On two charges (that) she was uncooperative, she cited her 20-year record.[8]

Again she was asked to resign; again, she refused.

Seventy interested citizens had appeared at the August board meeting. Nearly 200 attended the September meeting, but they were not allowed to speak. At that meeting, the trustees voted, three to two, to fire Layton, effective September 28.[9]

Layton appealed to the county merit council for determinations of whether her position as library director was part of the merit system and whether the trustees had acted properly in dismissing her. The council determined that it was the only body that could confer exempt status upon the library director's position, and that Layton was entitled to the protection of merit system grievance and dismissal procedures. It did not determine whether the library board had provided that protection to Layton before it fired her. The board contested the council's decision in state district court, but the court's ruling upheld it. Layton filed suit in federal district court on October 24, asking for damages and preliminary injunctive relief. The Freedom to Read Foundation aided her struggle by providing contributions to help defray her expenses. Relief was granted. The court observed that the requirements of due process must be met. "Implicit in the concept of 'due process' are two ideas: first, government, here Davis County government, must follow its own rules. Second, it must do so within a reasonable time."[10] Layton was reinstated to her position, and she won the 1980

Robert B. Downs Award given by the Graduate School of Library Science of the University of Illinois for "an outstanding contribution to intellectual freedom in libraries." Later she was awarded a $50,000 settlement for her legal expenses; from this settlement reimbursement was made to the Freedom to Read Foundation, to individual contributors, and to Layton herself for expenses incurred in the proceedings.

Despite her struggle to retain *Americana* she was later "forced to act on a majority opinion of a library review committee and a unanimous concurring vote by the Library board to remove copies" of the book. She said "it bothers me personally to have this happen, but I have no choice but to follow the decision of the board."[11]

## Fairhope, Alabama

Claire Oaks had served the city of Fairhope, Alabama as public library director for two controversial years before conflict with city officials ended in her leaving the post. Like Layton, she received financial support from the Freedom to Read Foundation for her legal battle.

As library director, Oaks's first meeting with the mayor (James Dix) was concerned, in part, with the presence of the books *The Joy of Sex* and *More Joy of Sex* in the library's collection.[12] Throughout her subsequent dispute with the mayor and the city council, Oaks maintained that an underlying cause of it was her refusal to remove the books from the library. Other differences between Oaks and city officials existed, including disagreement about library budget matters. She was fired in April 1979 when the city council dismissed the library board, which had supported Oaks, by rescinding the ordinance that had established it. The city council then fired Oaks and created a new library board.

Oaks filed suit in federal district court. An out-of-court settlement was reached, giving her legal costs, lost salary, and a guaranteed appointment to her position through September 1979. The library board dismissed her again at the end of September. Oaks decided to seek other employment while new legal action was pending. The federal district court for the Southern District of Alabama decided the second suit for the defendant city of Fairhope in May 1981.[13]

Both Layton and Oaks defended their positions and their principles in court at tremendous personal cost. Neither was forced to stand alone; both received the support from professional colleagues and other supporters of intellectual freedom and librarians' rights through the Freedom to Read Foundation and other professional groups. Both the Davis County commissioners and the officials of the city of Fairhope violated or changed existing ordinances or procedures in order to take action against the two directors. In neither case was victory complete for either side. In both cases, the censorship issues were articulated and the principles of intellectual freedom were defended, helping to create a public awareness of the challenges facing public libraries.

## LEGAL ISSUES IN A CASE OF CHILDREN'S ACCESS TO SEX EDUCATION MATERIALS

Leo Meirose, director of the Tampa-Hillsborough County (Florida) Library, also faced the challenge. In February 1981, parents of a seven-year-old Tampa girl gave her a public library copy of Peter Mayle's *Where Did I Come From?* to read. The child took the book to school, where a teacher overheard her discussing it with classmates and confiscated it. The teacher complained to the PTA president, who in turn complained to elected officials. Shortly afterwards, a county commissioner lodged a formal complaint against Mayle's and five other sex education books: *The Beauty of Birth* by Colette Portal, *How Babies are Made* by Andrew C. Andry and Steven Schepp, *Love and Sex in Plain Language* by Eric W. Johnson, *Where Do Babies Come From?* by Margaret Sheffield and Sheila Bowley, and *The Wonderful Story of How You Were Born* by Sidonie Matsner Gruenberg. The library received 145 complaint forms, many of which were photocopied duplicates of others. Complaints asserted that *Where Did I Come From?* was pornographic. One-third said that the book should be restricted. Of the remainder, half called for banning the book, and half called for its destruction or burning.

In response, librarians noted the many favorable reviews the books had received and that the books were not pornographic. Children's Services Coordinator Linda O'Connor-Levy defended the library's position when she wrote:

> Materials on the human body are selected for all children's collections in our library system, with care shown for the age-level of the presentation, accuracy, and appropriate method of presentation.[14]

Director Meirose formally recommended that the books be retained "with no restrictions except those imposed by individual parents on his or her child."[15] The city-county library board accepted his recommendation.

A 180-member "Taxpaying Parents against Kiddie Smut" was then formed to protest and prevent the provision of objectionable materials to children by libraries. The group conducted demonstrations against the library board's decision. The *Newsletter on Intellectual Freedom* recounted the events which followed:

> . . . things began to heat up. First, a local pharmacist, who claimed to have collected 3,000 signatures on a petition protesting the board's decision, publicly requested that the books be moved. Second, Shirley Correll, state director of the Pro-Family Forum, conyinced both the Hillsborough County Commission and the Tampa City Council to ask the city-county library board to move the six books from the children's section of the library to the adult section.* This meant that, although they could still be checked out by children at the main library, the books would be in another building, and thereby, relatively inaccessible to children.
>
> At this point, questions were raised about the authority of the library board to set library policy pertaining to selection and review of materials, the respective voting powers of city and county board members, and the ultimate control of the library by the city and the county. Upon examination of a 1969 statute, the Tampa city attorney found that the City Council did not have to ask the library board to move the offending books; the Council could *demand* it. It was also discovered that the equal voting rights allotted by tradition to county and city board members violated a 1961 city-county agreement, which gave full suffrage to Tampa members and only advisory powers to Hillsborough County representatives. In fact, although the county's contribution to library funding had risen to fifty-six percent of the budget, the county was found to have no control whatsoever over library policy.
>
> Then, the heat brought the issue to a boil. On the one hand, county commissioners claimed that because the county pays for more than half the library budget, it is entitled to [at] least half the voting power on the joint library board. City Council argued that the city has invested millions of dollars in buildings and facilities and is legally obligated only to share its resources with the county on a pay-for-services basis. Mayor Martinez entered the act by contending that neither the Hillsborough County Commission nor the Tampa City Council should have final authority over the library system. He said [it] should be completely under the control of the mayor, as are all other city services.
>
> In January, the City Council library subcommittee recommended that the mayor assume control of the library, with a ten-member board—appointed by the mayor—equally representing the city and the county. In protest, the [county] Commission voted to withhold its share of funding for the library. In February, however, after the city

---

*An earlier issue of the *Newsletter* had noted that Shirley Correll of Pro-Family Forum had led an unsuccessful attempt to have Eldridge Cleaver's *Soul on Ice* and Richard Wright's *Black Boy* removed from the state department of education's approved list of books.

threatened to shut down the library system by March 6 if the county didn't pay up, and commission relented and signed an agreement that tied the county to another year of city control of the library. Nevertheless, the Commission requested that the Council establish "a library board appointed on a population basis" and responsible to both the city and the county.

In March, the City Council rejected the county's request for a joint board independent of either city or county authority and rescinded its earlier representation on an advisory board. The new proposal created a library board consisting of seven members representing only the city. In the meantime, the county had developed a specific plan in which an independent board of fourteen members would be appointed by the county (six members), the city (six members), and Temple Terrace and Plant City (one member each). The commissioners also considered setting up a separate county library system and discussed asking state legislators to pass special laws that would take precedence over city ordinances.

In April, the County Commission again rejected the City Council proposal to make the library system a city department under the mayor. In a letter to Martinez, the Commission said it considered the transfer of authority to be a breach of the city-county agreement. The mayor, in turn, assured the county that the proposed library board would be free to set policy without mayoral interference. But the county refused to budge.

With threats and counterthreats flying, and the July budget deadline approaching, the city of Tampa threw one last ultimatum into the already sizzling brew. Either yield to the city's demands, city officials told the County Commission, or the city will sever its ties with the county and split up the library system. In this inauspicious setting, Library Director Meirose, who for more than a year had courageously defended what he eloquently called "the insecurity of freedom," as well as the autonomy of public libraries, resigned.[16]

The sequence of events in Tampa was remarkable for several reasons:

- It involved the confiscation by a teacher of a book given to a child by her parents.
- It involved the confiscation of public library material by a teacher.

In the face of political pressure, the governing authority apparently found itself unable to reach a decision without first experiencing considerable conflict about authority and responsibility for the decision. The library, however, was prepared to defend and did defend its selection of the materials that became controversial, and even in the disturbances that resulted, it remained firm in its defense of the principles of intellectual freedom.

## THE CONFIDENTIALITY OF LIBRARY RECORDS

In 1981, the Washington State Library proved to be an equally firm backer of intellectual freedom in its defense of the principle of confidentiality of library circulation records. It became necessary to do so when the Moral Majority of Washington brought suit against it to obtain the names of persons who had borrowed the film *Achieving Sexual Maturity*. According to Sue Fontaine, public information officer at the state library:

> The Moral Majority's ultimate goal was to learn which schools in Washington State had shown the film, so that the information could be used to bolster its proposed legislation calling for closer parental/ community control of sex education in the public schools.[17]

Fontaine's article in *Library Journal* (June 15, 1981) presents in detail the sequence of events which culminated in the Moral Majority's request that the suit be granted dismissal with prejudice.

On January 29, 1981, the Washington State Moral Majority's head, Michael Farris, phoned the state library's film department and asked for a list of the film's borrowers. He was informed that library policy held circulation records to be confidential. Farris then contacted the assistant attorney general assigned to the library and notified him of his intent to bring action to get the records. Farris was asked to make his request formally and in writing. Farris's formal request was made in a letter dated February 3, 1981. The request cited the Public Disclosure Act and asked for "all public school districts and their employees who have received from your library the film *Achieving Sexual Maturity*."[18] Since the state library had adopted a "Privacy of Library Circulation Records Policy" in 1972, the assistant attorney general reviewed the policy, along with Washington's Public Disclosure Act, and other related documents. It was found that film circulation records were an exception to the library's general practice of eliminating circulation records as soon as materials were returned: they were held for six months to allow time for processing and to be available should problems with the returned films come to light. Thus the information Farris requested could have been provided without a great burden of extra searching for the library staff.

On February 9 its attorney advised the state library to "stand firm in its denial." He further advised that library policy and regulations did not conflict with the Public Disclosure Act because library circulation records were excepted from disclosure.

On February 11 the Moral Majority filed its petition for disclosure in state court, asking for names of the school districts borrowing the film, dates of film showings, audience size, grade level, whether viewers were in

coeducational classes, and whether classes were compulsory. Accompanying the petition was a compromise "offer of settlement," which was later
rejected by the library.[19]

A hearing was scheduled for February 23. The assistant attorney
general's brief asserted that disclosure of the circulation records would be
an unconstitutional invasion of privacy and that disclosure would violate
the First Amendment's free speech clause. Shortly before the scheduled
start of the hearing, Farris announced that he was dropping the suit. His
stated reason was that " 'he got what he wanted' " and would pursue his
quest for information on sex education materials directly with the public
schools.[20] In response, the library's attorney stated that "the library did not
compromise its position in any way. We refused from the outset to divulge
the names of any individuals, and have not retreated one iota. We are
prepared to argue our case on its merits."[21]

Granting Farris's motion for "dismissal with prejudice" meant that
the library could not be taken to court again for this same cause. Mixed
reactions greeted the decision: on the one hand, the library was spared the
considerable expense of court proceedings, but on the other hand, the
opportunity to obtain a court decision which might set a precedent in favor
of the protection of patron privacy in library circulation records was, for the
moment, lost. The library's case was strong, however, and despite the fact
that it lost the chance to prevail in court, it prevailed in principle. The
principle of confidentiality of library circulation records was maintained,
and a possible attempt by the Moral Majority to censor the use of the film in
Washington schools was delayed, if not prevented, because the library
adhered to its policy and its procedures.

## A CHALLENGE TO GAY MATERIALS

The public library's free distribution of *Our Own*, a newspaper concerned with activities of the gay community and their parents and friends,
stirred a controversy in Virginia Beach, Virginia, which resulted in a
city-wide referendum and a lawsuit.

For two years *Our Own* had been available, along with other local
publications, in multiple copies for free distribution in the community
information section of the libraries. It was also available in libraries in
neighboring cities.[22] Library director Marcy Sims described it as "a well-
written, authoritative medium of communication for homosexual men and
women in Tidewater."[23]

In the spring of 1980, a local reporter saw the March issue, which contained a cartoon reprint from the *National Lampoon*. He wrote an article for his paper and included interviews with city council members about *Our Own*. The published article drew the attention of some fundamentalist ministers, who expressed concern about the presence of the newspaper in city libraries. Community reaction was felt in city council, and although no formal request for reconsideration was made, the mayor asked the library board for a recommendation for appropriate action.

The library board heard statements on the issue of removal and decided to cease free distribution of the newspaper because it was the only one still being received for distribution by that time. It recommended retaining one copy as part of the periodical collection. The city council could not agree on a recommendation, and the mayor ruled that the library board's decision would stand.

An organization called the Coalition for the Family was formed under the auspices of one of the fundamentalist churches. It obtained enough signatures to add this question to the November 1980 ballot: "Shall publications whose primary purpose is to depict or advocate, by picture or word, homosexual acts, be displayed, distributed, or received into the public libraries of Virginia Beach, Virginia?"[24] Sixty percent of the voters voted no, and 40 percent said yes or, following the library's recommendation, did not vote upon the question. Because it was an advisory referendum, city officials were not bound by the outcome, and no change was made in the library board's earlier decision to retain one copy in the periodical collection.

The American Civil Liberties Union and the Unitarian-Universalist Gay Community brought suit in federal district court, seeking a preliminary injunction ordering the library to continue to distribute copies. The injunction was not granted because the plaintiffs did not show a likelihood of success on the merits of their case. Later they dropped the suit.

## SUMMARY

The five cases covered in this chapter—Layton in Utah, Oaks in Alabama, Meirose in Florida, the state library in Washington, and the public library in Virginia Beach—share common elements:

1. All of the challenged materials dealt in some manner with human sexuality, and/or were considered to be pornographic or obscene. None had been judged obscene by the courts.

2. In each case, the decision making, as governed by library policy, was at issue.

3. Four of the five situations involved ex post facto changes in the ordinances or regulations that governed the library:
   - Layton's position was removed from the Utah merit system by action of the Davis County Commissioners, although it was later restored by the county's merit council.
   - The library board of the city of Fairhope was dismissed following a change in city ordinance.
   - The city of Tampa and the county of Hillsborough entered into a dispute over the governance of the city-county library.
   - A referendum was placed on the Virginia Beach ballot to determine whether the library could have materials on homosexuality in its collection.

4. Most involved the actions of organizations that had been formed to act, or did act, against the challenged materials: Citizens for True Freedom, to which one of Davis County's conservative library trustees belonged, Tampa's Taxpaying Parents against Kiddie Smut and Pro-Family Forum, Washington's Moral Majority, and Virginia Beach's Coalition for the Family.

5. The Utah Library Association, the Freedom to Read Foundation, the American Civil Liberties Union, and others rallied to the support of the libraries and librarians under challenge.

6. Two of the cases—Tampa-Hillsborough and the Washington State Library—were directly concerned with the question of children's access to materials on human sexuality. And, in each of the other three cases, the implication was there that children were in danger of being exposed to material being challenged as "obscene."

## REFERENCES

1. "Library Board Censured over Firing," *Wilson Library Bulletin* 57 (4) (December 1979): 216.
2. "Utah Librarian Fights Dismissal by Trustees over DeLillo's *Americana*," *American Libraries* (November 1979): 572.
3. Ibid.
4. Ibid.
5. Ibid.
6. 484 F. Supp. 956, 960 (1979).

7. *American Libraries* (November 1979): p. 572.
8. Ibid.
9. Ibid.
10. 484 F. Supp. 956, 961 (1979).
11. "Censorship Dateline: Davis County, Utah," *Newsletter on Intellectual Freedom* 29 (6) (November 1980): 127.
12. Calvin Trillin, "U.S. Journal: Fairhope, Alabama," *New Yorker* (June 11, 1979): 81.
13. 515 F. Supp. 1004, 1005 (1981).
14. "Tampa Library Boards Keep Controversial Books," *School Library Journal* (September 1981): 15–16.
15. Ibid.
16. "Tampa-Hillsborough County Library Director Resigns," *Newsletter on Intellectual Freedom* 31 (4) (July 1982): 115, 147.
17. Sue Fontaine, "Dismissal with Prejudice," *Library Journal* 106 (12) (June 15, 1981): 1273.
18. Fontaine, p. 1274.
19. Fontaine, p. 1276.
20. Fontaine, p. 1277.
21. Ibid.
22. Marcy Sims, "The Lessons of Virginia Beach," *Newsletter on Intellectual Freedom* 30 (6) (November 1981): 153.
23. "Fundamentalists Challenge Gay Rights Journal," *American Libraries* (September 1980): 465.
24. "Virginia Beach Referendum Results." *Newsletter on Intellectual Freedom* 30 (1) (July 1980): 6.

# Chapter 8
# Children's Access, "Dangerous" Materials, and Other Concerns in Public Libraries

Even when they do not result in legal action, complaints against public library materials are a recurring phenomenon in contemporary national life. The incidents described in this chapter, many of which concern children's access to information about human sexuality, all pose serious threats to intellectual freedom.

## CHALLENGES TO SEX EDUCATION MATERIALS

Certain materials, such as the sex education manual *Show Me!*, with its photographic illustrations and its broad coverage of sexual topics, have been attacked many times. Perhaps no attack was stronger than that directed at the Oak Lawn, Illinois, Public Library in 1980.

*Show Me!* had been shelved on the parents' shelf in the children's department for five years before the controversy began. Early in 1980, a mother, having brought her children to the library, happened to notice some young girls poring over the book, talking and laughing as they did so. She looked to see what was producing their reaction, and on seeing what it was, took the book away from them. She reported her experience to a friend, and eventually the story reached Oak Lawn resident Mary Ann Hardek. (Hardek's husband John was a village trustee.[1]) Early in August, Hardek telephoned library director Michael O'Brien to object to *Show Me!* as part of the library's collection. Upon checking, O'Brien discovered that both of the library's copies were missing. He conveyed this information and also told her that no additional copies would be purchased. Thus her complaint seemed to be rendered moot.

In September, Hardek appeared at the library board meeting, with one of the library's missing copies. She expressed her objections to the board and suggested that they take action to ban the book from the library. The board instead directed O'Brien to review the book, respond to Hardek in two weeks, review the library's sex education collection, and report back to the board in November.

Hardek's cause was taken up by the Oak Lawn Community Awareness for Life Group, Inc., which was run by Nancy Czerwiec, already known to the community for her fight against an abortion clinic. Local news media were alerted, and a room at a local motel was rented to serve as a place for the organization to display the book and gather signatures on a petition to remove it. The VFW hall was used for the same purpose. This strategy was effective in producing a full-blown controversy in the fall of the year, a time when the library board was also involved in a referendum to decide whether it would gain autonomy from the village board, and the controversy fueled opposition to library autonomy. As one writer has suggested: "The timing of these developments was more than coincidental. The opponents of *Show Me!* checked out the book from the library in February and then waited until September to express their complaints."[2]

At a special board meeting in early October, O'Brien reported that the courts had not found *Show Me!* to be obscene and suggested that a decision on the book be made in connection with the review of the library's other sex education holdings.

The library board's next meeting that month received full news media coverage. The book's opposition again took the opportunity to speak. From Nancy Czerwiec:

> "It is not educational," she declared, referring to *Show Me!* She went on to explain the book's impact: "In the final analysis, I see the destruction of marriage and I see a country being destroyed." Her comments won a standing ovation from a receptive audience of her supporters. To many residents, the book had come to symbolize the erosion of traditional American values, and they were fervently convinced that its retention would lead to the "moral decay of Oak Lawn youth."[3]

O'Brien's report, based on library staff reviews of the book, was due at the next meeting.

An overflow crowd attended the November meeting, held one week after the elections. Again, all news media were represented. Czerwiec launched her appeal:

> [She] stood up before the crowd at the library board meeting, wrapped in an American flag. Holding her stepson, she told the board that if *Show Me!* stayed in the library, her stepson Christopher would not

grow up to be a good man. Books like *Show Me!*, she said, create mass murderers like John Gacy.[4]

Other speakers defended the book, but the final speaker again called for its removal. O'Brien reported the results of the staff review of sex education books in the collection and its recommendation that *Show Me!* be retained, with restrictions. It would be shelved in the children's librarian's office and circulated in response to requests from adults. The board voted to accept this recommendation.[5]

Although the board's vote settled the question of the book's status in the public library, it did not settle the community controversy. Hardek and Czerwiec continued the fight together, if for somewhat different reasons. In Hardek's view, all books molded children's behavior: "*Show Me!* encourages teenagers to have sex and teaches them that homosexuality is normal, she says. Why should the Oak Lawn Public Library support those views?"[6] Czerwiec's opinion was stronger, as may be seen by this excerpt from an interview:

> "They'll take an open-minded child who is growing up and try to sway them to sexual promiscuity and sexual perversion and say that's normal."

Why?

> "To alter the family. Once you destroy the family, the country's gone."

Why would someone want to do that?

> "We know there's a tremendous struggle in the world to see who's going to dominate, the free world or not the free world. So how do you destroy any country? You must destroy the one element that holds the country strong, and that is the family," she explains.[7]

Czerwiec also assigned librarians their share of the responsibility for children's upbringing:

> "What the librarians are doing today is abdicating their responsibility to the child. Once a child is about to go into a public institution like the school or the library, those institutions must accept responsibility for what is available to them. Libraries don't want to assume that responsibility today. I don't think parents should be infringed upon because the libraries have moved into license, which is the abuse of freedom. If it is true freedom that is operating in the library, they will be answerable to the community, which means that if a child comes in and asks for a book there should be restrictions."[8]

Such views, despite their apparent contradictions, were persuasive to a great many people in the Oak Lawn community. Ultimately Hardek and Czerwiec succeeded in persuading an Illinois legislator to introduce a bill that would have toughened the state's obscenity law, by removing the librarians' exemption from the section that made the giving of "harmful materials" to persons under 18 illegal and made violation a misdemeanor punishable by up to 18 months in jail. The bill was later defeated. Unfortunately, so was the library's referendum in Oak Lawn.

Another chapter was added to *Show Me!*'s story when the Supreme Court's 1982 decision in *People v. Ferber* reached a decision that forced its publisher, St. Martin's Press, to cease publication of *Show Me!* The case was concerned with child pornography, and it arose from the complaint of a bookstore owner—who had been sentenced in 1978 to 45 days in jail for selling two nonobscene films—that his First Amendment rights had been violated.[9] A unanimous Court ruled against the use of children in sexually explicit pictures or live performances, not to protect the public, but to protect the children. In a letter addressed to booksellers, St. Martin's president Thomas J. McCormack observed:

> The Court ruefully concedes that the decision, aimed at deterring child abuse, could have an 'overbroad' application to which legitimate works—like *National Geographic* or *Show Me!*—might fall prey. But they could not bring themselves to find a way around this difficulty. The result is a vexing erosion of our First Amendment right to read and publish, and the loss of a superb and enlightened work of sexual orientation for young people. I have no illusions that everyone approves of *Show Me!,* but there are many parents, educators, librarians, and psychologists who feel as I do that it is the best available book for fostering in young people a healthy attitude towards sex.
> So I am deeply distressed that such a book must now be suppressed. But the Court tells me that it is the law of the land, and I hereby withdraw the title from the St. Martin's Press trade list.[10]

The Supreme Court has allowed very few exceptions to the rule of free speech, but with its decision in *People v. Ferber* made it clear that child pornography is a permissible exception.

## AN UNSATISFACTORY SOLUTION: RESTRICTING ACCESS FOR MINORS

In Oklahoma, controversy erupted over Wardell Pomeroy's *Boys and Sex* and *Girls and Sex,* two standard titles from sex education literature, and the Oklahoma County Libraries in Oklahoma City experienced a four-month ordeal that began in December 1975 with an open letter to library director Lee Brawner. The letter was published in the *Oklahoma Journal*, a daily newspaper with 70,000 circulation. The larger (280,000 circulation) *Daily Oklahoman* received but did not publish the letter, which was written by Ben Travis, who described himself as a "father, Sunday School teacher, and a public school teacher."[11] In his letter, Travis characterized the books as irresponsible and noted that *Boys and Sex* "advocated and encouraged" premarital sex.

The appearance of the letter coincided with the monthly meeting of the Metropolitan Library Commission. Although it lacked a quorum for official business, the meeting did provide a forum for discussion of the letter and the books. A *Journal* reporter covered the meeting and filed a report for the next morning's edition. In an atmosphere of high news media interest, the library staff reviewed the books in order to respond to the Travis letter. The library's response quoted from Pomeroy's introduction to *Boys and Sex,* in which he described his experience in seeing the human anguish that results from sexual mistakes because of misinformation and fears about sex. The response also noted that the library must leave parents free to select materials on sex for their children, and that the library must provide a wide variety of materials in order to serve all parents in the community. The books were retained. The library's policy on book selection and citizen complaints about library materials was clear: the library director and staff were responsible for carrying out both activities, within the framework provided by the established policies.

The library staff then decided to try to establish an optional card system, in which a limited access card for children could be obtained by parents if they chose to do so. At the January meeting of the Metropolitan Library Commission, the idea was presented, and the staff was instructed to explore the optional card concept. Under such a system, parents would be given a choice between an unlimited access card for their children, or in accompanying their children to the library to obtain a restricted card, which was available for children under the age of fifteen and a half.

Meanwhile public opinion was being molded, in part, through the efforts of one of the county commissioners, who disagreed with the library's decision to retain the books, and said that he favored "putting the books on the same basis as 'R' or 'X' rated movies by requiring parents to check out the books for their children."[12] The commissioner sent letters to ministers in the county and to elected officials, asking their participation in "what he called an all-out fight against the two books."[13]

In the resulting furor, the library director decided to restrict access to the two books to borrowers holding adult cards only. When announcement of this decision was made, public reaction from the other side—the side opposed to restrictions on access—became more pronounced, finally at least equalling the uproar over the library's refusal to ban the books. A special meeting of the library commission was called for February 19, and more than 20 citizens, angry about the restricted policy, attended. An attorney from the American Civil Liberties Union told the library commission,

> Limited access is a violation of your own policies. You adopted the Library Bill of Rights in 1969 and the Freedom to Read Statement in 1973. You don't even have to go as high as the U.S. Constitution. You don't seem to understand the broad impact of what you've done. You've made a terrible mistake. I hope you reconsider.[14]

A survey of other public libraries was suggested, in order to discover how many had an optional card system. The staff surveyed 227 public libraries serving populations of 100,000 or more. It received 186 responses. A minority of those responding (15%) issued more than one type of children's library card and a minority also restricted access to library materials. Thus the survey responses were of limited usefulness in resolving the issues before the commission. But it had other results.

> It did, however, show a questionable stance on the part of some libraries across the country. In answer to a question about what kinds of materials are restricted, one library . . . listed "six titles, including *Exorcist* and *Rebel without a Cause.*"
> The survey made one realize that possibly a third or more of our nation's libraries have bowed, in one way or another, to demands for restriction. Or, horrible thought, maybe they do their *own* restricting! Only five of those libraries admitting they had a restrictive policy said the policy was the result of *community* pressure.[15]

With public opinion apparently equally divided, the library director requested legal advice on several questions: whether under the state or federal constitutions the library commission had the authority to deny access to anyone any material not otherwise restricted by law to anyone on the basis of age, and if so at what age; and whether minors had any recourse if access was denied to them, and what penalities if any might the commission, administration, and staff have to pay if they violated a person's rights by forbidding access.[16]

The director and the library commission received the legal advice that the commission could deny access to anyone under 18 to library materials that they deemed unsuitable for minors. But the commission was also reminded that its mission was the provision of library service and not the protection of "the safety and morals of the community."[17] The commission must ensure that juveniles have equal access to all materials unless and until there were legally defensible rules which "discriminate against some citizens (juveniles) by denying them access to certain materials while allowing other citizens (adults) access to those same materials."[18] The attorney also noted the practical difficulties involved in establishing such rules. He raised questions concerning what criteria could be used to establish whether a particular book would be unsuitable for children and whether the commission itself would select materials or would delegate the job to the director. He also asked how the commission could assure parents that there would be no possibility that their children could inadvertently be exposed to unsuitable material and whether it was possible to physically segregate unsuitable materials from children in each library facility.

The commission appointed a committee to study all the available information and to recommend a course of action at the April 15 meeting. The committee voted to rescind the restrictive policy and to return to the open access policy, and, as a result, the commission accepted the recommendation.

The restrictions on access were removed from all except Pomeroy's books, which the commission required to be classified as adult, although they could be checked out by any patron. The long journey from December 18 to April 15 was over, and one librarian remarked, "Everyone was weary. There was no high hilarity on our part. I suppose we all realized that the struggle was just part of our jobs. . . . When you stop to think of it, that's a good part of what professionalism is all about."[19]

## RESTRICTING ACCESS TO A POPULAR CHILDREN'S AUTHOR

Although she is unquestionably among the most popular and best loved of children's authors, the works of Judy Blume are also among the most frequently challenged by censors. Recent objections in school libraries illustrate the controversy.

- A Florida minister, representing the Movement for Moral Decency, complained to school officials about several Blume novels, and *Deenie* in particular. Objecting because the books "described the act of masturbation . . . and that amounts to a 'how to' " for children, he asked school officials to remove *Deenie* and others from school libraries in the area.[20]
- An Elk River (MN) school board removed *Are You There God? It's Me, Margaret; Deenie;* and *Then Again Maybe I Won't* from the elementary school libraries. The books then became available in

a reserve library, where secondary students could borrow them, with parental permission. Rae Pace Alexander's *Young and Black in America* was also removed to the reserve library.[21]

- In Montana, parents requested that Blume's works, along with Norma Klein's, be removed from an elementary school library.[22]
- Pennsylvania parents wanted *Forever* banned from the junior-senior high school their children attended. They called the book "filth" and "pornography." One expressed the view that *Forever* suggests that "the best cure for teenage problems is promiscuity."[23]

Even among her supporters, there were those who felt that Blume had "gone too far," "let her readers down" or misled them, with the publications of *Forever* and *Wifey*, her two most controversial novels to date. One of the most widely noted controversies concerning *Wifey* took place in the public library of Columbus County, North Carolina, in 1980.

The issue started when the 12-year-old daughter of Elaine Cumbee, a rural resident of the county, brought *Wifey* home from the library. Cumbee's protest that the book contained "sexual filth" reached the county commissioners, who voted in secret session to order library director Amanda Bible to remove it. They were supported in their decision by 4,000 signers of a petition, who threatened not to pay their library tax if the book remained in the library.[24]

The library board of trustees, however, held firm and rejected the commissioners' action. They requested a ruling by the state attorney general. The ruling said that the county commissioners did have the right to formulate county library policy, and that minors could be denied access to adult books, unless accompanied by parents. It was suggested that the book be placed in an adult section, with circulation limited to patrons over 18 years old.[25]

A workable compromise was offered: parents wishing to restrict their children's reading could request cards for them which would bear the notation 'Restricted—J." The compromise proved satisfactory to all sides of the question, although comparatively few parents (less than 100 of a possible 6000 at one point) requested the special designation.

Because they take cognizance of parents' right to authority over their children's reading, restricted borrowers' cards for children are preferable to restricted shelves or book removal. They are a workable compromise, yes, but not a perfect solution. An extra burden is created for library staff who must enforce borrower restrictions. And, despite restrictions placed on loaned materials, children may still use materials while in the library of which their parents might disapprove. Open access for every child, with his/her parent/guardian monitoring use of the library, remains the best option and places responsibility where it should be, with the parent or guardian.

Speaking about the issue of restricting children's library access to her books, author Judy Blume had these comments for some of her Minnesota critics:

> Children write to me complaining of restrictions placed on certain books in their libraries. They say that it embarrasses them to ask for the books, it makes them feel as if there is something wrong with the books and with them. Placing books on a reserve shelf is not a solution.
>
> It's always the children who lose out in cases like this. . . . The librarian . . . seems to be the only person involved who is speaking out for them. . . . The real solution to books that are considered "controversial" lies in communication. If parents can talk to their kids about what they're reading, and if teachers promote the open discussion of ideas with their students, then there should be no threat from any book, and no need to remove it from the library shelf, or place it under restrictions, or be afraid of it at all.
>
> The problem with a censorship case like this is—where does it stop? Once the school board is willing to start removing books because they offend community members, they have opened up themselves to tremendous pressure, and a big job ahead. . . . Somebody in the community could decide to go to bat for the children.
>
> Censors don't seem to understand what is important to young people. They may not care. And they don't listen. Fortunately there are some, like the librarian, who do.[26]

## MINORS' ACCESS STATUTES

The issue of restricting free access to materials by minors has posed other difficulties and has received legislative attention in several states. In Colorado, a statute restricting minors' access was passed by the legislature but vetoed by the governor. Pennsylvania and Georgia passed similar statutes that took effect in 1980 and 1981 respectively. Georgia's was found unconstitutional in federal district court in 1981. Pennsylvania's was challenged in court but was allowed to stand after a December 1981 state court decision. Although not aimed at libraries only, such statutes have disturbing implications for children's use of library collections.

An earlier California case, *Moore v. Younger* (127 Cal. Rpt. 171, 1976) concerned the state's Harmful Matter Statute (Pen. Code, SS 313-313.5). The statute made criminal the distribution to minors of "harmful matter," defined as:

> . . . matter, taken as a whole, the predominant appeal of which to the average person, applying contemporary standards, is to prurient in-

terest, i.e., a shameful or morbid interest in nudity, sex, or excretion; and is matter which taken as a whole goes substantially beyond customary limits of candor in description or representation of such matters; and is matter which taken as a whole is utterly without redeeming social importance for minors.[27]

A complaint was filed in California superior court by individual city, county, public school, and university librarians; and by the American Library Association, the California Library Association, the Los Angeles Public Library Staff Association, and the board of Library Commissioners of Los Angeles. It sought a declaration that the statute was unconstitutional. This judgement was not granted. The trial court instead declared that:

. . . it was the intention of the Legislature to provide librarians with exemption from application of the Harmful Matter Statute when acting in the discharge of their duties; (and) . . . alternatively that the availability and distribution of books at public and school libraries is necessarily always in furtherance of legitimate educational and scientific purposes . . . and accordingly, librarians are not subject to prosecution.[28]

The plaintiffs appealed the judgement, but the appeals court dismissed the case, stating that they had ". . . achieved all that they could expect as a result of their attack on the statute as librarians. . . ."[29]

Georgia's minors' access statute enacted 5 years later stated in part that:

It shall be unlawful for any person knowingly to engage in the business of selling, lending, giving away, showing, advertising for sale, or distributing to any minor; or to have in his possession with intent to engage in the said business; or otherwise to offer for sale or commercial distribution to any minor; or to display in public or at newsstands or any other business establishment frequented by minors or where minors are or may be invited as a part of the general public, any motion picture or live show, or any still picture, drawing, sculpture, photography, or any book, pocket book, pamphlet, or magazine the cover or content of which contains descriptions or depictions of illicit sex or sexual immorality or which is lewd, lascivious, or indecent, or which contains pictures of nude or partially denuded figures posed or presented in a manner to provide or arouse lust or passion or to exploit sex lust or perversion for commercial gain, or any article or instrument of indecent or immoral use.[30]

Suit was filed by the American Booksellers Association, the Association of American Publishers, the Freedom to Read Foundation and others, who contended that the law was invalid because it was overbroad and vague; it constituted a prior restraint on speech and press; and that it unconstitutionally infringed their First, Fifth, and Fourteenth Amendment rights under the constitution. The Georgia Federal District Court's opinion stated that, because the law did not contain standards by which obscenity could be determined, it could result in the prohibition of nonobscene, constitutionally protected material. Thus it was unconstitutional. It also determined that the law was invalid for reasons of vagueness and overbreadth.

In Pennsylvania, by contrast, a state court judge ruled that the law was not unduly restrictive of adult access to nonobscene materials from which minors were restricted. The plaintiffs planned an appeal of that ruling.[31]

## "DANGEROUS" MATERIALS AND OTHER CONCERNS: EVENTS IN CALIFORNIA, MINNESOTA, AND VIRGINIA

Censors have by no means restricted their concerns to public library materials for children. Their numbers have included those who would also restrict the available choices of library materials for persons of all ages.

In California, for example, the book *Recreational Drugs* had to be temporarily restricted to the reference section of the Alameda County Library System. A county commissioner urged removing it, after hearing an objection from a constituent whose son had the book in his possession when he suffered a drug overdose. The library staff, however, recommended retaining the book. A compromise decision placed the book temporarily in the reference section, where it was available to all readers (although it could no longer circulate). At the end of a six-month period, library director Ginnie Cooper's final decision returned *Recreational Drugs* to the circulating collection.[32]

In Minnesota, the Superior Public Library's board decided to ban Michael Castleman's *Sexual Solutions: An Informative Guide* after a 67-year-old woman complained about its presence in the collection. Thus it became the first banned book in the library's 83-year history. But when the library board's decision occasioned complaints against the removal from the mayor, the Superior Federation of Labor, and the Douglas County Democratic Party, it was reconsidered, and the board decided to retain the book, but to restrict its circulation to young persons.[33]

The novels of Harold Robbins, Sidney Sheldon, Jacqueline Susann, and others were the objects of attempted censorship in Abingdon, Virginia during 1980. The long battle that ensued resulted in a triumphant victory for the Washington County Library and for intellectual freedom.

It began when the Rev. Tom Williams went to the library to discover whether it had copies of Sheldon's *Bloodline* and Robbins's *The Lonely Lady,* which had been used as evidence, by their defense, in a trial of three merchants accused of selling obscene materials. When he found them in the library, he demanded that the director, Kathy Russell, get rid of them and all other books by the two authors.

Russell responded according to policy and procedure by asking Williams to complete a complaint form about the books. He refused, and took his complaint to Bobby Sproles, chairman of the county board of supervisors, who agreed with his objections. Williams then returned to the library to ask once more for the books' removal. Russell again refused to comply with his request. Williams then demanded access to the library's circulation records in order to determine whether the books had been borrowed by minors and threatened criminal charges against Russell if that were so. Again, Russell refused.

Williams and Sproles responded by launching a public campaign against the library and against Russell: "They sought to publish the most 'objectionable' passages in a paid advertisement in a local paper. When this was refused, they distributed the excerpts on street corners."[34]

Kathy Russell's public response defended intellectual freedom in libraries, based on the Library Bill of Rights. She noted that Williams's request for circulation records was improper under Virginia law. She asked for a public apology to the library staff and to herself and for a retraction of "untrue and unfounded statements."[35] The library board, and its chairman, Dr. E.B. Stanley, defended Russell. A meeting was scheduled for November 17, then rescheduled for the next day, when Williams and Sproles said they could not attend the earlier meeting. Despite the attempt to accommodate their appearances, Williams and Sproles did not attend the November 18 meeting, contending that "a decision had already been made."[36] When they also advised their supporters not to attend, the way was left open for the library's supporters. Writing for the *Newsletter on Intellectual Freedom,* Henry Reichmann described the meeting:

> The library board met first in executive session. Thanks to Kathy Russell's diligent work, all members were well-informed about the principles of intellectual freedom in libraries. They had studied the Library Bill of Rights and its "interpretations" and were firm supporters of the First Amendment. Although the charge raised by Williams and Sproles that all decided secretly in advance did not appear true, clearly the two did not enjoy much support.
>
> The executive session was followed by a public meeting in which an overflow crowd of more than 200 people, all supporters of the library and free expression, packed the room. Individual after individual, civil group after civic group expressed opposition, many eloquently, to the censorship attempt. A petition signed by 1,900 of Abingdon's 5,000 residents in support of the library staff was presented. Resolutions of support came from Kiwanis, Civitan, Booklov-

ers and Rotary clubs in Abingdon, the faculties of neighboring Emory and Henry Colleges and Virginia Highlands Community College, the American Association of University Women's Abingdon Branch, People, Inc., the Head Start Policy Council, League of County Voters, Abingdon Jaycees, and the Washington County Ministerial Association. Lelia Saunders, President of the Virginia Library Association, Allen Bonney Brooks, chair of the VLA Intellectual Freedom Committee, and I were greeted with vigorous applause and exceptional warmth when we voiced our support.

A victory had been won. The meeting revealed that when the library stands firm against the censor, when community support is organized, and when the issues are made clear, supporters step forward.[37]

Libraries and librarians do not always resist censorship so forcefully, and the defenders of intellectual freedom are not always victorious. Reichmann also notes that a library nearby "quietly pulled the three titles questioned in Abingdon from the shelves and assigned them an 'under the counter' status."[38] But the examples of courage, intelligence, and good sense provided by the public librarians and their supporters described in these chapters afford every hope that the victory is possible and the certainty that it is worth every effort.

## REFERENCES

1. Anthony Schmitz, "The Purity Patrol," *Student Lawyer* 10 (2) (October 1981): 15.
2. Robert P. Doyle, "Library Censorship: Two Case Studies. Oak Lawn, Illinois," *Newsletter on Intellectual Freedom* 30 (1) (January 1981): 23.
3. Ibid.
4. Schmitz, p. 16.
5. Doyle, p. 24.
6. Schmitz, p. 16.
7. Ibid.
8. Schmitz, p. 40.
9. "The Court's Final Flurry," *Time* (July 12, 1982): 52.
10. Thomas J. McCormack to booksellers, August 16, 1982.
11. Duane H. Meyers, "Boys and Girls and Sex and Libraries," *Library Journal* 96 (4) (February 15, 1977): 458. This article provides a complete account of this Oklahoma censorship controversy.

12. Meyers, p. 460.
13. Ibid.
14. Meyers, p. 462.
15. Ibid.
16. Ibid.
17. Meyers, p. 463.
18. Ibid.
19. Ibid.
20. "Censorship Dateline: Lake County, Florida," *Newsletter on Intellectual Freedom* 31 (21) (March 1982): 43.
21. *Elk River News* (August 5, 1982): 1.
22. "Censorship Dateline: Whitehall, Montana," *Newsletter on Intellectual Freedom* 31 (2) (March 1982): 43.
23. "Censorship Dateline: Scranton, Pennsylvania," *Newsletter on Intellectual Freedom* 31 (3) (May 1982): 84.
24. Ibid.
25. "Amanda Bible Honored," *Newsletter on Intellectual Freedom* 31 (1) (January 1982): 5.
26. *Elk River News,* p. 2.
27. *California Penal Code, Section 313,* subdivision (a).
28. 127 Cal. Rptr. 171, 172 (1976).
29. 127 Cal. Rptr. 171, 173 (1976).
30. "Minors Access Laws," *Newsletter on Intellectual Freedom* 31 (4) (July 1982): 138.
31. "Pennsylvania Minors Access Statute Upheld," *BP Report* 7 (3) (December 1982): 7.
32. "Success Stories: Oakland, California," *Newsletter on Intellectual Freedom* 31 (5) (September 1982): 169.
33. "Success Stories: Superior, Wisconsin," *Newsletter on Intellectual Freedom* 31 (2) (March 1982): 58.
34. Henry Reichman, "Library Censorship: Two Case Studies. Washington County, Virginia," *Newsletter on Intellectual Freedom* 30 (1) (January 1981): 25.
35. Ibid.
36. Ibid.
37. Reichman, p. 26.
38. Ibid.

# Chapter 9
# Meeting Rooms, Exhibits, and Programs in the Library

**Libraries which make exhibit spaces and meeting rooms available to the public they serve should make such facilities available on an equitable basis, regardless of the beliefs or affiliations of individuals or groups requesting their use.**

**Article 6**
*Library Bill of Rights*

Public library meeting rooms and exhibit spaces serve as valuable resources for their communities. When used for events or displays which satisfy the informational, educational, cultural, or entertainment needs of citizens, they increase the public library's effectiveness as a community forum. Citizens who do not otherwise make use of the library's collection may still be drawn to the library for meetings, programs, classes, and displays or exhibits that interest them.

## MEETING ROOM USE

Libraries have traditionally permitted public use of their meeting rooms and exhibit spaces. Although the criteria for public use varies from library to library according to the availability and arrangement of physical space, and to the priorities for use that each library must set, policies should be established to permit equitable use. The American Library Association has recommended that:

Libraries maintaining exhibit and meeting room facilities for outside groups should develop and publish policy statements governing their use. These statements can properly define and restrict eligibility for use as long as the qualifications do not pertain to the content of a meeting or exhibit or to the beliefs or affiliations of the sponsors.[1]

Just as it is true that the majority of any library's collection is noncontroversial, it is also true that thousands of citizens are served each year, without complaint or incident, by the events and exhibits provided at public libraries. From time to time, however, controversy has arisen in connection with library-sponsored activities and with public use of library meeting or exhibit facilities, as the experiences of libraries in Minnesota, North Carolina, California, and Virginia demonstrate.

The Hennepin County (MN) Library provides meeting facilities in 16 of its 25 libraries. The library's meeting room policy and its accompanying regulations govern the use of all meeting facilities.

Meeting room use by the Transcendental Meditation Society has been the object of recurring controversy, and citizen complaints have cited objections that libraries should not "make possible the control of our young people's minds by Hindu gods" or support "the corrupting of the minds of little children."[2] While such statements have registered only the individual complainant's point of view, they have also raised a substantive issue: although the Transcendental Meditation Society, as a nonprofit organization, had qualified for use of the library's meeting facilities under its meeting room policy, was it a recognizable religion? If so, could it be permitted, along with other religious groups, to use library meeting rooms?

A 1976 county attorney's opinion had addressed the issue of rental of library meeting rooms for church services or other church purposes on an occasional basis at a fair rental value. The opinion cited *Pratt v. Arizona Board of Regents* (1974)[3], which held that it was constitutionally permissible under both state and federal constitutions for the Arizona Board of Regents to permit the rental of the Arizona State University football stadium for a series of religious meetings held by Dr. Billy Graham, as long as fair rental value was received and the rental was not undertaken on a permanent or indeterminate basis. Under these guidelines the Hennepin County library had permitted the short-term use of meeting rooms by churches whose congregations awaited the completion of new church buildings or the availability of other places for worship services.

The library had maintained records of several years of use by church groups. By late 1977 these records showed that church use took place at times when the libraries were not open for regular business, and that it appeared to be developing into a kind of ongoing use that could be regarded as at least semi-permanent. Because religious group use threatened to become permanent, its legality became questionable. Because it took place when the libraries were closed, there was difficulty in maintaining necessary building security measures. In addition, church use ran the risk of establishing a difficult precedent to follow: because church groups met each

Sunday, they were using library facilties for more time and with more regularity than could be permitted to other not-for-profit groups who wished to schedule meetings without charge at more usual or popular times of the week (e.g., weekday evenings).

With these facts in hand, Hennepin County Library administration recommended that church and religious groups' use of library meeting rooms be restricted to hours when the libraries were open to the public and staffed by employees competent to carry out all required building security measures. These same requirements were made for all other groups using meeting facilities. Criteria for free use of meeting rooms by religious groups were that their meetings be devoid of any religious worship, free and open to the public, and have as their basic intent the giving or exchange of information. The library board approved the recommendation, and it became library policy in 1977.

Citizens have objected to the use of Hennepin meeting rooms for Transcendental Meditation Society on the grounds that they are religious, and as such, forbidden by the establishment of religion clause of the First Amendment to take place on government-owned property. However, because the TM introductory lecture (the only one permitted—charges are made for attendance at subsequent lectures in the series) meets the requirements set forth by legal opinion and in the library's meeting room policy, it has continued to be permitted in Hennepin libraries, despite occasional controversy and complaint.

## CONTROVERSIAL EXHIBITS

Recurring controversy of a political and social nature challenged the Forsyth County (NC) Public Library's granting of permission for Ku Klux Klan exhibits in 1979 and 1981. On February 5, 1979, a local Klan leader, Vernon Logan, reserved the auditorium of the headquarters library for the evening of February 26 in order to exhibit Klan memorabilia. He followed regular library procedures by booking the auditorium through the library's audiovisual department, but he also notified library director William Roberts and the local press.[4] An article about the exhibit appeared in the next morning's paper.

A snow storm on February 7 prevented the regular library board meeting, but on February 16 an informal meeting of the director, the assistant director, and some members of the board took place, at which there was a discussion of the "Use of Library Auditoriums" policy. The policy provided that auditoriums could be used by outside organizations anytime during regular library hours, for programs that were of public interest, open to the public, and free of charge. Auditorium bookings were taken on a first-come-first-served basis, no more than 45 days in advance, and no group could make bookings for the same day and hour on a continuous basis.

On February 21 the library board met. Logan and another Klan member attended. The board took no action concerning the Klan exhibit, but it did approve a library staff request to have an exhibit elsewhere in the library building to counterbalance the Klan's exhibit. It also named a committee to study the auditorium use policy.

By February 23 the exhibit and the library began receiving national media attention, and on February 26 the Klan exhibit was installed as planned. That morning the National Association for the Advancement of Colored People (NAACP) began picketing the library. The library's own exhibit was set up. The library board and staff reviewed the Klan's exhibit at 6:00 p.m. and asked for the removal of one item because it was "offensive."[5]

The exhibit opened at 6:30 p.m. At 7:10 members of the (Communist) National United Workers Organization arrived and began shouting anti-Klan messages. At 7:15 p.m. members of the American Nazi Party arrived and returned the shouts. By 7:20 p.m. the auditorium had to be closed because of overcrowding and because of a shouting and shoving match that had developed. At 7:30 the library itself had to be closed to guarantee the safety of people there and to disperse the crowd of 300 people who had gathered.[6]

Despite the turmoil that had ensued, the library had remained firm in adhering to its own policy and in its defense of the right of the Klan to use library exhibit facilities under that policy. Its board and staff were supported in their courageous stand by the county attorney, whose memo on February 22 had stated, in part:

> As you know, the Library is a public facility and as such is available for the public's use for library purposes. The United States Constitution protects freedom of speech, assembly and association; and so long as individuals and organizations are allowed to provide displays at the Library, I do not believe that Government can pick and choose which individuals or organizations can participate and which ones cannot. This assumes, of course, that the organization abides by reasonable rules applying to all and conducts its display in a lawful manner. I further do not believe that the courts would sanction the use of a subjective standard of what is in "the public interest" in deciding which individuals or organizations to allow to utilize a public facility. There is always a difference of opinion as to the worth of a cause of association, but that has to remain a personal judgment which cannot

affect the situation referred to in the newspaper article. Government cannot make choices on this basis under the circumstances involved here. The same standards of availability must apply to everyone.[7]

Their stand was also praised by the press. From the *Raleigh Times:*

> Freedom isn't always pretty, and it wasn't Tuesday night at that Ku Klux Klan exhibit in the Winston-Salem public library. But it was still freedom . . . (and) however repugnant he undoubtedly found the show's substance, Forsyth County Library Director William H. Roberts III was right in permitting that show, and right in his reasons.
>
> It was a simple question of free speech for Roberts, who said any other group would have the same access to library facilities. "It's no different from the local Black Panthers group. If the Panthers wanted to come in, they certainly could."
>
> There is no freedom as hard to maintain and to act on as the freedom of the other man to have his say, no matter what or how disturbing that say may be. Whenever one man's voice is squelched, it becomes that much easier to squelch the next.
>
> Roberts understood this, and acted on it. He deserves his community's thanks.[8]

And from Winston-Salem's *Sentinel:*

> The library's board and administration acted quite properly in permitting a ku klux klan exhibit to be displayed in the main library auditorium. . . . The wisdom of the library staff was even more evident in the decision to offer elsewhere in the building its own display, countering the klan propaganda with facts about the sordid history of such organizations.
>
> . . . To turn the klan away would have been a popular decision, no doubt. No one with an ounce of humanity likes the idea of the group's hodgepodge of bigotry, misinformation and malicious fantasy being aired in a public forum.
>
> Yet is is just such airing that poses the greatest threat to a gospel of conspiracy and oppression, whether it be preached by klansman, pseudo-nazi or communist. Such things thrive only on suppression. In the competitive marketplace of ideas, under the full light of day, their shoddiness and silliness is plain to see.[9]

Two years later, the Klan again requested and received permission for an exhibit. This time the exhibit took place in the library's new auditorium, part of a multimillion dollar addition to the building. In the interim between the two exhibits, a new policy on the use of library meeting rooms and exhibit spaces was developed. It enhanced the earlier policy by the addition of three statements.

> Programs and exhibits may not disrupt the use of the library by others. Persons attending the meeting are subject to all library rules and regulations.

> Library facilities shall be left in a clean and orderly condition. Users shall pay the cost for repair of any damages to facilities. The library will not be responsible for materials or equipment left in the building by users.
> Granting of permission to use library facilities does not constitute an endorsement by the Library Staff or Board of the user or its beliefs.[10]

The Klan's proposed 1981 exhibit met all policy requirements and took place free of problems or public disturbance.

The concept that the granting of permission for the use of library meeting or exhibit facilities does not constitute library endorsements of a sponsoring group's ideas, policies, or activities is crucial to public acceptance of library meeting room and exhibit policies that guarantee constitutional rights of free expression. The experiences of public libraries in California and Virginia illustrate this point.

Early in 1980, the Hayward (CA) Library Commission granted permission for a display of homosexual books, photographs, and artwork to the Berkeley-based Pacific Center for Human Growth.[11] In the fall of the year when the display went on view, citizens objected to it, arguing that it promoted homosexuality. The library commission affirmed its earlier stand and the display remained in the library. In Fairfax County (VA) the public library's display "The Lavender Life," which included books supporting and explaining homosexual lifestyles, encountered objections for similar reasons. The library did not withdraw the exhibit because of the objections; rather, it augmented it with the addition of other books on homosexuality in order to provide balance to what was seen by some as a display advocating homosexuality.[12]

"Exhibit Spaces and Meeting Rooms; an interpretation of the Library Bill of Rights" addresses the issue of fair representation of all points of view when it states:

> Exhibits and meetings sponsored by the library itself should be organized in a manner consistent with the Library Bill of Rights, especially Article II which states that "libraries should provide materials and information presenting all points of view." . . . Those who object to or disagree with the content of any exhibit or meeting held at the library should be entitled to submit their own exhibit or meeting proposals which should be judged according to the policies established by the library.[13]

Adherence to these guidelines furthers the guarantees of constitutional freedoms as they apply to the use of public library meeting and display facilities.

## LIBRARY-INITIATED PROGRAMS

Programs or meetings sponsored or initiated by public libraries can also be controversial, as the following examples attest:

- A Minnesota public library informational program on life insurance, oriented to the needs of the consumer, drew fire from local insurance salespersons who accused the presenter of ignorance and incompetence and objected to the library's sponsorship of the presentation. Library staff were assured of the presenter's competence by prior review of the program, and, although opposition was expressed by local insurance representatives during the program, it was permitted to be held.
- A North Carolina public library screening of *La Cage Aux Folles,* which centers on a homosexual couple, encountered public objection and had to be cancelled because the library did not have a policy which dealt with the presentation of R-rated films in its facilities.[14]
- The inclusion of the game *Dungeons and Dragons* in Dubuque, Iowa's Carnegie-Stout Public Library's summer program for children met with protest from a religious pressure group. Supported by petitions signed by adults, the library director continued the program.[15]

"Library-Initiated Programs as a Resource; an Interpretation of the Library Bill of Rights" states:

> Selection of library program topics, speakers, courses, classes, and resource materials should be made by library staff on the basis of the interests and needs of library users and the community. Library programming should not exclude topics, books, speakers, media, and other resources because they might be controversial.[16]

Once selected, programs should not be removed or cancelled "because of partisan or doctrinal disapproval." The rights of persons to attend library-sponsored programs are analogous to their rights to have access to other library resources; thus, they "should not be denied or abridged because of (their) origin, age, background, or views."[17]

The American Library Association recommends that libraries develop and publish policies governing exhibit spaces, meeting rooms, and library-sponsored programing. Explicit statements of library objectives and priorities serve to keep the library's public and staff properly informed as to the nature of appropriate meeting room or exhibit space use and library programing. Citing ALA's statements in the policies can provide a valuable link between the individual libraries and accepted professional opinion on these topics. (For sample policies, see Appendix 1; for ALA's statements on "Exhibit Spaces and Meeting Rooms" and "Library Initiated Programs as a Resource," see Appendix 2.)

## REFERENCES

 1. American Library Association, "Exhibit Spaces and Meeting Rooms; An Interpretation of the Library Bill of Rights" (Chicago: Office for Intellectual Freedom, American Library Association, 1981). See Appendix 2 for the statement.
 2. Hennepin County Library, Staff memoranda describing citizens' complaints concerning meeting room use by the Transcendental Meditation Society.
 3. *Pratt v. Arizona Board of Regents.* 110 Ariz. 466 (1974).
 4. Forsyth County Public Library, "Chronology of Klan Exhibit, February 26, 1979."
 5. Ibid.
 6. Ibid.
 7. P. Eugene Price, Jr., County Attorney, to William H. Roberts, Director of Libraries, "Memorandum," February 22, 1979.
 8. "Protect KKK's Rights" (editorial), *Raleigh Times* (February 28, 1979).
 9. "Disquiet at the Library" (editorial), Winston-Salem *Sentinel* (February 28, 1979).
10. Forsyth County Public Library, "Policy on the Use of Library Meeting Rooms and Exhibit Space for Groups." See Appendix 1 for the full policy.
11. "Censorship Dateline: Hayward, California," *Newsletter on Intellectual Freedom,* 30 (1) (January 1981): 9.
12. Virginia Library Seeks Compromise in Gay Display," *Newsletter on Intellectual Freedom,* 30 (3) (May 1981): 59.
13. American Library Association, "Exhibit Spaces and Meeting Rooms."
14. "R-rated Film Airing Halted by N.C. Library," *Library Journal* 106 (6) (March 15, 1981): 598.
15. "Dungeons & Dragons in Dubuque," *LJ Hotline* (September 13, 1982): XI–28.

16. American Library Association, "Library Initiated Programs as a Resource; An Interpretation of the Library Bill of Rights" (Chicago: Office for Intellectual Freedom, American Library Association, 1982). See Appendix 2 for the full statement.
17. Ibid.

# Coping with Conflict

# Chapter 10
# Internal Censorship:
# Putting Principles into Practice

Several studies undertaken to determine the nature and extent of censorship in school and public libraries share one conclusion: library censorship has its origins in the libraries themselves, or in their parent organizations, the schools, as well as the communities they serve.

## SURVEYING THE PROBLEM

In the late 1950s, Marjorie Fiske directed a landmark study of California school and public librarians. Her report of the results of that study clearly indicated that the majority of objections to library materials came from within the organizations in which the libraries were located or from the libraries themselves. In the school libraries under study, 42 percent of the objectors to books were librarians; 23 percent were administrative staff; and 8 percent were teachers. In public libraries, 65 percent of the objectors were found to be librarians.[1]

Charles Busha's 1970 investigations into midwestern public librarians' attitudes towards intellectual freedom and censorship found "a marked disparity between the attitudes of some librarians toward intellectual freedom as a concept and their attitude toward censorship as an activity."[2] He concluded that, although many librarians expressed agreement with intellectual freedom principles, many of them "apparently did not feel strong enough as professionals to assert these principles in the face of real or anticipated censorship pressures."[3]

In 1977 the National Council of Teachers of English (NCTE) surveyed secondary school teachers among its membership. While not as large as Fiske's or Busha's, the survey nevertheless revealed that 23 percent of known objections to school materials came from within the school organization: 10.4 percent were offered by administrators; 8.6 percent by teachers or department chairpersons; 2.9 percent by librarians; and less than one percent from boards of education.[4]

In 1980 the Association of American Publishers, the American Library Association, and the Association for Supervision of Curriculum Development jointly sponsored a questionnaire survey of more than 7,000 public elementary and secondary school librarians, library-supervisors, principals, and district superintendents in the United States. The questionnaire elicited information concerning challenges that had occurred during the previous 2 years. Approximately 1,900 responses were returned, and 494 responses reported challenges. One interesting finding was that, although administrators responded that fewer than 10 percent of the challenges came from the staff, librarians reported that over 30 percent of the challengers were staff members.[5]

Politics, religion, violence, negative images of family life or of parents, undermining of the traditional family, secular humanism, criticism of American history, Darwinism and evolution, and values clarification— all have prompted censorship challenges to materials in school and public libraries. But references to sex and human sexuality, perceived obscenity, and the use of objectionable language have prompted almost as many challenges as the others combined. Fiske reported in the 1950s that 49 percent of library objections occurred for these reasons.[6] And in 1980, the AAP/ALA/ASCD study found that 48 percent of challenges were attributed to sex, sexuality, obscenity, and language in the challenged materials.[7]

Fiske reported that, while approximately 50 percent of responding librarians expressed freedom-to-read convictions, approximately 60 percent had decided against book purchases because of actual or potential controversy.[8] Approximately 25 percent of the respondents to the ALA/AAP/ASCD survey reported that selection of materials was influenced as a result of challenges.[9]

From these results it is apparent that there is some professional uncertainty about putting intellectual freedom principles into practice in library materials selection, and that school and public library staffs might benefit from a clearer understanding of the differences between selection and censorship.

## SELECTION VERSUS CENSORSHIP

Lester Asheim in his classic article, "Not Censorship, but Selection," points out the differences. Censorship, he says, is negative. Its intention is to exclude. Selection is positive; it seeks to include material if it can, after determining honestly whether it meets library standards. He notes intent of the author, literary excellence, effect upon the reader, and the time and the customs of the community as standards for selection. He cautions, however, that these standards may be too vague to be reliable at all times, and that they may be the very standards employed by the censor. Asheim writes about the differences in intention which distinguish selectors from censors:

> For the selector the important thing is to find reasons to keep the book.
> . . . For the censor, on the other hand, the important thing is to find
> reasons to reject the book; his guiding principle leads him to seek out
> the objectionable features, the weaknesses, the possibilities for mis-
> interpretation.[10]

Such stringency inevitably leads the censor to examining parts of works more heavily than the entire work and to the problem common to many, if not most, acts of censorship: that some part of the work—its language, one or two isolated scenes or incidents—is objected to, and as a result, the entire work is challenged.

The selector, by contrast, views the work in its entirety and is able to assess the appropriateness of the inclusion of each of its elements within the context of the entire work. The selector seeks to expand the intellectual possibilities for users of the library. The censor almost always seeks to limit them.

The selector expresses implicit belief in the intelligence of the library's clientele and in its potential for growth through the experiences provided by library materials. The censor is fearful that readers lack intelligence, judgment, and virtue.

The censor is elitist; the selector knows that the provision of many intellectual options is the only appropriate behavior in a democratic environment.

Asheim's article was published in 1953 and his analysis is as timely 30 years later as it was at the time of writing.

## TYPES OF PRESELECTION CENSORSHIP

Internal censorship in libraries can be divided, for discussion purposes, into two categories: selection avoidance or *preselection censorship* practices and *postselection censorship* practices.

Preselection censorship occurs when works are not selected because they are controversial in the opinion of library selectors; when too few copies of controversial works are purchased to meet the demand for them; when reviews do not appear in the most frequently consulted review sources; when materials are not selected for the collection because of their subjects or formats; and when specific categories of materials are not selected because of selectors' beliefs that library users lack background to use or appreciate them.

## Controversial Titles

A variety of reasons and justifications are advanced to support pre-selection practices, and the argument that materials are or may become too controversial is frequently the basis for decisions not to select materials whose social, political, religious, or sexual content is seen as objectionable. This criticism has been applied equally to children's and adult materials, to fiction and nonfiction, and to print and nonprint materials. A familiar, if spurious, "greater good principle" is often expressed in support of the argument not to select controversial materials. It suggests that it is of greater benefit to the library or school to keep it free from controversy, opposition, or bad feeling than it is to select materials that might provoke them. This belief also implies, if only indirectly, that the school or public library somehow endorses or promotes the ideas found in all the material selected for its collection. Relying upon these misguided and wrong "principles," many assert that harm to the school's or library's public relations might result if certain materials are selected. Another, more specific, harmful result that is often predicted is that reduction in the library's budget may occur if the selection of controversial material places the library in conflict with funding authorities. Even when these fears are real and justified, it is important to recognize, in order to keep these apprehensions in balance, that selection avoidance thwarts the library's mission to provide an open forum for ideas and fair access to them.

Even if the goal of unbiased selection is at times unattainable, it is still a goal worth pursuing. Failure to select a controversial item that has a rightful place in the library's collection is the first step away from the goal, and that particular opportunity to move towards the goal is lost forever. There have always been censors. The problem is not how to avoid them—"the ostrich is not the . . . library's mascot"[11]—the problem is how to deal with them. There is no better starting place than with the school or library staff and their governing authorities for the teaching of established principles of selection and for developing an awareness of the threat of censorship.

Also advanced in support of the "greater good principle" is the assertion that members of the library's public are not prepared by intelligence or maturity for controversial materials. While such a decision may justifiably be taken at certain times and in certain circumstances (e.g., when proper authority determines that specific items are not appropriate for inclusion in school library collections), it is not justified when it is merely the expression of professional arrogance towards public library users. There is no acceptable argument that public library users are less intelligent or mature than public library staff.

An insidious, quiet, yet very real form of selection censorship is limiting the number of copies of controversial works added to the collection. The purchase of just one copy of a controversial, in-demand title, for example, is tantamount to censorship if other noncontroversial titles are purchased in sufficient copies to meet existing demand.

## Lack of Reviews

Libraries may also justify their failure to select controversial, nontraditional or partisan materials by reasoning that they were not reviewed, or that they did not receive enough reviews. At least one study has concluded, however, that controversial materials are selected more often (in the libraries surveyed) when they receive many reviews than when reviews are less available.[12] While the adherence to a regular practice of using reviews as one external standard for selection of library materials is generally laudable, it must also be recognized that the standard review sources in common use do not review all materials, and that there may be "little or no exposure among selectors to alternative media and appropriate review/announcement vehicles"[13] for other materials. It will take conscientious and sincere efforts by selecting librarians to become aware of the many small press and alternative media producers' review sources, but such sources are available.[14]

Heavy reliance on the "standard" review sources may, in fact, lead to the inadvertent, but habitual or consistent, avoidance of selection in certain subject areas. Materials on labor unions and collective bargaining have been cited as one example, and Sanford Berman has noted the lack of availability of materials on how to organize a union or how to strike or boycott. He states:

> Typically, libraries spend heavily on books, magazines, and services of direct value to investors and business people. . . . However, they spend next-to-nothing for material on how to organize a union, how to strike, how to boycott, how to run a co-op, how to form a collective. . . ."[15]

This lack of inclusion of materials on labor is particularly noteworthy. School and public libraries serve communities of working people in greater numbers than people of high economic status. Many unions can and do supply information to meet workers' economic, social and educational needs at little or no cost to libraries. Yet such materials are underrepresented in most libraries. This is a form of censorship.

## Nonprint Materials

Nonprint media can cause trouble in some libraries. Some librarians are uncomfortable with nonprint media, and conscious or subconscious precensorship of these formats may result. Nonprint materials may be avoided by selectors for any of the following reasons:

- A lack of recognition that some ideas, experiences, and information are given more appropriate and meaningful expression using media other than the printed word.
- A lack of recognition that not all library users are willing to use printed sources.
- A lack of recognition that not all library users are capable of using printed sources.
- A lack of familiarity with the range of materials available.
- A lack of familiarity with review sources.

Experience and awareness remedy these deficiencies. The requirements of unbiased selection necessitate that the experience be gained, and the awareness be attained, in order to avoid a print bias in library collections.

Two other problems arise in relation to selection of nonprint media. Some selectors may be reluctant to purchase from small producers or distributors for fear that replacements for film footage or damaged/missing parts of multimedia works may not be obtainable, should they be needed. Although such concern is certainly understandable, it is not sufficient justification for the failure to include unique or otherwise unobtainable works in the collection.

Selectors may also be reluctant to select media for which the library has no playback facilities, but this reluctance can result in abridgement of the public's right to obtain them for use elsewhere.

## Prejudging Library Patrons

Finally, the attitude that public library users are not "sophisticated" or "intelligent" enough to require or use materials above the beginners' level in certain subject areas warrants careful examination if it is not to become censorship. The subject of mathematics affords a convenient hypothetical example. The library that buys freely in the areas of beginning or business mathematics but balks at purchasing materials for the study of calculus may have failed to realize that for some, the study of calculus is also a beginning.

While it is true that most public library collections are not intended to support scholarly or research needs, it is also true that:

> The librarian's education of demand should *release,* not control, the curiosities and interests of its readers; it will *increase* the diversity of materials to be read, viewed, and heard, not limit the range; it will *improve* the skill with which the library user makes independent judgments, not substitute the librarian's judgment for his own.[16]

## TYPES OF POSTSELECTION CENSORSHIP

Postselection censorship practices limit or constrain library users' access to library materials in other ways. Problems arise from inadequate catalog access to materials, discriminatory service patterns, labeling and expurgation, and physical locations within the library.

### Inadequate Cataloging and Discriminatory Service Patterns

Sanford Berman discusses inadequate catalog access:

> due, variously, to insufficient or imprecise subject tracings; too few title added entries; biased or offensive descriptors that prejudice a person's approach to the material; and awkward or archaic terminology that may frustrate searching, (and) the arbitrary exclusion of whole classes of material. . . .[17]

Among the problems caused by physical location of materials in the collection, Berman notes too many places to look; too many sequences, not all of which may be understandable or even apparent to the library user; locating sensitive materials in unusual or inaccessible spots; scattering material on the same subject in many different nonfiction classes; burying material in unlikely classification numbers; and stack areas that are physically inaccessible for some persons.[18]

Sanford Berman also names discriminatory service patterns, such as library cards that restrict the use of adult material by children, or the restriction of interlibrary loan service to adults only. Finally he lists "meagre and frequently outmoded signage that fails to instantly and understandably signal where things are."[19]

A postselection practice that may discourage young readers in public libraries is that of assigning adult status to works written for a younger audience because of known or anticipated controversy connected with the works. It seems particularly unfair to place such obstacles in the way of younger readers, yet as has been seen in incidents described in this book, such practices are not uncommon.

## Labeling and Expurgation

Another postselection practice, one specifically addressed by the ALA's *Intellectual Freedom Manual,* is the practice of labeling. Labeling is defined as:

> the practice of describing or designating certain library materials by affixing a prejudicial label to them or segregating them by a prejudicial system.[20]

Labeling is regarded as "an attempt to prejudice attitudes and as such, it is a censor's tool." The "Statement on Labeling" continues:

> Some find it easy and even proper according to their ethics, to establish criteria for judging publications as objectionable. However, injustice and ignorance rather than justice and enlightenment result from such practices, and the American Library Association opposes the establishment of such criteria.[21]

Specifically excluded from ALA's opposition, however, are "organizational schemes designed as directional aids or to facilitate access to materials."[22] Thus the affixing of a label designating a work of fiction as a mystery or a romance is not labeling in the sense described here. Labeling works as controversial or objectionable either by some sign to the reader on the works themselves or in their cataloging is an attempt to prejudice the reader and results in censorship.

Expurgation is another form of postselection censorship dealt with by the ALA. It is defined as "any deletion, excision, alteration, or obliteration of any part(s) of books or other library resources by the library."[23] Access to the complete work is denied when it is expurgated, thus censorship occurs. Removal of illustrations from books or magazines is a common form of expurgation.

Labelers and expurgators arrogate to themselves the roles of intermediaries or intervenors by inserting themselves between the creators of a work—its authors, illustrators, editors, publishers, et al.—and its audience. There is no place for such intervention in an intellectually honest and democratically free environment.

## Restricting Access

The common practice of restricting access to certain titles or classes of library materials by locating them in locked cases, on closed shelves or behind the reference librarian's desk, may be a form of postselection censorship if it is done in order to sequester materials that might be considered objectionable. ALA's statement "Restricted Access to Library Materials" advises:

> When restricted access is implemented solely to protect materials from theft or mutilation, the practice may be legitimate. However, segregation of materials to protect them must be administered with extreme attention to the reason for restricting access. Too often only "controversial" materials are the subject of such segregation, indicating that factors other than theft and multilation—including content— were the true considerations.[24]

The statement also notes that restricting access may violate the *Library Bill of Rights*. Because restricted access may suppress materials, it may also violate Article 2, which states that "no library materials should be proscribed . . . because of partisan or doctrinal disapproval."[25] Because it may restrict access to materials by young persons, it may violate Article 5, which states that "a persons rights to use a library should not be denied or abridged because of . . . age. . . ."[26]

Even when a work is accessible through the library's catalog, there may be a barrier to obtaining it for the patron.

> Because a majority of materials placed in restricted collections deal with controversial, unusual, or "sensitive" subjects, asking a librarian or circulation clerk for them may be embarrassing for patrons desiring the materials. Because restricted collections are often composed of materials which some library patrons consider "objectionable," the potential user is predisposed to thinking of the materials as "objectionable," and may be reluctant to ask for them. Although the barrier between the materials and the patron is psychological, it is nonetheless a limitation on access to information.[27]

In sum, such restriction of access implies a judgment of suitability or appropriateness on the materials that is improper once materials have been selected according to established selection guidelines.

## GUIDELINES FOR DEALING WITH INTERNAL CENSORSHIP

While the problems created by internal censorship are serious, they may also be easier to solve than problems created by censorship from external sources, because they are to a great extent under the library's control. Some guidelines for dealing with internal censorship follow:

1. *It is essential to recognize that internal censorship does happen despite the best professional efforts to prevent it.* It may occur, for example, when some member of the organization experiences personal difficulty in accepting and living with the requirements of intellectual freedom when they are operationalized in the form of selection of works distasteful or objectionable to that person. Or it

may occur because of misunderstanding, lack of understanding, or incomplete understanding of the library's service goals and policies.

2. *Internal censorship may lead to, or even be caused by, conflict on the library staff.* Regardless of the specific issues in the conflict, its interpersonal aspects cannot be ignored. The sources of conflict must be located in order to resolve it.

- Differences in *personal values* are a probable source of conflict. A staff member who perceives her- or himself as a political liberal might experience conflict with others whose orientation is to a politically conservative point of view, if, for example, a book or film of liberal political intent is rejected in a selection meeting.
- When staff members cannot agree on *priorities* they will experience conflict. A high priority assigned by one librarian to providing quality literature may collide with the priorities of another librarian, who thinks it is more important to satisfy public demand for popular literature.
- *Role pressures* are a source of conflict. A staff member who is perceived and who perceives her- or himself as a winner, for example, will attach importance to having his/her point of view prevail in censorship matters. Similarly, a loss in a conflict may be perceived as a serious threat to his/her status. A senior staff member of conservative orientation, for example, may perceive such a threat when less-experienced staff members urge a more liberal approach to library selection in order to avoid censorship.
- Individual *differences in perception* may be at the base of conflict. An important issue for some on the staff may not be viewed as important by all. For example, a staff member involved in a right-to-life organization may attach far greater importance to the inclusion of all materials representing the organization's point of view than any other members of the staff do.
- Finally, *divergent goals* are a source of conflict. One staff member who is particularly concerned about the goal of intellectual freedom may seek to defend the presence of a controversial work in the collection, while another, enmeshed in crucial financial problems of the library, may be far more concerned about not stirring up controversy in order to ensure the success of a library-supporting bond issue.

3. *A workplace atmosphere in which open discussion can take place is a necessary prerequisite to conflict resolution.* Censorship is too

sensitive and too fundamental a professional matter to be ignored, and any conflict resulting from it will, like any other conflict, affect staff relationships. If agreement upon the specific issues cannot be reached even when all points of view are thoroughly aired, it may at least be possible to agree to disagree. Though this may be less than satisfactory, it can still serve to keep communication channels open. In time that openness may lead to a wider sharing of perceptions, values, and goals and thus unite the library staff in support of intellectual freedom.

4. *The importance of selection policies cannot be overstated.* The drafting, ratification, and putting into practice of a good materials selection policy provides the most effective weapon to combat censorship, both internal and external. To be effective, selection policies should provide clear and comprehensible statements of the library's goals in collection development and of its intention to uphold intellectual freedom. An endorsement of the Library Bill of Rights and of the statements on "The Freedom to Read" and "The Freedom to View" in selection policies provides a vital link to national library policy on censorship and intellectual freedom and should be included. There are many excellent sources of help in preparing selection policies. Some guidelines and sample policies, as well as ALA statements on intellectual freedom, are provided in Appendixes 1 and 2.

5. *The selection policy should be supported by appropriate written procedures.* Staff members should know precisely which actions of behavior are in keeping with organizational policy, and conversely, which are not. And, it cannot be overemphasized that the best selection policies and procedures are useless unless the entire library staff is familiar with them. Unhappily, many librarians have no idea or only a vague idea of what the library's policies may be. It is the library director's duty to see that all staff members, from professional librarians to clerical employees, know and understand these policies. And, firm knowledge of procedure will help the staff member more confidently deal with the censor, whether s/he comes from within or without the library.

6. *Special staff training is an excellent way to enable staff to cope effectively with censorship issues.* Workshops, conferences, classes, etc. are important for two reasons. First, they can bring awareness of censorship, both internal and external, to a large number of library staff members in an effective way. Second, inservice training can be a particularly good way of defusing or

preventing internal censorship in a professional, nonjudgemental manner. This is especially true if the leader of the inservice training (or out-of-library workshop) is not a member of the attending library's staff.

Regardless of who leads the training, inservice education is not difficult to design. One model (the author's) for a training workshop for professional and clerical staff, which has been used over a three-year period in the Hennepin County (MN) Library, used the *Intellectual Freedom Manual* (1974) as a guide. In this workshop, the presenter discusses the Library Bill of Rights; the Intellectual Freedom Statement; and the statements on expurgation, free access for minors, labeling, and sexism, racism, etc., in library materials—linking them to real, known examples of censorship challenges, which serve as springboards for discussion. Participants are strongly encouraged to add to the discussion by providing their own examples. Despite its simplicity, this training model has received very favorable participant evaluations and has been presented over 30 times to school and public library staffs. See Appendix 5 for an outline of this workshop.

Experience in presenting the workshop has clearly shown that:

- Participants are genuinely concerned about library censorship.
- They are eager both to gain and to share information about censorship problems.
- They are willing to learn from one another's experiences and ideas and, most important, to support one another under challenge.

Library schools, as well as colleges and universities, also offer training in dealing with censorship as part of degree programs and as continuing education. Further training opportunities are available through library and education professional associations, either at their regular meetings or as special events. It goes without saying that membership in professional associations should be encouraged, both for the training opportunities they can provide, and for the support that can be found in association with others of common purpose.

Coping with internal censorship is difficult and complex, but it is possible through patient and painstaking effort to adhere to professional principle, supported and encouraged by other librarians. Recognition that it exists and a willingness to promote and support thoughtful and appropriate policies, procedures, and training will most effectively combat the problem of censorship within the library.

# REFERENCES

1. Marjorie Fiske, *Book Selection and Censorship* (Berkeley, CA: University of California Press, 1968), p. 123.
2. Charles Busha, "Intellectual Freedom and Censorship: The Climate of Opinion in Midwestern Public Libraries," *Library Quarterly* 42 (3) (July 1972): 300.
3. Ibid.
4. Lee Burress, "A Brief Report of the 1977 NCTE Censorship Survey," in *Dealing with Censorship,* ed. by James E. Davis (Urbana, IL: National Council of Teachers of English, 1979), p. 16.
5. "Limiting What Students Shall Read, Summary Report on the Survey 'Book and Materials Selection for School Libraries and Classrooms: Procedures, Challenges, and Responses' " (New York: American Association of Publishers/American Library Association/Association for Supervision and Curriculum Development, 1981), pp. 3–4.
6. Fiske, p. 123.
7. "Limiting What Students Shall Read," p. 4.
8. Fiske, p. 124.
9. "Limiting What Students Shall Read," p. 4.
10. Lester Asheim, "Not Censorship but Selection," *Wilson Library Bulletin* 28 (September 1953): 66.
11. Ronald A. Landor, "The Fallacy of 'Balance' in Public Library Book Selection," in *Book Selection and Censorship in the Sixties,* ed. by Eric Moon (New York: Bowker, 1969), p. 39.
12. Judith Serebnik, "Book Reviews and the Selection of Potentially Controversial Books in Public Libraries," *Library Quarterly,* 51 (4) (1981): 405.
13. Sanford Berman, " 'Inside' Censorship," *Wisconsin Library Bulletin* (Spring 1982): 22.
14. See, for example, the sources given in Berman's article, cited above.
15. Berman, p. 21.
16. Monroe, Margaret. "Meeting Demands: A Library Imperative," in *Book Selection and Censorship in the Sixties,* p. 36.
17. Berman, p. 22.
18. Berman, p. 23.
19. Ibid.

20. "Statement on Labeling; An Interpretation of the Library Bill of Rights" (Chicago: Office for Intellectual Freedom, American Library Association, 1981). See Appendix 2 for the full statement.

21. Ibid.

22. Ibid.

23. "Expurgation of Library Materials: An Interpretation of the Library Bill of Rights" (Chicago: Office for Intellectual Freedom, American Library Association, 1981). See Appendix 2 for the full statement.

24. "Restricted Access to Library Materials: An Interpretation of the Library Bill of Rights" (Chicago: Office for Intellectual Freedom, American Library Association, 1981). See Appendix 2 for the full statement.

25. Ibid.

26. Ibid.

27. Ibid.

# Chapter 11
# Responsible Planning and Effective Response: Meeting the Challenge of Censorship

Attempts to answer the questions who censors; what is censored; and where, when, and why censorship occurs are frustrated by the lack of reliable available data on censorship attempts. Even the question of whether censorship attempts are increasing in America's libraries has no definitive answer. Although many perceive that censorship is increasing, surveys undertaken recently to determine whether this is so suffer from a lack of earlier studies of the same population groups upon which comparisons may be based. Several studies have been made (and are noted in other chapters); unfortunately, despite their merits, they are all limited in the information they can provide. Reports in the national and library press are useful for obtaining information about specific cases or incidents, but they do not provide the reader with a detailed national picture of all forms of censorship that occur or are likely to occur in America's school and public libraries. What is clear from recorded censorship cases, however, is that some citizen attempts to censor library materials have drawn considerable public attention and comment; thus, one available inference is that such public notice may serve to encourage other citizens to exercise their rights to question or challenge their own libraries on similar grounds. These rights, of course, have always been available. Public and school librarians must stand in readiness to answer the questions and meet the challenges, if they are to deal with censorship effectively.

## WHAT CENSORSHIP IS, WHAT IT IS NOT

The term censorship has been used to describe a variety of actions taken in regard to library materials. Before outlining any strategy for dealing with censorship, it is important to list those actions that are correctly categorized as censorship and those that are not. Among the terms frequently used in relation to censorship are *question, objection,* and *complaint.* In this discussion, the terms are used as described below:

*Questioning* is used to describe the act of inquiring about the reasons for material being or not being in the library's collection. Questioning is not in itself an attempt to censor. The library patron who wants to know why *The Joy of Sex* is in the collection has a right to an answer that gives a comprehensible explanation of the criteria used to select it and of its place or function in the collection. The distinction between questioning a selection decision and attempting to censor it is an essential distinction. The public or school library, as a tax-supported institution, is accountable for its decisions, and those decisions are open to public scrutiny. The library's role as a public forum renders it a particularly appropriate location for open discussion. Openness and willingness to engage in discussion concerning selection decisions is one way to garner public trust and support for them. By contrast, refusal to respond to citizen questions may arouse suspicion or resentment and encourage the citizen to more assertive action in order to obtain the information s/he wants.

*Objections* and *complaints* differ from questions in that they state an opinion or belief that the library's decision to include or exclude specific materials was incorrect. Objections and complaints may also state the opinion or belief that the material objected to is intrinsically unsuitable, inappropriate, or just plain bad and should not be available to anyone anywhere; but the availability of the material in the library is what is of concern to the staff who must deal with objections or complaints.

Objections may be formal or informal. Informal objections reach the library in a variety of ways. They may be:

- Brief, apparently offhand comments made to the staff when a book is returned, e.g., "This is trash!" "I don't know why the library buys this stuff!" "Why don't they buy any good books anymore?"
- Written comments left in books or other materials, e.g., "This book is filthy and should not be in the library." One public library has employed a patron comment card left in the book pockets in order to elicit feedback on the reading experience. Although Norma Klein's *Domestic Arrangements* drew three consecutive comments of "absolute junk," "should be burnt," "Sex at 14 years? How cheap!," no formal objection to it was ever made.

Formal objections or complaints are usually lodged in writing, and many libraries wisely provide specific guidelines and special forms for registering formal objections. The forms may be called "citizens' complaint forms'' or ''requests for reconsideration of library materials,'' or other names, but they share the common purposes of gathering information concerning:

- Whether the objection/complaint concerns materials in the collection, or materials not found in the collection.
- The specific item (book, film, record, etc.) or type of material that has occasioned the objection/complaint.
- Specific reasons for the objection/complaint.
- What action is requested of the library.
- Whether the objector has read, viewed or listened to the entire work.
- The name, address and phone number of the person stating the objection/complaint.

Sample forms are found in Appendixes 1 and 2.

Objections and complaints that are lodged in accordance with guidelines provided by the library are not, in and of themselves, censorship. As a practical matter, the process of censorship most often includes the following elements:

1. Citizens who use unlawful or irregular means of removing materials from the collection, or who alter materials in the collection. An example of irregular removal of materials is borrowing and not returning them; an example of an unlawful means could be removing the materials from the library without using regular borrowing procedures. One example of censorship by altering materials is excision, or the removal of parts of books, e.g., illustrations. Another is the addition of written comments, such as comments labeling the materials as false, inaccurate, or obscene. Such acts may also qualify as acts of vandalism; but they are distinct from other vandalism in that their apparent intention is to modify or influence others' experience of the works because of dislike for or disagreement with their contents.

2. Citizens who bring unusual administrative, political, or legal pressure on library decision makers in order to ensure that the results they want are achieved, without regard for established library policy, procedures, or guidelines. Examples of this form of censorship occur in the cases described in earlier chapters.

3. The library that responds to questions or objections/complaints by removing materials that were properly selected in the first place.

It is essential to note that not all book removals are censorship. Libraries are human organizations; humans make mistakes; and libraries can make genuine mistakes in selection. An even greater mistake, however, is failing to defend a work which has a rightful place in the library collection.

## DEALING WITH CENSORSHIP THROUGH PLANNING

No effective preventive reaction against censorship is possible without advance planning. Careful planning will not eliminate censorship attempts, but it will ensure that the library's responsibility to resist them is fulfilled. Responsible planning includes the steps listed below.

1. Provide a written policy for the selection and acquisition of library materials. (Guides to the writing of selection policies may be found in "Recommended Reading," and sample selection policies are found in Appendix 1.) Citing ALA's Library Bill of Rights, and its "Interpretations," as well as the "Intellectual Freedom," "Freedom to Read," and 'Freedom to View" statements in selection policies provides them with additional substance in addition to making them a vital link to national professional policy. (See Appendix 2 for these statements.) Policies should also note that the library does not endorse the contents of every item in its collection. Good selection policies accomplish three important objectives: they assist the staff in making effective and appropriate selection decisions; they increase staff understanding of selection decisions; and they improve public understanding of the purpose of the library's collection and the role played by selection decisions in developing the collection.
2. Supplement policy statements with written selection procedures that provide clear descriptions of specific selection tasks and responsibilities, selection criteria, and methods of selection.
3. Ensure that the materials selected provide a balance of information, opinion, and belief on all topics represented in the collection, including topics of known or anticipated controversy.
4. Establish a process that gives citizens the opportunity to question, object to, and complain about materials included in or excluded from the collection, and make the process known to library staff and patrons alike. The inclusion of a complaint or request for reconsideration form is recommended as part of the process.

5. Provide written procedures, based on the library's experience, for dealing with citizen questions, objections, or complaints. Well-written procedures can and should specify areas and levels of responsibility, i.e., they should note specifically who or which positions on the staff are responsible for each step in the process of handling questions, objections, or complaints. They might state, for example, that circulation desk staff responsibility for responding to questions, objections, or complaints is limited to a courteous offer to locate a librarian to discuss them, or to providing a complaint or request for reconsideration form; that nonsupervisory librarians may discuss complaints and convey the results of the discussion to supervising staff but should take no formal action to resolve complaints; and that supervising staff may resolve complaints in consultation with selectors, administrators, or governing boards. No procedures, no matter how well-written, will anticipate every circumstance that may arise, but by giving thorough coverage to the more common ones, they will be of inestimable help to the staff.

6. Provide the library staff with training in order to increase their understanding of the library's selection policy, its procedures, and of their roles in the handling of citizens' questions, objections, and complaints.

7. Become informed about and supportive of the work of organizations that can assist libraries in resisting censorship. (A list of organizations is provided in Appendix 4.)

8. Inform and educate library and school governing boards in the principles of intellectual freedom expressed in the Library Bill of Rights and other relevant professional sources.

## HANDLING THE CHALLENGE WHEN IT COMES

With appropriate policies and procedures in place and thoroughly understood by the library staff, further thought can be given to meeting censorship challenges. Censorship studies indicate, as do the cases described in earlier chapters, that the majority of objections and complaints are made initially by individual citizens. Thus the library's effectiveness in dealing with censorship may rest to a great extent upon the ability of its staff to communicate effectively with individual citizens about their concerns. For this reason, some guidelines for the communication process are offered.

1. *Active listening is the first step.* Hearing words and statements is not enough, because they alone do not convey the speaker's full meaning. Careful observation of behavior that reveals the speaker's emotional state is equally, if not more, important, as is sensitivity to the tone of voice used. Being open and receptive to all of these observations is essential to a complete understanding of the intended meaning. Without such understanding it is easy to mistake a question for an objection or a complaint, or to mistake an informal objection—one that requires no formal action from the library—for a serious formal complaint. The opposite sort of confusion may also occur, with the result that the library may take no immediate action when it is needed, and conflict may escalate unnecessarily.

Cross-checking or verification of understanding of the intended meaning may be necessary. This can be accomplished by restating the citizen's concern and then asking him/her if the understanding is correct. The process can be repeated, if necessary, until a successful understanding is reached.

It is important to listen for any expression that reveals concerns that underly those expressed to the library staff member. For example, a parent worried about a child reading "vulgarity" or "obscenity" of which she or he disapproves may in fact be far more concerned about a gap in communication or understanding that is being experienced with the child. If the library is not also to bear the greater pressures caused by underlying concerns, these must be sorted out, so that only concerns directly related to library materials remain to be acted upon.

It is equally important to discern whether there are unspoken, underlying objections. The stated reasons may not be the only reasons for complaints or objections to books and other materials. The language used in *Manchild in the Promised Land* or *Down These Mean Streets* may cause less shock than their revelations of human poverty and racial discrimination. *365 Days* may be less objectionable for its language than for its description of the inhuman consequences of an unpopular war. And *Are You There, God? It's Me, Margaret* "is not about a girl who wants a bra, any more than *Hamlet* is about a man who is in love with a woman who goes crazy."[1]

Active listening is not easy and can be very difficult indeed in an atmosphere that is emotion-charged or threatening. But the informed and active listener can retain control in such situations by remaining calm and responding only to appropriate library concerns. Inservice training, involving techniques such as role playing, can help library staff members be prepared for active listening.

2. *Assuring the citizen that his/her concerns are being heard and that a response to them will be forthcoming is the next step.* This is especially important if the staff member who first engages in conversation about the question or complaint is not the one charged with the authority and responsibility for resolving it.

3. *Responding to questions, objections, or complaints is essential.* Response may take the form of further conversation to clarify concerns or of a written response to a complaint or request for reconsideration. Responses should adhere to guidelines established by library policy and procedure. Whatever form they take, they are essential to maintain citizen trust in the library's institutional integrity and competence.

   Left unresolved, citizen concerns may remain a continuing irritant; and the citizen may then feel that library inaction warrants increased action on his/her part, thus leading to greater censorship difficulties.

Some approaches may render library responses less effective than they can be.

1. *Apologies are not in order.* It may be tempting to express an apology on the library's behalf to the concerned citizen, but the temptation should be resisted. An apology may indicate that there is some wrongdoing on the library's part. Unless it is later shown that this is so, an apology is unnecessary and inappropriate. On the other hand, expressing regret that a citizen is concerned about or disappointed in the library can be a show of courtesy and tact that may encourage greater openness and understanding of the library's position.

2. *Expressing disagreement with the citizen's assessment or opinion of library materials is rarely effective.* It usually serves only to escalate conflict. Even if strong, cogent arguments can be advanced against the citizen's position, it is not likely that the conflict will be resolved by compelling her/him to admit to being wrong. On the contrary, such embarrassment may lead to further retaliation.

3. *Citing "expert" opinion is only slightly effective.* Even if the expert's credentials are genuinely impressive, it can still be asserted that the expert does not know what is good for this school, library, or individual.

4. *Personal attacks on library staff need not be tolerated, but they obviously should not be answered in kind.* Because the library does not endorse the contents of materials in its collection, any attempt to link what the citizen finds objectionable in them to the individual beliefs, opinions, or characteristics of library staff members is inappropriate and irrelevant. Should it be necessary, a polite but firm statement to this effect can and should be given in response.

Effective responses address those citizen concerns which the library can and does act upon. They may include (but are not limited to):

- A statement that the materials meet the requirements of the library's selection policy.
- A statement that the library does not endorse the contents of the materials in its collection.
- An acknowledgement that not all library materials will be read or approved by all citizens, but that the library attempts to provide a wide variety of materials, in order to serve the entire school or community.

It is recommended that a copy of the library's selection policy be given to the citizen or included with a written response when it is sent.

A word about selection errors: if upon examination it is determined that materials that have encountered objection or complaint do not meet the criteria established by the library's selection policy, the material should be withdrawn. It should not be feared that acknowledging that the library could and did err in selection is capitulating to censorship pressure. On the contrary, willingness to admit a genuine error may serve to strengthen arguments for retaining material when future censorship controversies arise. Because the library's willingness to take responsibility for a selection error will have been demonstrated, its judgement that subsequent objections are not the result of selection error will probably be regarded as sound and respected.

Despite their staffs' best efforts, not all censorship challenges may be successfully met in libraries, and censorship controversy may reach out to involve school or public library governing authority and others in the community. When this occurs, support and help are available, and the staff need not stand alone. Its interest in intellectual freedom and in resisting censorship is shared by many, and help will come to those who ask for it. State library associations, state education associations and departments, state libraries, schools of library science, and local American Civil Liberties Union chapters are all good places to start. (See Appendix 4 for a selected list of helpful organizations.) And, since the defense of First

Amendment principles and of those expressed in the Library Bill of Rights is undertaken in the best interest of all, many citizens, understanding this, will rise to assist the library in fighting the challenge.

Recent censorship controversies have been likened to a war between darkness and light. No conflict of this magnitude can be successfully undertaken singlehandedly. Librarians are not alone, but even were this so, one voice alone can be sufficient to signal the threat of censorship oppression, and to lead others in defense of First Amendment freedoms. Censorship conflicts may appear to be dangerous, but today's real danger lies—as it always has—in failing to recognize when the loss of First Amendment freedoms threatens, and in failing to fight to defend against such loss.

In his autobiography Justice William O. Douglas wrote:

> The First Amendment sets us apart from most other nations. It marks the end of all censorship, it allows the ability of the mind to roam at will over the entire spectrum of ideas, and the sanctity of one's beliefs. . . . A symbol of our health is the respect we show to First Amendment values.[2]

America's school and public libraries contribute significantly to the health and well-being of the nation. Their contribution is never greater than when they uphold and defend the ideal of intellectual freedom and resist censorship.

## REFERENCES

1. Judith M. Goldberger, "Judy Blume: Target of the Censor," *Newsletter on Intellectual Freedom* 30 (3) (May 1981): 62.
2. William O. Douglas, *The Court Years: 1939–1975* (New York: Random House, 1980): 266.

# Appendixes

# Appendix 1
# Sample Policies and Guidelines

## POLICIES AND GUIDELINES FOR SCHOOL LIBRARIES

### Guidelines for Writing a Materials Selection Policy

Prepared by the Intellectual Freedom Department of OELMA, 1982*

A Materials Selection Policy should contain:

I.   Philosophy, goals and objectives of the school district.
    A. The selection policy and all criteria should conform to the school system's philosophy
    B. Educational objectives of the media center should be delineated

II.  Statement concerning selection personnel.
    A. Who should be included
    B. What their responsibilities are
    C. Emphasize that final selection rests with media center professionals (librarians and/or media specialists)

III. Criteria for selection of print and nonprint materials.
    A. Curricula
    B. High artistic quality and/or literary style
    C. Representative of many viewpoints
    D. Various maturity and ability levels considered
    E. Needs of school
    F. Accuracy and scope of coverage

IV.  Inclusion of selection aids.
    A. Lists of reviewing sources
    B. Staff and student suggestions

---

*Reprinted by permission of the Ohio Library Association.

V.   Characteristics of the collection.
   A.  Scope
   B.  Size
   C.  Reasons for special emphasis
   D.  Statement on development
   E.  Fulfillment of standards (i.e. ALA, AECT, North Central, State of Ohio)

VI.   Policies on maintenance of the collection.
   A.  Weeding
   B.  Replacing
   C.  Binding
   D.  Multiple copies

VII.  Policies on controversial materials.

IX.   [Sic] Procedure for handling challenged materials.

X.   Special Areas.
   A.  Gifts.
   B.  Sponsored materials
   C.  Expensive materials
   D.  Ephemeral materials
   E.  Jobbers and salesmen
   F.  Archival, special requests etc.

## Model Challenged Materials Policy for Maine Secondary Schools*

### I. STATEMENT OF POLICY

A. Secondary school libraries exist for the support, enrichment, implementation, and supplementation of the curriculum and educational programs of the school system. To that end, books, periodicals and other library resources exist:

a. to provide materials that will stimulate growth in factual knowledge, appreciation of literature, aesthetic values, and ethical standards;

b. to provide a varied and diverse background of information which will enable students to make intelligent judgments in their daily lives;

c. to provide materials presenting a variety of points of view concerning literary and historical issues in order to develop, under guidance, critical examination, thinking, and informed judgment;

d. to provide materials which realistically represent our pluralistic society and reflect the contributions made by many groups and individuals to our American heritage;

e. to generate an understanding of American freedoms and a desire to preserve those freedoms through the development of informed and responsible citizenship;

f. to promote a critical appreciation for, as well as skills in, reading, viewing, listening, and learning which will continue as a lifetime source of education and enjoyment; and,

g. to provide a planned program which will arouse in students an interest in books and other types of media and to broaden this interest through service and guidance in a pleasant atmosphere.

B. Criteria employed for selection and retention of library resources are: overall purpose and scope; currentness or permanence; importance of the subject matter; accuracy; quality of the writing/production; significance, impact and intent of the author/artist/producer; reputation of the publisher/producer; authoritativeness; readability/visual or audio effectiveness; suitability to age and grade level; interest and appeal; freedom from stereotyping; presentation of different points of view; format and price.

C. In order to implement this Policy it is necessary to place principle above personal opinion and reason above prejudice in the selection, including gifts, of materials of the highest quality in order to assure a comprehensive print and non-print collection appropriate for the students.

---

*This policy was prepared by plaintiffs' attorney Ronald R. Coles for submission in *Sheck vs. Baileyville School Committee* (1982). Reprinted by permission.

D. Pursuant to 20 M.R.S.A. §856: "Administrative Units shall provide school books . . . for the use of pupils . . ."

## II. PROCEDURES DEALING WITH CHALLENGED MATERIALS

### A. INITIAL STATEMENT

Any adult resident or resident organization of the school district may challenge learning resources used in any of the district's educational libraries on the basis of appropriateness to all students. This procedure is designed for the purpose of considering the opinions of those persons who were not directly involved in the initial resource selection process. However, it is the policy of the School Board to support and respect the initial presumed valid library materials acquisition decisions made by the education professionals, i.e., teachers, librarians, etc. to whom that role has been historically assigned.

### B. REQUEST FOR INFORMAL RECONSIDERATION

a. The school receiving a complaint regarding a library learning resource shall try to resolve the issue informally.

1. The librarian shall explain to the complainant the school's selection procedure, criteria, and the STATEMENT OF POLICY as per I above.

2. Thereafter, if the complaint has not been resolved, the Principal shall also explain to the complainant the particular place the questioned resource occupies in the educational program and its intended educational usefulness.

### C. REQUEST FOR FORMAL RECONSIDERATION

a. If the complainant wishes to file a formal challenge, a copy of a "Request for Review of Library Materials" form, (hereinafter referred to as "Request"), as annexed hereto as Exhibit "A," shall be handed to the complainant for completion and signature.

b. Upon request of the completed and signed "Request" form from the complainant, the principal shall refer the Request to the Superintendent of the school administrative unit. The Superintendent shall refer the Request to the School Board at the next regularly scheduled Board meeting.

c. The School Board shall refer the Request immediately to a standing Reconsideration Committee, chosen by a majority of the School Board, which shall be composed of the following seven members:

1. The principal of the school involved;
2. English Department Chairperson of the school involved;
3. An English Teacher of the School involved;

4. Chairman of the School Board;

5. Male student of the school involved;

6. Female student of the school involved;

(both students shall be those in the highest grade level at the school involved, exhibiting high academic scholarship)

7. A parent having a student child in the school involved.

d. Within thirty (30) days of the School Board meeting mentioned in (b) above, the reconsideration committee shall meet, and within thirty (30) days thereafter shall:

1. Completely read and review thoroughly the challenged material and available reviews. Passages or parts of the material shall not be pulled out of context and the committee evaluation shall be made on the material as a whole.

2. The evaluation shall be in light of the needs and interests of all of the students, the school, the curriculum and the community.

3. The material shall further be evaluated in the light of, and governed by, the criteria for initial selection and purchase as provided for in STATEMENT OF POLICY, per I above.

4. The material shall be further reviewed in the light of the rights guaranteed under the Constitution of the United States, the Constitution of the State of Maine, and pursuant to the guidelines in *Sheck vs. Baileyville School Committee*, 530 F. Supp 679 (DC, ME 1982).

e. From initial receipt of the Request until final decision by the School Board hereafter, the challenged material shall not be removed from the library, nor placed upon any restricted shelf, nor in any other manner be made unavailable to students. Notwithstanding any other provision contained herein, no restrictions of any kind or manner may restrict any student from reading, carrying or otherwise possessing on school grounds and facilities any learning resource, from whatever source derived, utilized by the student for his/her own personal use.

f. The Reconsideration Committee shall hold at least one (1) previously advertised and announced public meeting to which any person may attend and comment as to the challenged material at issue. The committee shall also accept and consider any written comments received within ten (10) days after the last hearing.

g. Within thirty (30) days of the last public hearing aforementioned, the reconsideration committee shall issue a written decision of its majority findings which shall be signed by all members of the reconsideration committee. Any dissenting findings, if any, shall be signed by those committee members in the minority. The findings shall be forwarded directly to the Chairman of the School Board, and shall be presented to the

School Board at the next regularly scheduled Board meeting; the pre-Board meeting agenda shall specifically identify the decision to be acted upon. A copy of the committee findings shall also be mailed to the complainant, to all persons commenting at the committee's public hearing(s) or in writing and to any other area resident requesting a copy in writing.

h. The School Board shall adopt the findings of the reconsideration committee absent [of] any clear and convincing proof that the committee findings were capricious or arbitrary. The School Board's adoption of the committee's findings shall be administratively final, binding and conclusive.

i. Any person aggrieved by the adoption or rejection of the committee findings by the School Board may pursue any and all legal remedies thereafter available.

### D.  INDIVIDUAL PARENTAL RESTRICTION

Notwithstanding any other provisions of this Policy, any parent or guardian of his/her minor child student may absolutely restrict said child from reading/viewing any specific library resource to be utilized by the student as an extra-curricular activity. Should the parent/guardian desire to exercise this restriction, he/she shall:

1. Advise, in writing, to the librarian of the school library involved, that certain specific library resources be made unavailable to the child. The writing shall include the name and author of each book or title of the resource.

2. One copy of the written restriction request received from the parent/ guardian shall be placed in the student's file, another copy shall be delivered to the student by the librarian, and the original retained by the librarian.

3. The written restriction request shall be effective only during the academic school year in which the restriction request is received by the librarian, and shall become null and void on the last day of the academic school year, usually in the month of June. Should the student attain the age of eighteen (18) years during the academic school year in which the parental restriction is in effect, the restriction request shall become null and void on the student's 18th birthday.

Dated: June 7, 1982

## REQUEST FOR REVIEW OF LIBRARY MATERIALS

Author _____

Title _____

Publisher/Producer _____

Request initiated by _____

Telephone _____ Address _____

City _____ State _____ Zip Code _____

Complainant represents: _____

_____ him/herself _____

_____ (name of organization) _____

_____ (identify other group) _____

1. To what in the material do you object? Please be specific. _____
_____

2. What do you feel might be the result of reading or viewing the material? _____
_____

3. For what age group would you recommend the material? _____
_____

4. Did you read or view the entire work? If "NO," why not? _____
_____

5. Are you aware of the judgment of the material by reviewers or evaluators? _____
_____

6. What do you believe is the theme of the material? _____
_____

7. What would you like the library to do about the material? _____
_____

8. In its place, what material would you recommend? _____
_____

_____          _____
(date)                           (Signature of Complainant)

EXHIBIT "A"

## POLICIES AND GUIDELINES FOR PUBLIC LIBRARIES

### Hennepin (MN) County Library Materials Selection Policy*

The purpose of this policy is to guide librarians and to inform the public about the principles upon which decisions are made. A policy cannot replace the judgment of librarians, but stating goals and indicating boundaries will assist them in choosing from the best array of available materials.

One of the Library's goals is the provision of materials which best meet the community's information, recreation and education needs. Basic to this policy is the Library Bill of Rights adopted by the Hennepin County Library Board April 24, 1980.

The future of the Library will depend upon its ability to provide information to the public it serves. Free speech and the open exchange of information cannot depend solely on the traditional producers of mass communications. The Library recognizes a responsibility to support the production and translation of library materials by patrons, community groups and library staff in order to ensure the open exchange of information in the communities served.

DEFINITIONS

The word "materials" as it occurs in this policy has the widest possible meaning; hence it is implicit that every format is included, whether printed or in manuscript; bound or unbound; photographed or otherwise reproduced or recorded.

"Selection": the decision that must be made either to add material to the collection or to retain or withdraw material already in the collection. It does not refer to the guidance of an individual patron.

"Production": the mechanical and creative processes involved in the preparation of library materials by patrons as groups or individually, and by Library staff.

"Translation": the changing of library materials from one medium to another.

"Transmission": the sending of the contents of library materials from one place to another by electrical or optical means.

OBJECTIVES

The primary objectives of the Library are to collect, produce and make easily available materials of contemporary significance and of long term value. The Library will always be guided by a sense of responsibility to both

*Reprinted by permission of the Hennepin County (Minnesota) Library.

present and future in adding materials which will enrich the collection and maintain an overall balance. The Library also recognizes an immediate duty to make available materials for enlightenment and recreation, even though such materials may not have enduring interest or value.

All staff members selecting, producing, translating and transmitting library materials or authorizing the same, will be expected to keep the objectives in mind and apply their professional knowledge and experience in making decisions.

Final responsibility lies with the Director. The Director delegates to staff members the authority to interpret and guide the application of the policy in making day-to-day decisions. Unusual problems will be referred to the Director for resolution.

GUIDELINES FOR SELECTION

The Library recognizes that many materials are controversial and that any given item may offend some patrons. Decisions will not be made on the basis of any anticipated approval or disapproval, but solely on the merits of the work in relation to the building of the collection and to serving the interests of patrons.

Responsibility for children's use of library materials rests with their parents or legal guardians. Selection decisions will not be inhibited by the possibility that material may be accessible to use by children.

The Library recognizes the purposes and resources of other libraries in the Twin Cities, particularly those of the Minneapolis Public Library and Information Center and shall not needlessly duplicate functions and materials.

The Library does not attempt to acquire textbooks or other curriculum-related materials except as such materials also serve the general public.

The Library acknowledges a particular interest in local, county and state history. It will take a broad view of works by and about Minnesota authors as well as general works relating to the State of Minnesota. However, the Library is not under obligation to add to its collection everything about Minnesota or produced by authors, printers or publishers with Minnesota connections.

The Library will always seek to select materials of varying complexity and format because it has a potential public embracing a wide range of ages, educational backgrounds, interests, sensory preferences, and reading skills.

The Library will pay due regard to the special civic, commercial, cooperative, cultural, industrial and labor activities of each of the communities it serves.

Library materials will not be marked or identified to show approval or disapproval of the contents and materials will not be sequestered except for the purpose of protecting them from damage or theft.

The Library will reconsider any material in its collection upon written request of a patron.

## GIFTS

The Library accepts gifts of library materials with the understanding that the same standards of selection are applied to gifts as to materials acquired by purchase. The Library reserves the right to evaluate and to dispose of gifts in accordance with the criteria applied to purchased materials.

## REVISION

This policy will be reviewed by the Library Board at least every two years.

**Request for Reconsideration—Hennepin County Library***

Author _____

Title _____

Request initiated by _____

Telephone _____ Address _____

City _____ Zone _____

Library _____ Date _____

Please answer the following questions if your request is that the book be *removed* from the library.

1. To what in the book do you object? (Please be specific; cite pages.)

_____

2. Did you read the entire book? _____
If not, which portion did you read? _____

Please answer the following questions if your request is that the book be *added* to the library:

1. What is the subject of the book? _____

_____

2. Have you read the book? _____

3. Why do you think it should be added to the library? _____

_____

4. Do you know of any reviews? (Please cite source, date and page).

_____

*Reprinted by permission of the Hennepin County (Minnesota) Library.

## Hennepin County (MN) Library Meeting Room Policy*

"As an institution of education for democratic living, the library should welcome the use of its meeting rooms for socially useful and cultural activities and discussion of current public questions. Such meeting places should be available on equal terms to all groups in the community regardless of the beliefs and affiliations of their members, provided that the meeting be open to the public." . . . From American Library Association, LIBRARY BILL OF RIGHTS.

The Hennepin County Library is a public institution whose facilities are available to all. The intent of this policy is to make the Library's limited meeting room space available on as wide-spread and equitable a basis as possible for educational and informational community meetings and programs.

Meetings held in the Community Libraries must be open to the public and be free of charge, and are limited to non-profit organizations and groups.

Meeting rooms in the Area Libraries are also open on a fee basis to non-profit tax exempt organizations or institutions which charge a fee or tuition, and to profit-making organizations, subject to Library approval.

*First Priority* for use of meeting rooms will be given to Library produced or sponsored programs. The library reserves the right to revoke permission to use a meeting room if the room is needed for library purposes.

*Second Priority* will be given to meetings of an educational, cultural, civic, political or professional nature. The use is to be on an occasional basis for general public meetings. It is not the intent of the Library to provide space on a frequent and permanent basis to support the primary activities of a group or organization.

In the Area Libraries only, *Third Priority* will be given to meetings of any non-profit organization or institution which charges a fee or tuition.

In the Area Libraries only, *Fourth Priority* will be given to meetings of any profit-making organization.

Meeting rooms will not be available for commercial purposes, fund raising or sale of items. Exceptions shall be:

1. programs or sales conducted by non-profit Library Friends groups, the proceeds of which will go to the direct benefit of the Library;
2. sale of material directly related to library sponsored programs which has had prior approval of the Library Director.

---

*Reprinted by permission of the Hennepin County (Minnesota) Library.

Meetings which may interfere with the regular use of a library because of noise, activity, etc., will not be permitted.

At Area and Community Libraries meeting rooms will be available free to non-profit organizations during the scheduled open times.

At both Area and Community Libraries fees have been established for set-up and cleaning of meeting rooms, and for use of meeting rooms prior to or after library open hours. Hourly fees have been established at the Area Libraries for use by non-profit organizations which charge a fee or tuition or by profit-making organizations. In addition, there is a fee for the provision of audio-visual equipment at the Area Libraries.

The Library Director will establish and publish specific regulations based on this adopted policy statement. The Library Board will be the final authority in granting or refusing permission for use of Library facilities.

## REGULATIONS FOR THE USE OF LIBRARY MEETING ROOMS

1. Reservations may be taken beginning one month prior to the start of the booking period. The booking periods are January through May, June through August, September through December. These booking periods are necessary in order to allow access by the maximum number of users to the limited space available.

2. For prime time when there is more than one potential user for a meeting room, an individual library may restrict use by a group or individual to once a month. Every effort will be made to schedule such use at acceptable non-prime times. In the event a prime time period has not been booked, any qualified user may reserve it seven or less days in advance of the day of use.

3. Meeting rooms may be booked for hours which that Library is open. In libraries where staff are present, the Librarian may allow a meeting to begin prior to open hours. In libraries where the security system permits, the Librarian may allow a meeting which started during open hours to continue after the Library has closed, provided arrangements are made at the time the room is booked. The individual making application for the meeting room use will be held responsible for securing the lights and exit door. In no event will a meeting room be used beyond eleven p.m. Arrangements can be made to use the Southdale meeting rooms beginning at eight a.m. Monday through Friday.

4. The Library reserves the right to revoke permission to use a meeting room if the scheduled room is needed for library purposes. Every

attempt will be made to provide an acceptable alternate time. A four-week notice will be given the booked organization.

5. After reading the Hennepin County Meeting Room Policy and Regulations, the requesting individual will complete an application for approval and filing by the Librarian in charge.

6. If there is to be a program at a meeting (speaker, film, etc.), this information is to be designated on the application so that telephone and other inquiries may be answered by the Library. Groups with regularly scheduled meetings should provide this information well in advance of each program. Groups can be of further assistance to the Library by including a group member's name and telephone number in meeting notices so that direct contact with the group can be made.

7. The Hennepin County Library or any of its area community libraries may not be used as the official address or headquarters of any organization. No equipment or material may be stored at the Library.

8. The Librarian in charge must be notified as soon as possible if it is necessary to cancel a reservation for a meeting room. Failure to notify a library of a canceled meeting may result in cancellations of future meeting room reservations for the organization.

9. Permission for the use of Library meeting rooms for courses of an educational or cultural nature sponsored by a college, university, school, governmental agency, or by the Library for which a charge or tuition is necessary to support the program must be approved by the Library Director. All regulations of the meeting room policy apply to meetings falling within this cateogry.

10. The group will be responsible for setting up, rearranging and taking down needed tables and chairs. All furniture arrangements requiring extra custodial assistance or rearrangement of meeting rooms must be made known to the Community Librarian at the time application is made and may be billed at the rate of $10.00 per hour, with a minimum fee of $5.00 per half-hour or portion thereof.

11. The individual submitting the application for meeting room use will be responsible for discipline and reasonable care of the room and furnishings and is expected to pay for any damage.

12. The Librarian may require a supervising adult to be in charge and present whenever a group of children or young people uses the meeting room.

13. Light refreshments only may be served where facilities permit. Permission must be secured at the time the application is approved. No alcoholic beverages may be served.

14. Rooms will be left in an orderly condition. A cleanup charge at the rate of $10.00 per hour must be paid if such service is required.

15. Rulings of the local Fire Department as to smoking and the capacity of rooms and other matters will be observed in all meetings.

16. Organizations requesting the use of library A-V equipment may do so according to the conditions in Procedure 95: Projectionist for Non-Library Programs.

17. Failure to observe these regulations will result in the loss of meeting room privileges.

## Forsyth County Public Library Policy on the Use of Library Meeting Rooms and Exhibit Space for Groups*

As a public institution dedicated to the free expression and free access to ideas presenting all points of view concerning the problems and issues of our times, all meeting rooms and exhibit space in the Forsyth County Public Library System are available on equal terms for the lawful activities of all groups, regardless of their beliefs or affiliations.

PROCEDURES GOVERNING THE USE OF LIBRARY MEETING ROOMS AND EXHIBIT SPACE FOR GROUPS

1. Meeting rooms and exhibit space may be used anytime during the regular hours of the library.
2. No fees, dues, or donations may be charged or solicited by the user for any program or exhibit. All programs and exhibits shall be free.
3. All programs and exhibits shall be open to the public.
4. Booking will come on a first come, first served basis. No group may reserve meeting rooms or exhibit space for the same time continually.
5. Meeting rooms and exhibit space may be booked no more than forty-five days in advance. Exceptions will be considered upon receipt of a written request.
6. Programs and exhibits may not disrupt the use of the library by others. Persons attending the meeting are subject to all library rules and regulations.
7. Library facilities shall be left in a clean and orderly condition. Users shall pay the cost for repair of any damages to facilities. The library will not be responsible for materials or equipment left in the building by users.
8. Granting of permission to use library facilities does not constitute an endorsement by the Library Staff or Board of the user or its beliefs.

---

*Reprinted by permission of the Forsyth County (North Carolina) Public Library.

# Appendix 2
# Intellectual Freedom Statements

## LIBRARY BILL OF RIGHTS*

The American Library Association affirms that all libraries are forums for information and ideas, and that the following basic policies should guide their services.

1. Books and other library resources should be provided for the interest, information, and enlightenment of all people of the community the library serves. Materials should not be excluded because of the origin, background, or views of those contributing to their creation.

2. Libraries should provide materials and information presenting all points of view on current and historical issues. Materials should not be proscribed or removed because of partisan or doctrinal disapproval.

3. Libraries should challenge censorship in the fulfillment of their responsibility to provide information and enlightenment.

4. Libraries should cooperate with all persons and groups concerned with resisting abridgment of free expression and free access to ideas.

5. A person's right to use a library should not be denied or abridged because of origin, age, background, or views.

6. Libraries which make exhibit spaces and meeting rooms available to the public they serve should make such facilities available on an equitable

---

*Unless otherwise noted, all statements in Appendix 2 are reprinted by permission of the American Library Association.

basis, regardless of the beliefs or affiliations of individuals or groups requesting their use.

*Adopted June 18, 1948.*
*Amended February 2, 1961, June 27, 1967, and January 23, 1980,*
*by the ALA Council\**

---

\*In 1975, the American Association of School Librarians endorsed the Library Bill of Rights.

## INTELLECTUAL FREEDOM STATEMENT

### An Interpretation of the Library Bill of Rights

The heritage of free men is ours. In the Bill of Rights to the United States Constitution, the founders of our nation proclaimed certain fundamental freedoms to be essential to our form of government. Primary among these is the freedom of expression, specifically the right to publish diverse opinions and the right to unrestricted access to those opinions. As citizens committed to the full and free use of all communications media and as professional persons responsible for making the content of those media accessible to all without prejudice, we, the undersigned, wish to assert the public interest in the preservation of freedom of expression.

Through continuing judicial interpretations of the First Amendment to the United States Constitution, freedom of expression has been guaranteed. Every American who aspires to the success of our experiment in democracy—who has faith in the political and social integrity of free men—must stand firm on those constitutional guarantees of essential rights. Such Americans can be expected to fulfill the responsibilities implicit in those rights.

We, therefore, affirm these propositions:

1. We will make available to everyone who needs or desires them the widest possible diversity of views and modes of expression, including those which are strange, unorthodox or unpopular.

   Creative thought is, by its nature, new. New ideas are always different and, to some people, distressing and even threatening. The creator of every new idea is likely to be regarded as unconventional—occasionally heretical—until his idea is first examined, then refined, then tested in its political, social or moral applications. The characteristic ability of our governmental system to adapt to necessary change is vastly strengthened by the option of the people to choose freely from among conflicting opinions. To stifle nonconformist ideas at their inception would be to end the democratic process. Only through continuous weighing and selection from among opposing views can free individuals obtain the strength needed for intelligent, constructive decisions and actions. In short, we need to understand not only what we believe, but why we believe as we do.

2. We need not endorse every idea contained in the materials we produce and make available.

We serve the educational process by disseminating the knowledge and wisdom required for the growth of the mind and the expansion of learning. For us to employ our own political, moral, or esthetic views as standards for determining what materials are published or circulated conflicts with the public interest. We cannot foster true education by imposing on others the structure and content of our own opinions. We must preserve and enhance the people's right to a broader range of ideas than those held by any librarian or publisher or church or government. We hold that it is wrong to limit any person to those ideas and that information another believes to be true, good, and proper.

3. We regard as irrelevant to the acceptance and distribution of any creative work the personal history or political affiliations of the author or others responsible for it or its publication.

A work of art must be judged solely on its own merits. Creativity cannot flourish if its appraisal and acceptance by the community is influenced by the political views or private lives of the artists of the creators. A society that allows blacklists to be compiled and used to silence writers and artists cannot exist as a free society.

4. With every available legal means, we will challenge laws or governmental action restricting or prohibiting the publication of certain materials or limiting free access to such materials.

Our society has no place for legislative efforts to coerce the taste of its members, to restrict adults to reading matter deemed suitable only for children, or to inhibit the efforts of creative persons in their attempts to achieve artistic perfection. When we prevent serious artists from dealing with truth as they see it, we stifle creative endeavor at its source. Those who direct and control the intellectual development of our children—parents, teachers, religious leaders, scientists, philosophers, statesmen—must assume the responsibility for preparing young people to cope with life as it is and to face the diversity of experience to which they will be exposed as they mature. This is an affirmative responsibility that cannot be discharged easily, certainly not with the added burden of curtailing one's access to art, literature, and opinion. Tastes differ. Taste, like morality, cannot be controlled by government, for governmental action, devised to suit the demands of one group, thereby limits the freedom of all others.

5. We oppose labeling any work of literature or art, or any persons responsible for its creation, as subversive, dangerous, or otherwise undesirable.

Labeling attempts to predispose users of the various media of communication, and to ultimately close off a path to knowledge. Labeling rests on the assumption that persons exist who have a special wisdom, and who, therefore, can be permitted to determine what will have good and bad effects on other people. But freedom of expression rests on the premise of ideas vying in the open marketplace for acceptance, change, or rejection by individuals. Free men choose this path.

6. We, as guardians of intellectual freedom, oppose and will resist every encroachment upon that freedom by individuals or groups, private or official.

It is inevitable in the give-and-take of the democratic process that the political, moral and esthetic preferences of a person or group will conflict occasionally with those of others. A fundamental premise of our free society is that each citizen is privileged to decide those opinions to which he will adhere or which he will recommend to the members of a privately organized group or association. But no private group may usurp the law and impose its own political or moral concepts upon the general public. Freedom cannot be accorded only to selected groups, for it is then transmuted into privilege and unwarranted license.

7. Both as citizens and professionals, we will strive by all legitimate means open to us to be relieved of the threat of personal, economic, and legal reprisals resulting from our support and defense of the principles of intellectual freedom.

Those who refuse to compromise their ideals in support of intellectual freedom have often suffered dismissals from employment, forced resignations, boycotts of products and establishments, and other invidious forms of punishment. We perceive the admirable, often lonely, refusal to succumb to threats of punitive action as the highest form of true professionalism: dedication to the cause of intellectual freedom and the preservation of vital human and civil liberties.

In our various capacities, we will actively resist incursions against the full exercise of our professional responsibility for creating and maintaining an intellectual environment which fosters unrestrained creative endeavor and true freedom of choice and access for all members of the community.

We state these propositions with conviction, not as easy generalizations. We advance a noble claim for the value of ideas, freely expressed, as embodied in books and other kinds of communication. We do this in our belief that a free intellectual climate fosters creative endeavors capable of enormous variety, beauty, and usefulness, and thus worthy of support and preservation. We recognize that application of these propositions may encourage the dissemination of ideas and forms of expression that will be frightening or abhorrent to some. We believe that what people read, view, and hear is a critically important issue. We recognize, too, that ideas can be dangerous. It may be, however, that they are effectually dangerous only when opposing ideas are suppressed. Freedom, in its many facets, is a precarious course. We espouse it heartily.

*Adopted by the American Library Association Council, June 25, 1971.*

## FREE ACCESS TO LIBRARIES FOR MINORS

### An Interpretation of the Library Bill of Rights

Some library procedures and practices effectively deny minors access to certain services and materials available to adults. Such procedures and practices are not in accord with the LIBRARY BILL OF RIGHTS and are opposed by the American Library Association.

Restrictions take a variety of forms, including, among others, restricted reading rooms for adult use only, library cards limiting circulation of some materials to adults only, closed collections for adult use only, collections limited to teacher use, or restricted according to a student's grade level, and interlibrary loan service for adult use only.

Article 5 of the LIBRARY BILL OF RIGHTS states that, "A person's right to use a library should not be denied or abridged because of origin, age, background, or views." All limitations on minors' access to library materials and services violate that Article. The "right to use a library" includes use of, and access to, all library materials and services. Thus, practices which allow adults to use some services and materials which are denied to minors abridge the use of libraries based on age.

Material selection decisions are often made and restrictions are often initiated under the assumption that certain materials may be "harmful" to minors, or in an effort to avoid controversy with parents. Libraries or library boards who would restrict the access of minors to materials and services because of actual or suspected parental objections should bear in mind that they do not serve *in loco parentis*. Varied levels of intellectual development among young people and differing family background and child-rearing philosophies are significant factors not accommodated by a uniform policy based upon age.

In today's world, children are exposed to adult life much earlier than in the past. They read materials and view a variety of media on the adult level at home and elsewhere. Current emphasis upon early childhood education has also increased opportunities for young people to learn and to have access to materials, and has decreased the validity of using chronological age as an index to the use of libraries. The period of time during which children are interested in reading materials specifically designed for them grows steadily shorter, and librarians must recognize and adjust to this change if they wish to serve young people effectively. Librarians have a responsibility to ensure that young people have access to a wide range of informational and recreational materials and services that reflects sufficient diversity to meet the young person's needs.

The American Library Association opposes libraries restricting access to library materials and services for minors and holds that it is the parents—and only parents—who may restrict their children—and only their children—from access to library materials and services. Parents who would rather their children did not have access to certain materials should so advise their children. The library and its staff are responsible for providing equal access to library materials and services for all library users.

The word "age" was incorporated into Article 5 of the LIBRARY BILL OF RIGHTS because young people are entitled to the same access to libraries and to the materials in libraries as are adults. Materials selection should not be diluted on that account.

*Adopted June 30, 1972; amended July 1, 1981, by the ALA Council.*

## EXHIBIT SPACES AND MEETING ROOMS

### An Interpretation of the Library Bill of Rights

As part of their program of service, many libraries provide meeting rooms and exhibit spaces for individuals and groups. Article VI of the LIBRARY BILL OF RIGHTS states that such facilities should be made available to the public served by the given library "on an equitable basis, regardless of the beliefs or affiliations of individuals or groups requesting their use."

In formulating this position, the American Library Association sought to accommodate the broad range of practices among public, academic, school and other libraries, while upholding a standard of fairness. Libraries maintaining exhibit and meeting room facilities for outside groups and individuals should develop and publish policy statements governing their use. These statements can properly define and restrict eligibility for use as long as the qualifications do not pertain to the content of a meeting or exhibit or to the beliefs or affiliations of the sponsors.

It is appropriate for a library to limit access to meeting rooms or exhibit space to members of the specific community served by the library or to groups of a specific category. It is not proper to apply such limitations in ways which favor points of view or organizations advocating certain viewpoints. For example, some libraries permit religious groups to use meeting facilities, while others do not. According to Article VI, both policies are acceptable as long as all religious groups are treated in the same way, irrespective of their doctrines.

Exhibits and meetings sponsored by the library itself should be organized in a manner consistent with the LIBRARY BILL OF RIGHTS, especially Article II which states that "libraries should provide materials and information presenting all points of view." However, in granting meeting or exhibit space to outside individuals and groups, the library should make no effort to censor or amend the content of the exhibit or meeting. Those who object to or disagree with the content of any exhibit or meeting held at the library should be entitled to submit their own exhibit or meeting proposals which should be judged according to the policies established by the library.

The library may properly limit the use of its meeting rooms to meetings which are open to the public, or it may make space available for both public and private sessions. Again, however, the same standard should be applicable to all.

*Adopted February 4, 1981 by the ALA Council.*

## LIBRARY INITIATED PROGRAMS AS A RESOURCE

### An Interpretation of the Library Bill of Rights

Library initiated programming is a library resource that provides information, education, and recreation to library users. Library initiated programming utilizes library staff, books, library and community resources, resource people, displays, and media presentations. The library often incorporates cooperative programming with other agencies, organizations, and educational institutions, as well as other resources, to communicate with library users. Library initiated programs should provide "for the interest, information, and enlightenment of all the people of the community the library serves," as stated in Article 1 of the LIBRARY BILL OF RIGHTS.

The American Library Association believes that library sponsored programs, as well as library resources, "should not be proscribed or removed (or canceled) because of partisan or doctrinal disapproval" (Article 2 of the LIBRARY BILL OF RIGHTS).

A person's right to attend a library initiated program "should not be denied or abridged because of origin, age, background, or views" (Article 5 of the LIBRARY BILL OF RIGHTS).

A written policy on library initiated programming, approved by the library's policy-making body, should reflect the library's philosophy regarding free access to information and ideas. Similarly, concerns expressed regarding library initiated programs should be handled as they are for library resources.

Selection of library program topics, speakers, courses, classes, and resource materials should be made by library staff on the basis of the interests and needs of library users and the community. Library programming should not exclude topics, books, speakers, media, and other resources because they might be controversial.

*Adopted January 27, 1982 by the ALA Council.*

## STATEMENT ON LABELING

### An Interpretation of the Library Bill of Rights

Labeling is the practice of describing or designating certain library materials by affixing a prejudicial label to them or segregating them by a prejudicial system. The American Library Association opposes this as a means of predisposing people's attitudes towards library materials for the following reasons:

1. Labeling is an attempt to prejudice attitudes and as such, it is a censor's tool.

2. Some find it easy and even proper, according to their ethics, to establish criteria for judging publications as objectionable. However, injustice and ignorance rather than justice and enlightenment result from such practices, and the American Library Association opposes the establishment of such criteria.

3. Libraries do not advocate the ideas found in their collections. The presence of books and other resources in a library does not indicate endorsement of their contents by the library.

   The American Library Association opposes efforts which aim at closing any path to knowledge. This statement does not, however, exclude the adoption of organizational schemes designed as directional aids or to facilitate access to materials.

*Adopted July 13, 1951. Amended June 25, 1971; July 1, 1981,*
*by the ALA Council.*

## EXPURGATION OF LIBRARY MATERIALS

### An Interpretation of the Library Bill of Rights

Books and other library resources are selected for their value, interest, and importance to the people of the community the library serves. Since books and other library resources are acquired for these reasons and in accordance with a written statement on materials selection, then expurgating them must be interpreted as a violation of the LIBRARY BILL OF RIGHTS. Expurgation as defined by this interpretation includes any deletion, excision, alteration, or obliteration of any part(s) of books or other library resources by the library. By such expurgation, the library is in effect denying access to the complete work and the entire spectrum of ideas that the work intended to express; such action stands in violation of Articles 1, 2, and 3 of the LIBRARY BILL OF RIGHTS, which state that "Materials should not be excluded because of the origin, background, or views of those contributing to their creation," that "Materials should not be proscribed or removed because of partisan or doctrinal disapproval," and that "Libraries should challenge censorship in the fulfillment of their responsibility to provide information and enlightenment."

The act of expurgation has serious implications. It involves a determination that it is necessary to restrict complete access to that material. This is censorship. When a work is expurgated, under the assumption that certain portions of that work would be harmful to minors, the situation is no less serious.

Expurgation of any books or other library resources imposes a restriction, without regard to the rights and desires of all library users, by limiting access to ideas and information.

*Adopted February 2, 1973; amended July 1, 1981, by the ALA Council.*

## RESTRICTED ACCESS TO LIBRARY MATERIALS

### An Interpretation of the Library Bill of Rights*

Restricting access of certain titles and classes of library materials is a practice common to many libraries in the United States. Collections of these materials are referred to by a variety of names such as "closed shelf," "locked case," "adults only," or "restricted shelf."

Three reasons generally advanced to justify restricted access are:

1. It provides a refuge for materials that belong in the collection but which may be considered "objectionable" by some library patrons;

2. It provides a means for controlling distribution of materials to those who are allegedly not "prepared" for such materials, or who have been labeled less responsible, because of experience, education, or age;

3. It provides a means to protect certain materials from theft and mutilation.

Restricted access to library materials is frequently in opposition to the principles of intellectual freedom. While the limitation differs from direct censorship activities, such as removal of library materials or refusal to purchase certain publications, it nonetheless constitutes censorship, albeit in a subtle form. Restricted access often violates the spirit of the LIBRARY BILL OF RIGHTS in the following ways:

1. It violates that portion of Article 2 which states that ". . . no library materials should be proscribed . . . because of partisan or doctrinal disapproval."

   "Materials . . . proscribed" as used in Article 2 includes "suppressed" materials. Restricted access achieves *de facto* suppression of certain materials.

   Even when a title is listed in the catalog with a reference to its restricted status, a barrier is placed between the patron and the publication. Because a majority of materials placed in restricted collections deal with controversial, unusual, or "sensitive" subjects, asking a librarian or

---

*See also FREE ACCESS TO LIBRARIES FOR MINORS, adopted June 30, 1972; amended July 1, 1981, by the ALA Council.

circulation clerk for them may be embarrassing for patrons desiring the materials. Because restricted collections are often composed of materials which some library patrons consider "objectionable," the potential user is predisposed to thinking of the materials as "objectionable," and may be reluctant to ask for them. Although the barrier between the materials and the patron is psychological, it is nonetheless a limitation on access to information.

2.  It violates Article 5, which states that, "A person's right to use a library should not be denied or aridged because of . . . age. . . ."

Limiting access of certain materials only to adults abridges the use of the library for minors. Access to library materials is an integral part of the right to use a library. Such restrictions are generally instituted under the assumption that certain materials are "harmful" to minors, or in an effort to avoid controversy with adults who might think so.

Libraries and library boards who would restrict the availability of materials to minors because of actual or anticipated parental objection should bear in mind that they do not serve *in loco parentis*. The American Library Association holds that it is parents—and only parents—who may restrict their children—and only their children—from access to library materials and services. Parents who would rather their children not have access to certain materials should so advise their children.

When restricted access is implemented solely to protect materials from theft or mutilation, the practice may be legitimate. However, segregation of materials to protect them must be administered with extreme attention to the reason for restricting access. Too often only "controversial" materials are the subject of such segregation, indicating that factors other than theft and mutilation—including content—were the true considerations. When loss rates of items popular with young people are high, this cannot justify the labeling of all minors as irresponsible and the adoption of prejudiced restrictions on the right of minors to use library services and materials.

Selection policies, carefully developed to include principles of intellectual freedom and the LIBRARY BILL OF RIGHTS, should not be vitiated by administrative practices such as restricted access.

*Adopted February 2, 1973; amended July 1, 1981, by the ALA Council.*

## DIVERSITY IN COLLECTION DEVELOPMENT

### An Interpretation of the Library Bill of Rights

Throughout history, the focus of censorship has vacillated from generation to generation. Books and other materials have not been selected or have been removed from library collections for many reasons, among which are prejudicial language and ideas, political content, economic theory, social philosophies, religious beliefs, and/or sexual forms of expression.

Some examples of this may include removing or not selecting materials because they are considered by some as racist or sexist; not purchasing conservative religious materials; not selecting materials about or by minorities because it is thought these groups or interests are not represented in a community; or not providing information on or materials from non-mainstream political entities.

Librarians may seek to increase user awareness of materials on various social concerns by many means, including, but not limited to, issuing bibliographies and presenting exhibits and programs.

Librarians have a professional responsibility to be inclusive, not exclusive, in collection development and in the provision of interlibrary loan. Access to all materials legally obtainable should be assured to the user and policies should not unjustly exclude materials even if offensive to the librarian or the user. Collection development should reflect the philosophy inherent in Article 2 of the LIBRARY BILL OF RIGHTS: "Libraries should provide materials and information presenting all points of view on current and historical issues. Materials should not be proscribed or removed because of partisan or doctrinal disapproval." A balanced collection reflects a diversity of materials, not an equality of numbers. Collection development and the selection of materials should be done according to professional standards and established selection and review procedures.

There are many complex facets to any issue, and variations of context in which issues may be expressed, discussed, or interpreted. Librarians have a professional responsibility to be fair, just, equitable, and to give all library users equal protection in guarding against violation of the library patrons' liberty to read, view, or listen to materials and resources protected by the First Amendment, no matter what the viewpoint of the author, creator, or selector. Librarians have an obligation to protect library collections from removal of materials based on personal bias or prejudice, and to select and support the access to materials on all subjects that meet, as closely as possible, the needs and interests of all persons in the community which the library serves. This includes materials that reflect political, economic, religious, social, minority, and sexual issues.

Intellectual freedom, the essence of equitable library services, promotes no causes, furthers no movements, and favors no viewpoints. It only provides for free access to all expressions of ideas through which any and all sides of a question, cause, or movement may be explored. Toleration is meaningless without tolerance for what some may consider detestable. Librarians cannot justly permit their own preferences to limit their degree of tolerance in collection development, because freedom is indivisible.

(Note: This policy replaces the policy, RACISM, SEXISM, AND OTHER -ISMS IN LIBRARY MATERIALS.)

*Adopted July 14, 1982 by the ALA Council.*

## EVALUATING LIBRARY COLLECTIONS

### An Interpretation of the Library Bill of Rights

The continuous review of library materials is necessary as a means of maintaining an active library collection of current interest to users. In the process, materials may be added and physically deteriorated or obsolete materials may be replaced or removed in accordance with the collection maintenance policy of a given library and the needs of the community it serves. Continued evaluation is closely related to the goals and responsibilities of libraries and is a valuable tool of collection development. This procedure is not to be used as a convenient means to remove materials presumed to be controversial or disapproved of by segments of the community. Such abuse of the evaluation function violates the principles of intellectual freedom and is in opposition to the Preamble and Articles 1 and 2 of the LIBRARY BILL OF RIGHTS, which state:

> The American Library Association affirms that all libraries are forums for information and ideas, and that the following basic policies should guide their services.
>
> 1. Books and other library resources should be provided for the interest, information, and enlightenment of all people of the community the library serves. Materials should not be excluded because of the origin, background, or views of those contributing to their creation.
>
> 2. Libraries should provide materials and information presenting all points of view on current and historical issues. Materials should not be proscribed or removed because of partisan or doctrinal disapproval.

The American Library Association declares as a matter of firm principle that it is the responsibility of every library to have a clearly defined materials selection policy in written form which reflects the LIBRARY BILL OF RIGHTS, and which is approved by the appropriate governing authority.

Challenged materials which meet the materials selection policy of the library should not be removed under any legal or extra-legal pressure. The LIBRARY BILL OF RIGHTS states in Article 1 that "Materials should not be excluded because of the origin, background, or views of those contributing to their creation," and in Article 2, that "Materials should not be proscribed or removed because of partisan or doctrinal disapproval." Freedom of expression is protected by the Constitution of the United States, but constitutionally protected expression is often separated from unprotected expression only by a dim and uncertain line. The Constitution requires a procedure designed to focus searchingly on challenged expression before it can be suppressed. An adversary hearing is a part of this procedure.

Therefore, any attempt, be it legal or extra-legal, to regulate or suppress materials in libraries must be closely scrutinized to the end that protected expression is not abridged.

*Adopted June 25, 1971; amended July 1, 1981, by the ALA Council.*

## ADMINISTRATIVE POLICIES AND PROCEDURES AFFECTING ACCESS TO LIBRARY RESOURCES AND SERVICES

### An Interpretation of the Library Bill of Rights

The right of free access to information for all individuals is basic to all aspects of library service regardless of type of library. Article 5 of the LIBRARY BILL OF RIGHTS protects the rights of an individual to use a library regardless of origin, age, background, or views. The central thrust of the LIBRARY BILL OF RIGHTS is to protect and encourage the free flow of information and ideas. The American Library Association urges that all libraries set policies and procedures that reflect the basic tenets of the LIBRARY BILL OF RIGHTS.

Many libraries have adopted administrative policies and procedures regulating access to resources, services, and facilities, i.e., specific collections, reference services, interlibrary loan, programming, meeting rooms, exhibit space. Such policies and procedures governing the order and protection of library materials and facilities, and the planning of library programs and exhibits, could become a convenient means for removing or restricting access to controversial materials, limiting access to programs or exhibits, or for discriminating against specific groups of library patrons. Such abuse of administrative procedures and policies is in opposition to the LIBRARY BILL OF RIGHTS.

The American Library Association recommends that all libraries with rare or special collections formulate policies and procedures for such collections so as not to restrict assess and use due to age or the nature of the patron interest in the materials. Restricted access to such collections is solely for the protection of the materials, and must in no way limit access to the information and ideas contained in the materials.

The Model Interlibrary Loan Code of the American Library Association recommends that all library patrons be eligible for interlibrary loan, in accordance with Article 5 of the LIBRARY BILL OF RIGHTS and the statement FREE ACCESS TO LIBRARIES FOR MINORS. The Model Interlibrary Loan Code states the importance of considering the needs and interests of all users, including children and young adults. Borrowing libraries should provide the resources to meet the ordinary needs of all of its primary clientele, and any members of its clientele should be eligible for interlibrary loan. When libraries adhere to the Model Interlibrary Loan Code, access to information is protected.

Library administrative policies should examine all restrictions to resources or services associated with age, as all are violations of Article 5 or the LIBRARY BILL OF RIGHTS and the statement on restricted access to library materials. For example, privileges associated with library cards should be consistent for all library users, no matter what the age. Library policies in which certain patrons, usually minors, are denied library privileges available to other library patrons are not endorsed by the American Library Association, as they violate Article 5 of the LIBRARY BILL OF RIGHTS, as well as the statement on FREE ACCESS TO LIBRARIES FOR MINORS. It is parents and only parents who may restrict their children—and only their children—from access to library materials and services.

Reference service policies and procedures, such as library policies limiting the time spent on answering telephone reference questions, should provide for equitable service to all library patrons, regardless of age or type of question. These policies must apply to both adult and child patrons.

Policies governing the use of meeting rooms and exhibits should be examined to ensure that minors are not excluded from a program of interest to them based on age. Meeting rooms and exhibit spaces should also be available on an "equitable basis, regardless of the beliefs or affiliations of individuals or groups requesting their use," and should not be denied to anyone based solely on age.

Policies should reflect that a person's right to attend a library initiated program "should not be denied or abridged because of origin, age, background, or views," as stated in LIBRARY INITIATED PROGRAMS AS A RESOURCE, an Interpretation of the LIBRARY BILL OF RIGHTS.

*Adopted January 27, 1982 by the ALA Council.*

## DEALING WITH COMPLAINTS ABOUT RESOURCES

All libraries are pressured from groups and individuals who wish to use the library as an instrument of their own tastes and views.

It is the responsibility of every library to take certain measures to clarify policies and establish community relations. They will provide a firm and clearly defined position if selection policies are challenged. As normal operating procedure, each library should:

1. *Maintain a materials selection policy.* It should be in written form and approved by the appropriate governing authority. It should apply to all library materials equally.

2. *Maintain a clearly defined method for handling complaints.* The complaint must be filed in writing and the complainant must be properly identified before action is taken. A decision should be deferred until fully considered by appropriate administrative authority. [A sample form follows.]

3. *Maintain in-service training.* Conduct periodic in-service training to acquaint staff, administration, and the governing authority with the materials selection policy and method for handling complaints.

4. *Maintain lines of communication with civic, religious, educational, and political bodies of the community.* Library board and staff participation in local civic organizations and presentations to these organizations should emphasize the library's selection process and intellectual freedom principles.

5. *Maintain a vigorous public information program on behalf of intellectual freedom.* Newspapers, radio and television should be informed of policies governing materials selection and use, and of any special activities pertaining to intellectual freedom.

6. *Maintain familiarity with any local, municipal and state legislation pertaining to intellectual freedom and First Amendment rights.*

Adherence to these practices will not preclude confrontations with pressure groups or individuals but should provide a base from which to resist efforts to place restraints on the library. If a confrontation does occur, take one or more of the steps listed below:

1. Listen calmly and courteously to the complaint and advise the complainant of the library's procedure for reconsideration of materials. Don't confuse noise with substance. Handle the complaint according to established rules. Treat the group or individual who complains with dignity and courtesy.

2. Take immediate steps to notify the administration and/or the governing authority (library board, etc.) of the complaint and assure them that the library's procedures are being followed. Present full, written information giving the nature of the complaint and identifying the source.

3. When appropriate, seek the support of the local media. Freedom to read and freedom of the press go hand in hand.

4. When appropriate, inform local civic organizations of the facts and enlist their support. Meet negative pressure with positive pressure.

5. Defend the *principle* of the freedom to read as a professional responsibility. Only rarely is it necessary to defend the individual item. Laws governing obscenity, subversive material, and other questionable matter are subject to interpretation by courts. Library materials found to meet the standards set in the selection policy should not be removed from public access until after an adversary hearing resulting in a final judicial determination.

6. Contact the ALA Office for Intellectual Freedom and your state intellectual freedom committee to inform them of the complaint and to enlist their support in appropriate ways. Even though censorship must be fought at the local level, there is value in the support and assistance of agencies outside the area which have no personal involvement. They can often cite parallel cases and suggest methods of meeting an attack.

The principles and procedures discussed above apply to all kinds of censorship attacks and are supported by groups such as the National Education Association, the American Civil Liberties Union, and the National Council of Teachers of English, as well as the American Library Association. While the practices provide positive means for preparing for and meeting pressure group complaints, they serve the more general purpose of supporting the LIBRARY BILL OF RIGHTS, particularly Article 3, which states that: "Libraries should challenge censorship in the fulfillment of their responsibility to provide information and enlightenment."

## **Request for Reconsideration of Library Materials**

Title _____ Book ____ Periodical ____ Other ____

Author _____

Publisher _____

Request initiated by _____

Address _____

City _____ State _____ Zip _____ Telephone _____

Do you represent:

_____ Yourself _____

_____ An Organization (name)_____

_____ Other group (name) _____

1. To what in the work do you object? (Please be specific. Cite pages.) _____
_____

2. Did you read the entire work?_____What parts?_____
_____

3. What do you feel might be the result of reading this work?_____
_____

4. For what age group would you recommend this work?_____
_____

5. What do you believe is the theme of this work? _____
_____

6. Are you aware of judgments of this work by literary critics?_____
_____

7. What would you like your library/school to do about this work? __
__ Do not assign/lend it to my child.
__ Return it to the staff selection committee/department for reevaluation.
__ Other. Explain._____
_____

8. In its place, what work would you recommend that would convey as valuable a picture and perspective of the subject treated? _____
_____
_____

Signature                                        Date

## POLICY ON CONFIDENTIALITY OF LIBRARY RECORDS

The Council of the American Library Association strongly recommends that the responsible officers of each library in the United States:

1. Formally adopt a policy which specifically recognizes its circulation records and other records identifying the names of library users to be confidential in nature.
2. Advise all librarians and library employees that such records shall not be made available to any agency of state, federal, or local government except pursuant to such process, order, or subpoena as may be authorized under the authority of, and pursuant to, federal, state, or local law relating to civil, criminal, or administrative discovery procedures or legislative investigative power.
3. Resist the issuance or enforcement of any such process, order, or subpoena until such time as a proper showing of good cause has been made in a court of competent jurisdiction.*

*Adopted January 20, 1971; revised July 4, 1975, by the ALA Council.*

---

*Note: Point 3, above, means that upon receipt of such process, order, or subpoena, the library's officers will consult with their legal counsel to determine if such process, order, or subpoena is in proper form and if there is a showing of good cause for its issuance; if the process, order, or subpoena is not in proper form or if good cause has not been shown, they will insist that such defects be cured.

## THE STUDENTS' RIGHT TO READ*

The right to read, like all rights guaranteed or implied within our constitutional tradition, can be used wisely or foolishly. In many ways, education is an effort to improve the quality of choices open to man. But to deny the freedom of choice in fear that it may be unwisely used is to destroy the freedom itself. For this reason, we respect the right of individuals to be selective in their own reading. But for the same reason, we oppose efforts of individuals or groups to limit the freedom of choice of others or to impose their own standards or tastes upon the community at large.

The right of any individual not just to read but to read whatever he wants to read is basic to a democratic society. This right is based on an assumption that the educated and reading man possesses judgment and understanding and can be trusted with the determination of his own actions. In effect, the reading man is freed from the burden of discovering all things and all facts and all truths through his own direct experiences for his reading allows him to meet people, debate philosophies, and experience events far beyond the narrow confines of his own existence.

In selecting books for reading by young people, English teachers consider the contribution which each work may make to the education of the reader, its aesthetic value, its honesty, its readability for a particular group of students, and its appeal to adolescents. English teachers, however, may use different works for different purposes. The criteria for choosing a work to be read by an entire class are somewhat different from the criteria for choosing works to be read by small groups. For example, a teacher might select John Knowles' *A Separate Peace* for reading by an entire class, partly because the book has received wide critical recognition, partly because it is relatively short and will keep the attention of many slow readers, and partly because it has proved popular with many students of widely differing abilities. The same teacher, faced with the responsibility of choosing or recommending books for several small groups of students, might select or recommend books as different as Nathaniel Hawthorne's *The Scarlet Letter,* Jack Schaefer's *Shane,* Alexander Solzhenitsyn's *One Day in the Life of Ivan Denisovitch,* Pierre Boulle's *The Bridge over the River Kwai,* Charles Dickens' *Great Expectations,* or Paul Zindel's *The Pigman,* depending upon the abilities and interests of the students in each group. And the criteria for suggesting books to individuals or for recommending something worth reading for a student who casually stops by after class are different from selecting material for a class or group. But the

---

*Reprinted by permission of National Council of Teachers of English.

teacher selects books; he does not censor them. Selection implies that a teacher is free to choose this or that work, depending upon the purpose to be achieved and the student or class in question, but a book selected this year may be ignored next year, and the reverse. Censorship implies that certain works are not open to selection, this year or any year.

Many works contain isolated elements to which some individuals or groups may object. The literary artist seeks truth, as he is able to see and feel it. As a seeker of truth, he must necessarily challenge at times the common beliefs or values of a society; he must analyze and comment on people's actions and values and the frequent discrepancy between what they purport to live by and what they do live by. In seeking to discover meaning behind reality, the artist strives to achieve a work which is honest. Moreover, the value and impact of any literary work must be examined as a whole and not in part—the impact of the entire work being more important than the words, phrases, or incidents out of which it is made.

Wallace Stevens once wrote, "Literature is the better part of life. To this it seems inevitably necessary to add, provided life is the better part of literature." Students and parents have the right to demand that education today keep students in touch with the reality of the world outside the classroom. Much of classic literature asks questions as valid and significant today as when the literature first appeared, questions like "What is the nature of humanity?" "Why do people praise individuality and practice conformity?" "What do people need for a good life?" and "What is the nature of the good person?" But youth is the age of revolt, and the times today show much of the world in revolt. To pretend otherwise is to ignore a reality made clear to young people and adults alike on television and radio, in newspapers and magazines. English teachers must be free to employ books, classic or contemporary, which do not lie to the young about the perilous but wondrous times we live in, books which talk of the fears, hopes, joys, and frustrations people experience, books about people not only as they are but as they can be. English teachers forced through the pressures of censorship to use only safe or antiseptic works are placed in the morally and intellectually untenable position of lying to their students about the nature and condition of mankind.

The teacher must exercise care to select or recommend works for class reading and group discussion which will not embarrass students in discussion with their peers. One of the most important responsibilities of the English teacher is developing rapport and respect among students. Respect for the uniqueness and potential of the individual, an important facet of the study of literature, should be emphasized in the English class. For students to develop a respect for each individual, no matter what his race or creed or values may be, multiethnic materials must become a part of the literature program in all schools, regardless of the ethnic composition of the school population. It is time that literature classes reflect the cultural contributions of many minority groups in the United States, just as they should acquaint students with contributions from the peoples of Asia, Africa, and Latin America.

What a young reader gets from any book depends both on the selection and on the reader himself. A teacher should choose books with an awareness of the student's interests, his reading ability, his mental and emotional maturity, and the values he may derive from the reading. A wide knowledge of many works, common sense, and professional dedication to students and to literature will guide the teacher in making his selections. The community that entrusts students to the care of an English teacher should also trust that teacher to exercise professional judgment in selecting or recommending books.

## The Threat to Education

Censorship leaves students with an inadequate and distorted picture of the ideals, values, and problems of their culture. Writers may often be the spokesmen of their culture, or they may stand to the side attempting to describe and evaluate that culture. Yet, partly because of censorship or the fear of censorship, many writers are ignored or inadequately represented in the public schools, and many are represented in anthologies not by their best work but by their "safest" or "least offensive" work.

The censorship pressures receiving the greatest publicity are those of small groups who protest the use of a limited number of books with some "objectionable" realistic elements, such as *Brave New World, Lord of the Flies, Catcher in the Rye, The Stranger, Johnny Got His Gun, The Assistant, Catch-22, Soul on Ice,* or *Stranger in a Strange Land.* The most obvious and immediate victims are often found among our best and most creative English teachers, those who have ventured outside the narrow boundaries of conventional texts. Ultimately, however, the real victims are the students, denied the freedom to explore ideas and pursue truth wherever and however they wish.

Great damage may be done by book committees appointed by national or local organizaions to pore over anthologies, texts, library books, and paperbacks to find sentences which advocate, or seem to advocate, causes or concepts or practices these organizations condemn. As a result, some publishers, sensitive to possible objections, carefully exclude sentences or selections that might conceivably offend some group somehow, sometime, somewhere.

Many well-meaning people wish to restrict reading materials in schools to books that do not mention certain aspects of life they find offensive: drugs, profanity, Black Power, antiwar marches, smoking, sex, racial unrest, rock music, politics, pregnancy, school dropouts, peace rallies, drinking, Chicano protests, or divorce. Although he may personally abhor one or more of these facets of modern life, the English teacher has the responsibility to encourage students to read about and reflect on many aspects, good and bad, of their own society and of other cultures.

## The English Teacher's Purposes and Responsibilities

The purpose of education remains what it has always been in a free society: to develop a free and reasoning human being who can think for himself, who understands his own and, to some extent, other cultures, who lives compassionately and cooperatively with his fellow man, who respects both himself and others, who has developed self-discipline and self-motivation and exercises both, who can laugh at a world which often seems mad, and who can successfully develop survival strategies for existence in that world.

The English teacher knows that literature is a significant part of the education of man, for literature raises problems and questions and dilemmas that have perplexed and intrigued and frustrated man since the dawn of time. Literature presents some solutions to complex problems and some answers to abiding questions, perhaps incomplete but the best we have found. Even more important, literature continues to raise questions man can never wholly answer: What is the relationship between power and moral responsibility? Why does the good man sometimes suffer and the evil man sometimes go untouched by adversity? How can man reconcile the conflict of duty between what he owes society and what he owes his own conscience? The continued search for answers, tentative as they must prove, is a necessary part of the educated man's life, and the search for answers may in part be found through reading.

Aware of the vital role of literature in the education of mankind, the English teacher has unique responsibilities to his students and to adults in the community. To his students, he is responsible for knowing many books from many cultures, for demonstrating a personal commitment to the search for truth through wide reading and continual critical questioning of his own values and beliefs, for respecting the unique qualities and potential of each student, for studying many cultures and societies and their values, and for exhibiting the qualities of the educated man. To adults, he is responsible for communicating information about his literature program;

for explaining, not defending, what books he uses with what students, for what reasons, and with what results; and for communicating the necessity of free inquiry and the search for truth in a democratic society and the dangers of censorship and repression.

## The Community's Responsibility

American citizens who care about the improvement of education are urged to join students, teachers, librarians, administrators, boards of education, and professional and scholarly organizations in support of the students' right to read. Only widespread and informed support in every community can assure that:

1. Enough citizens are interested in the development and maintenance of a superior school system to guarantee its achievement.
2. Malicious gossip, ignorant rumors, deceptive letters to the editor will not be circulated without challenge and correction.
3. Newspapers will be convinced that the public sincerely desires objective school news reporting, free from slanting or editorial comment which destroys confidence in and support for schools.
4. The community will not permit its resources and energies to be dissipated in conflicts created by special interest groups striving to advance their ideologies or biases.
5. Faith in democratic traditions and processes will be maintained.

*National Council of Teachers of English, Urbana, IL 61820.*

## THE FREEDOM TO READ

The freedom to read is essential to our democracy. It is continuously under attack. Private groups and public authorities in various parts of the country are working to remove books from sale, to censor textbooks, to label "controversial" books, to distribute lists of "objectionable" books or authors, and to purge libraries. These actions apparently rise from a view that our national tradition of free expression is no longer valid; that censorship and suppression are needed to avoid the subversion of politics and the corruption of morals. We, as citizens devoted to the use of books and as librarians and publishers responsible for disseminating them, wish to assert the public interest in the preservation of the freedom to read.

We are deeply concerned about these attempts at suppression. Most such attempts rest on a denial of the fundamental premise of democracy: that the ordinary citizen, by exercising his critical judgment, will accept the good and reject the bad. The censors, public and private, assume that they should determine what is good and what is bad for their fellow-citizens.

We trust Americans to recognize propaganda, and to reject it. We do not believe they need the help of censors to assist them in this task. We do not believe they are prepared to sacrifice their heritage of a free press in order to be "protected" against what others think may be bad for them. We believe they still favor free enterprise in ideas and expression.

We are aware, of course, that books are not alone in being subjected to efforts at suppression. We are aware that these efforts are related to a larger pattern of pressures being brought against education, the press, films, radio and television. The problem is not only one of actual censorship. The shadow of fear cast by these pressures leads, we suspect, to an even larger voluntary curtailment of expression by those who seek to avoid controversy.

Such pressure toward conformity is perhaps natural to a time of uneasy change and pervading fear. Especially when so many of our apprehensions are directed against an ideology, the expression of a dissident idea becomes a thing feared in itself, and we tend to move against it as against a hostile deed, with suppression.

And yet suppression is never more dangerous than in such a time of social tension. Freedom has given the United States the elasticity to endure strain. Freedom keeps open the path of novel and creative solutions, and enables change to come by choice. Every silencing of a heresy, every enforcement of an orthodoxy, diminishes the toughness and resilience of our society and leaves it the less able to deal with stress.

Now as always in our history, books are among our greatest instruments of freedom. They are almost the only means for making generally available ideas of manners of expression that can initially command only a small audience. They are the natural medium for the new idea and the untried voice from which come the original contributions to social growth. They are essential to the extended discussion which serious thought requires, and to the accumulation of knowledge and ideas into organized collections.

We believe that free communication is essential to the preservation of a free society and a creative culture. We believe that these pressures towards conformity present the danger of limiting the range and variety of inquiry and expression on which our democracy and our culture depend. We believe that every American community must jealously guard the freedom to publish and to circulate, in order to preserve its own freedom to read. We believe that publishers and librarians have a profound responsibility to give validity to that freedom to read by making it possible for the readers to choose freely from a variety of offerings.

The freedom to read is guaranteed by the Constitution. Those with faith in free men will stand firm on these constitutional guarantees of essential rights and will exercise the responsiilities that accompany these rights.

## We therefore affirm these propositions:

*1. It is in the public interest for publishers and librarians to make available the widest diversity of views and expressions, including those which are unorthodox or unpopular with the majority.*

Creative thought is by definition new, and what is new is different. The bearer of every new thought is a rebel until his idea is refined and tested. Totalitarian systems attempt to maintain themselves in power by the ruthless suppression of any concept which challenges the established orthodoxy. The power of a democratic system to adapt to change is vastly strengthened by the freedom of its citizens to choose widely from among conflicting opinions offered freely to them. To stifle every nonconformist idea at birth would mark the end of the democratic process. Furthermore, only through the constant activity of weighing and selecting can the democratic mind attain the strength demanded by times like these. We need to know not only what we believe but why we believe it.

*2. Publishers, librarians and booksellers do not need to endorse every idea or presentation contained in the books they make available. It would conflict with the public interest for them to establish their own political, moral or aesthetic views as a standard for determining what books should be published or circulated.*

Publishers and librarians serve the educational process by helping to make available knowledge and ideas required for the growth of the mind and the increase of learning. They do not foster education by imposing as mentors the patterns of their own thought. The people should have the freedom to read and consider a broader range of ideas than those that may be held by any single librarian or publisher or government or church. It is wrong that what one man can read should be confined to what another thinks proper.

*3. It is contrary to the public interest for publishers or librarians to determine the acceptability of a book on the basis of the personal history or political affiliations of the author.*

A book should be judged as a book. No art or literature can flourish if it is to be measured by the political views or private lives of its creators. No society of free men can flourish which draws up lists of writers to whom it will not listen, whatever they may have to say.

*4. There is no place in our society for efforts to coerce the taste of others, to confine adults to the reading matter deemed suitable for adolescents, or to inhibit the efforts of writers to achieve artistic expression.*

To some, much of modern literature is shocking. But is not much of life itself shocking? We cut off literature at the source if we prevent writers from dealing with the stuff of life. Parents and teachers have a responsibility to prepare the young to meet the diversity of experiences in life to which they will be exposed, as they have a responsibility to help them learn to think critically for themselves. These are affirmative responsibilities, not to be discharged simply by preventing them from reading works for which they are not yet prepared. In these matters taste differs, and taste cannot be legislated; nor can machinery be devised which will suit the demands of one group without limiting the freedom of others.

*5. It is not in the public interest to force a reader to accept with any book the prejudgment of a label characterizing the book or author as subversive or dangerous.*

The ideal of labeling presupposes the existence of individuals or groups with wisdom to determine by authority what is good or bad for the citizen. It presupposes that each individual must be directed in making up his mind about the ideas he examines. But Americans do not need others to do their thinking for them.

*6. It is the responsibility of publishers and librarians, as guardians of the people's freedom to read, to contest encroachments upon that freedom by individuals or groups seeking to impose their own standards or tastes upon the community at large.*

It is inevitable in the give and take of the democratic process that the political, the moral, or the aesthetic concepts of an individual or group will occasionally collide with those of another individual or group. In a free society each individual is free to determine for himself what he wishes to read, and each group is free to determine what it will recommend to its freely associated members. But no group has the right to take the law into its own hands, and to impose its own concept of politics or morality upon other members of a democratic society. Freedom is no freedom if it is accorded only to the accepted and the inoffensive.

*7. It is the responsibility of publishers and librarians to give full meaning to the freedom to read by providing books that enrich the quality and diversity of thought and expression. By the exercise of this affirmative responsibility, bookmen can demonstrate that the answer to a bad book is a good one, the answer to a bad idea is a good one.*

The freedom to read is of little consequence when expended on the trivial; it is frustrated when the reader cannot obtain matter fit for his purpose. What is needed is not only the absence of restraint, but the positive provision of opportunity for the people to read the best that has been thought and said. Books are the major channel by which the intellectual inheritance is handed down, and the principal means of its testing and growth. The defense of their freedom and integrity, and the enlargement of their service to society, requires of all bookmen the utmost of their faculties, and deserves of all citizens the fullest of their support.

We state these propositions neither lightly nor as easy generalizations. We here stake out a lofty claim for the value of books. We do so because we believe that they are good, possessed of enormous variety and usefulness, worthy of cherishing and keeping free. We realize that the application of these propositions may mean the dissemination of ideas and manners of expression that are repugnant to many persons. We do not state these propositions in the comfortable belief that what people read is unimportant. We believe rather that what people read is deeply important; that ideas can be dangerous; but that the supprssion of ideas is fatal to a democratic society. Freedom itself is a dangerous way of life, but it is ours.

**A Joint Statement by:**
*American Library Association*
*Association of American Publishers*

**Subsequently Endorsed by:**

*American Booksellers Association*
*American Civil Liberties Union*
*American Federation of Teachers AFL-CIO*
*Anti-Defamation League of B'nai B'rith*
*Association of American University Presses*
*Bureau of Independent Publishers & Distributors*
*Children's Book Council*
*Freedom of Information Center*
*Freedom to Read Foundation*
*Magazine Publishers Association*
*Motion Picture Association of America*
*National Association of College Stores*
*National Book Committee*
*National Council of Negro Women*
*National Council of Teachers of English*
*National Library Week Program*
*National Board of the Young Women's Christian Association of the U.S.A.*
*P.E.N.-American Center*
*Periodical and Book Association of America*
*Sex Information & Education Council of the U.S.*
*Women's National Book Association*

This statement was originally issued in May of 1953 by the Westchester Conference of the American Library Association and the American Book Publishers Council, which in 1970 consolidated with the American Educational Publishers Institute to become the Association of American Publishers.

## FREEDOM TO VIEW*

The FREEDOM TO VIEW, along with the freedom to speak, to hear, and to read, is protected by the First Amendment to the Constitution of the United States. In a free society, there is no place for censorship of any medium of expression. Therefore, we affirm these principles:

1. It is in the public interest to provide the broadest possible access to films and other audiovisual materials because they have proven to be among the most effective means for the communication of ideas. Liberty of circulation is essential to insure the constitutional guarantee of freedom of expression.
2. It is in the public interest to provide for our audiences films and other audiovisual materials which represent a diversity of views and expression. Selection of a work does not constitute or imply agreement with or approval of the content.
3. It is our professional responsibility to resist the constraint of labeling or prejudging a film on the basis of the moral, religious or political beliefs of the producer or filmmaker or on the basis of controversial content.
4. It is our professional responsibility to contest vigorously, by all lawful means, every encroachment upon the public's freedom to view.

*Educational Film Library Association 1979.*

---

*Reprinted by permission of the Educational Film Library Association.

# Appendix 3
# Banned Books

## CAUTION! A LIST OF BOOKS SOME PEOPLE CONSIDER DANGEROUS*

Compiled by the staff of the American Booksellers Association, edited by Mary Ann Tennenhouse and Jan De Deka, from the following sources, which may be consulted for more in-depth discussions of the issues involved with each title listed here.

Haight, Ann Lyon and Grannis, Chandler B., *Banned Books, 387 B.C. to 1978 A.D.*, R.R. Bowker Co.

Nelson, Randy F., "Banned in Boston and Elsewhere," *The Almanac of American Letters*, William Kaufmann, Inc.

Stanek, Lou Willett, *Censorship: A Guide for Teachers . . .*, Dell Publishing Co.

*The New York Times*, Monday, April 5, 1982

*The New York Times Book Review*, December 20, 1981

*Time*, April 19, 1982

*Censorship News*, National Coalition Against Censorship, various issues

*Newsletter on Intellectual Freedom*, Office for Intellectual Freedom, American Library Association

*Social Education*, April, 1982

*Limiting What Students Shall Read*, Summary report on survey sponsored by Association of American Publishers, American Library Association, Association for Supervision and Curriculum Development, National Coalition Against Censorship

Ken Donelson, "Censorship," a tape recording prepared by the Children's Book Council

American Library Association Traveling Exhibit

American Society of Journalists and Authors, various publications

Children's Book Council

Media Coalition

*Reprinted by permission of the American Booksellers Association.

For more complete bibliographic information consult *Books in Print, British Museum Catalog, Cumulative Book Index,* and *National Union Catalog* of the Library of Congress, particularly for those titles no longer in print.

Before the birth of Christ, even before the time of Homer (approximately 850 B.C.), writers and their writings were questioned. Although objections vary, foremost grounds have usually been religious, political or obscene or pornographic. Penalties have ranged from censure and removal of books, to fines and/or imprisonment for writers, booksellers and publishers, to the burning of books and even a few authors.

Where possible, the following list is coded (See Legend below) to indicate the reason(s) that have been given to seek the banning of each title. In the case of juvenile titles, many were questioned as to suitability at particular grade levels. With regard to obscenity, that category includes some titles thought to be objectionable if not actually obscene. Uncoded titles came from several sources and the reasons were not specified.

## LEGEND

1. Ethnic
2. Inappropriate for young readers, including improper grade level
3. Objectionable language
4. Obscene
5. Political
6. Pornographic
7. Religious
8. Special interest groups
9. Cultural
10. Ethical
11. Literary standards

## CENSORED TITLES

*The American Cartoon Album* [2]
*American Heritage Dictionary,* Dell, Houghton Mifflin [2, 3, 4]
*Baby Brother* [2]
*The Bible—Midrash* [1, 7, 9]
*Childhood Growth and Development,* McGraw-Hill
*Civics,* Follett

*Double Cross*, Chick
*Earth Science*, American Book
*Families*
*The Gospel*, Arbor House, Baker Books [7]
*The Koran*, Penguin, Tahrike Tarsile Quran [7]
*Level 1 Reader*, Harcourt Brace Jovanovich [2]
*Literature 7 and Literature 8*, Ginn & Co. [2]
*Living Law: Civil Justice*, Scholastic
*Living Law: Criminal Justice*, Scholastic
*New Voices*, vols. 1–4, Ginn & Co.
*Our Freedom*, Weekly Reader
*People, Places, and Change*, Holt, Rinehart & Winston
*Scholastic American Citizenship*, Scholastic Book Service
*Scholastic Book of Ghosts*, Scholastic [2]
*The Talmud*, Soncino Press [5]
*War Year*, Holt Rinehart & Winston
*We the People—History of the U.S.*, D.C. Heath
Abelard, Pierre. *Lettres d'Heloise et Abelard*, Cooper Square [4, 7, 9]
Agee, Philip. *Inside the Company: CIA Diary*, Bantam, Stonehill Pub. [5]
Aho and Petras. *Learning About Sex*, Holt, Rinehart & Winston [2]
Allard, Harry. *The Stupids Step Out*, Houghton Mifflin [2, 8]
Allen, Donald, Ed. *The New American Poetry*, Grove Press
Altman, Thomas. *Kiss Daddy Goodbye*, Bantam [2]
Andersen, Hans, Christian. *Wonder Stories* (2, 4)
Anderson, Sherwood. *Dark Laughter*, Dynamic Learning Corp., Liveright
Andress, Lesley. *Caper*, Pocket Books, Putnam [2]
Andry and Schepp. *How Babies are Made*, Time-Life [2]
Anonymous. *The Arabian Nights' Entertainment*, Dover Books, Grosset &
    Dunlap
Anonymous. *Go Ask Alice*, Avon, Prentice-Hall [2, 4]
Anson, Jay. *The Amityville Horror*, Bantam [2]
Archer, J. and Schwartz, A. *A Reader for Writers*, McGraw Hill [1, 2, 4, 7,
    10]
Aristophanes. *Lysistrata*, New American Library, Penguin, University
    Press of Virginia [4]
Arms and Camp. *Biology*, Holt, Rinehart & Winston [1]
Armstrong, William. *Sounder*, Harper & Row [1]
Arrick, Fran. *Steffie Can't Come Out to Play*, Bradbury
Asher, Don. *Blood Summer*, Putnam [2, 10]
Asimov, Issac. *Issac Asimov's Treasury of Humor*, Houghton Mifflin; [2]
    In the Beginning: Science Faces God in the Book of Genesis, Crown [7]

Babbitt, Natalie. *The Devil's Storybook*, Bantam [2]; Farrar, Straus & Giroux

Bacon, Francis. *Advancement of Learning* Humanities, Rowman & Littlefield [7]

Bailey and Kennedy. *The American Pageant: A History of the Republic*, D.C. Heath

Baldwin, James. *Another Country* [4]

Balzac, Honore de. *Droll Stories*, French & European [4]

Bannerman, Helen. *Little Black Sambo*, Lippincott, Platt & Munk, Western [1]

Baraka, Imamu Amiri (Leroi Jones). *The Toilet* [1, 2]

Baudelaire, Charles. *The Flowers of Evil*, New Directions, Norton [9, 10]

Baum, Frank L. *The Wizard of Oz*, Grosset & Dunlap [2, 11]

Beaumarchais, Pierre. *Barber of Seville*, Penguin [5, 7, 10]; *Marriage of Figaro*, Penguin [5, 7, 10]

Bell, Ruth et al. *Changing Bodies, Changing Lives*, Random House

Benchley, Peter. *Jaws*, Bantam, Doubleday [2, 3, 4]

Benford, Gregory. *In the Ocean of Night*, Dell [2]

Bently, Thomas. *Adventures of a Young Outlaw* [2]

Berrigan, Daniel. *Trial of the Catonsville Nine* [2]

Bishop, Claire H. *The Five Chinese Brothers* [1, 2]

Blatty, William P. *The Exorcist*, Bantam, Harper & Row [2, 4, 11]

Blume, Judy. *Are You There God? It's Me, Margaret*, Bradbury [2]; *Blubber*, Dell, Dutton [2]; *Deenie*, Bradbury [2, 4]; *Forever*, Bradbury, Pocket Books [2]; *It's Not the End of the World*, Bantam, Bradbury [2]; *Starring Sally J. Freedman as Herself*, Bradbury, Dell [2]; *Then Again, Maybe I Won't*, Bradbury [2]; *Wifey*, Pocket Books, Putnam [2, 6]

Boccaccio. *The Decameron*, AMS Press, Johns Hopkins, Norton, Penguin [4, 6]

Bomans, Godfried. *Wily Witch and All the Other Fairy Tales and Fables*, Stemmer House [2]

Bonham, Frank. *Gimme an H, Gimme an E, Gimme an L, Gimme a P*, Scribner

Bonners, Susan. *Panda*, Delacorte [2]

Boston Women's Health Book Collective. *Our Bodies, Ourselves*, Simon & Schuster [2]

Bower, William C. *The Living Bible*, Arno [7]

Branscum, Robbie. *Johnny May*, Doubleday [2]

Brautigan, Richard. *The Abortion: An Historical Romance*, Pocket Books, Simon & Schuster; *A Confederate General from Big Sur*, Delta/Seymour Lawrence; *The Pill vs. the Springhill Mine Disaster*, Dell [2, 4];

*The Revenge of the Lawn*, Pocket Books [2]; *Rommel Drives on Deep into Egypt*, Delacorte, Dell [2, 4]; *Trout Fishing in America*, Delacorte

Bredes, Don. *Hard Feelings,* Atheneum, Bantam

Bricklin, Mark. *The Practical Encyclopedia of Natural Healing*, Rodale Press [2]

Briggs, Raymond. *Father Christmas*, Coward [2, 9]

Brodsky, Mimi. *The House at 12 Row Street*, Archway [2]

Brown, Claude. *Manchild in the Promised Land*, Macmillan, New American Library [2, 3, 4]

Browning, Elizabeth Barrett. *Aurora Leigh*, Academy Chicago [4]

Buck, Pearl S. *The Good Earth*, Crowell, Harper & Row, Pocket Books [2]

Burgess, Anthony. *A Clockwork Orange*, Ballantine, Norton [2, 4, 11]

Burroughs, William. *Naked Lunch*, Grove Press [4]

Burroughs, William and Ginsberg, Allen. *The Yage Letters*, City Lights [4]

Buryn, Ed. *Vagabonding in the U.S.A.*, And/Or Press [2]

Cabell, James Branch. *Jurgen*, Dover Books [4]

Caldwell, Erskine. *God's Little Acre*, New American Library [4, 6]; *Tobacco Road*, New American Library [4, 6]

Calvin, John. *Civil and Canonical Law* [5, 7]

Carroll, Lewis. *Alice's Adventures in Wonderland*, Ace, Bantam, Crown, Delacorte, Dover, New American Library, Norton, Penguin, Random House, St. Martin's [9, 10, 11]

Casanova de Seingalt. *Memoires (History of My Life)*, Harcourt Brace Jovanovich [4, 7, 9, 10]

Cervantes, Saavedra, Miguel de. *Don Quixote*, Methuen, New American Library, Norton, Random House [7, 10]

Chamberlain, Wilt. *Wilt Chamberlain* [2]

Chelminsky, Rudolph. *Paris*, Time-Life [2, 4]

Chick, Jack T. *The Big Betrayal*, Chick [2]

Childress, Alice. *A Hero Ain't Nothin' but a Sandwich*, Avon, Coward, Putnam [1, 2, 4, 7, 10]

Chittum, Ida. *Tales of Terror* [2]

Chopin, Kate O'Flaherty. *The Awakening*, Avon, Bantam, Norton [4, 9, 10]

Clark, Walter Van Tilburg. *The Ox Bow Incident,* New American Library

Cleaver, Eldridge. *Soul on Ice*, Dell, McGraw Hill [1, 2, 5, 7, 11]

Cleland, John. *Fanny Hill*, Dell, Grove Press [4]

Clifton, Lucille. *AMIFSKA*, Dutton [2]

Colby, C.B. *Colby—Second World War Aircraft*, Coward [2]

Colman, Hila. *Diary of a Frantic Kid Sister*, Archway, Crown [2]

Comfort, Alex. *The Facts of Love*, Ballantine, Crown [2, 4]; *Joy of Sex*, Crown, Simon & Schuster [2, 4]; *More Joy of Sex*, Crown [2, 4]

Confucius. *Analects*, Dover Books, Random House [5, 9]

Connelly, Marc. *The Green Pastures*, Holt, Rinehart & Winston [7]

Coombs, Patricia. *The Magic Pot*, Lothrop [2]

Coppel, Alfred. *Thirty-Four East* [2]

Corley, Edwin. *The Genesis Rock*, Dell, Doubleday [2]

Cormier, Robert. *The Chocolate War*, Dell, Pantheon [2]

Cox, R. David. *Student Critic*, Winthrop Publishers

Dalrymple, D. and Parsons, L. *Marketing Management; Text and Cases*, Wiley

Daniell, Rosemary. *Fatal Flowers*, Avon, Holt, Rinehart & Winston [4, 9]

Dante, Alighieri. *The Divine Comedy*, Norton, Pocket Books, Random House, Regnery Gateway [4, 5, 6]

D'Arch, Anne Jeanne. *One Woman's War on VD in the Nursery School* [2]

Darrow, Whitney. *I'm Glad I'm a Boy, I'm Glad I'm a Girl* [2]

Darwin, Charles B. *On the Origin of Species*, Harvard University Press, Littlefield, Macmillan, New American Library, Norton, Rowman [2, 7]

Davenport, Basil. *Famous Monster Tales* [2]

Davies, Hunter. *The Beatles*, McGraw Hill [2]

Davies, Peter. *Fly Away Paul*, Crown [2]

Davis, Terry. *Vision Quest*, Bantam, Viking

DeFelitta, Frank Paul. *Audrey Rose*, Warner [2]

DeFoe, Daniel. *Adventures of Robinson Crusoe*, Bantam, Grosset & Dunlap, New American Library, Norton [1]; *Moll Flanders*, Houghton Mifflin, Modern Library, New American Library, Penguin [4]; *Political History of the Devil*, Oxford University Press [5]; *Roxana*, Viking [4]; *The Shortest Way with the Dissenters* [5, 7]

Diagram Group. *Man's Body: An Owner's Manual*, Bantam, Paddington Press [2]; *Woman's Body: An Owner's Manual*, Bantam, Paddington Press, Pocket Books [2]

Dickey, J. *Deliverance*, Dell [2, 3]

Donleavy, J.P. *The Ginger Man*, Delacorte, Dell; *Schultz*, Delacorte, Dell

Donovan, John. *I'll Get There. It Better Be Worth the Trip*, Dell, Harper & Row [2]

Dorson, Richard M. *America in Legend*, Pantheon Books [5, 6]

Doyle, Sir Arthur Conan. *The Adventures of Sherlock Holmes*, Avon, Berkley, Harper & Row [7]

Dreiser, Theodore. *An American Tragedy*, New American Library [4]; *Dawn* [4]; *Genius*, Lightyear, New American Library [4]; *Sister Carrie*, Airmont; Bantam; Bobbs-Merrill; Holt, Rinehart & Winston; Houghton Mifflin; Norton; Penguin [4]

Du Jardin, Rosamond. *Senior Prom*, Lippincott

Dumas, Alexandre. *La Dame au Camelias*, French & European [4]

Durrell, Lawrence. *The Black Book*, Dutton [4]

Dworkin, Andrea. *Pornography: Men Possessing Women*, Putnam

Eagan, Andrea B. *Why Am I So Miserable if These Are the Best Years of My Life* [2]

Ehrlich, Max. *The Reincarnation of Peter Proud*, Bobbs Merrill

Elfman, Blossom. *The Girls of Huntington House*, Bantam, Houghton Mifflin [2]

Eliot, George. *Adam Bede*, Houghton Mifflin, New American Library, Penguin [4]; *Silas Marner,* Bantam [2], New American Library, Zodiac Press [2]

Ellis, Havelock. *Studies in the Psychology of Sex* [3, 4]

Ellison, Ralph. *Invisible Man*, Random House, Vintage [1]

Elwood, Roger. *Future City*, Trident [2]

Emery, Anne. *Sorority Girl*, Westminster

Enger, Gibson, Kormelink, Ross, Smith. *Concepts in Biology*, William C. Brown Pub. [2, 4]

Eyerly, Jeannette. *He's My Baby Now*, Archway, Harper & Row, Pocket Books [2]

Farrell, James. *Studs Lonigan: A Trilogy*, Avon, Vanguard [3, 4, 9, 10]

Fast, Howard. *Citizen Tom Paine* [2, 5]

Faulkner, William. *The Hamlet*, Random House [4]; *Mosquitoes*, Liveright [4]; *Pylon* [4]; *Sanctuary*, Random House, Vintage [4]; *Soldier's Pay*, Liveright [4]; *Wild Palms*, Random House [4]

Felsen, Henry Gregor. *Hot Rod*, Dutton

Ferlinghetti, Lawrence. *Coney Island of the Mind*, New Directions [2, 4, 11]; *Starting from San Francisco*, New Directions [2, 4, 11]

Fielding, Henry. *Tom Jones*, New American Library, Norton, Penguin [4, 7]

Fields, Jeff. *A Cry of Angels*, Atheneum, Ballantine [2]

Fitzgerald, F. Scott. *The Great Gatsby*, Scribner [3, 4]

Fitzgerald, John D. *The Great Brain*, Dell, Dial [2]

Fitzhugh, Louise. *Bang, Bang, You're Dead*, Harper & Row [2]

Flaubert, Gustave. *Madame Bovary*, Bantam, Houghton Mifflin, Modern Library, New American Library, Norton, Penguin [4, 9, 10]

Fox, Paula. *The Slave Dancer*, Bradbury [1]

Forbes, Esther. *Johnny Tremain*, Dell, Houghton Mifflin

Frank, Anne. *Anne Frank: The Diary of a Young Girl,*, Doubleday, Pocket Books, Random House [2, 4]

French, Marilyn. *The Women's Room*, Jove, Summit [2]

Friday, Nancy. *Men in Love*, Delacorte, Dial

Fromm, Erich. *The Art of Loving*, Harper & Row [2]

Gaines, Donald. *Whoreson,* Holloway

Galilei, Galilei. *Dialogo Sopra I Due Massini Sistemi del Mondo*, University of California Press [7]

Gardner, Benjamin Franklin. *Black*, Books for Libraries Press [2, 6]

Gates, Doris. *Two Queens of Heaven*, Viking [2, 4]

Gautier, Theophile. *Mademoiselle de Maupin*, French & European, Penguin [4]

Genet, Jean. *Our Lady of the Flowers*, Grove Press [4]

George, Jean Craighead. *Julie of the Wolves*, Harper & Row

Gibbon, Edward. *History of the Decline and Fall of the Roman Empire*, Modern Library [5, 7]

Gide, Andre. *If It Die* [4]

Ginsberg, Allen. *Howl and Other Poems*, City Lights [2]; *Kaddish and other Poems*, City Lights

Glasser, Ronald J. *365 Days*, Braziller [2, 3]

Godey, John. *The Snake*, Putnam [2]

Goethe, Johann Wolfgang von. *Faust*, Doubleday, Macmillan, Norton, Oxford University Press, Penguin [5, 7]; *The Sorrows of Werther*, Ungar [7]

Golding, William. *Lord of the Flies*, Coward [2]

Goode, Erich and Troiden, Richard, eds. *Sexual Deviance and Sexual Deviants*, Morrow [6]

Gordon, Sol. *You: The Teenage Survival Book*, Times Books [2]

Graves, Robert. *I, Claudius*, Random House [4]

Grawunder, Ralph and Steinmann, Marion. *Life and Health* [2, 10]

Griffin, John Howard. *Black Like Me*, Houghton Mifflin, New American Library [2]

Gruenberg, Sidonie M. *The Wonderful Story of How You Were Born*, Doubleday [2]

Guest, Judith. *Ordinary People,* Ballantine, G.K. Hall, Viking

Guthrie, A.B., Jr. *The Big Sky*, Bantam [5]; *The Way West*, Bantam [5]

Guy, Rosa. *Ruby*, Viking

Haining, Peter. *Necromancers* [2]

Hall, Lynn. *Sticks and Stones*, Dell, Follett [2]

Hall, Radclyffe. *The Well of Loneliness*, Avon [4, 10]

Hannam, Charles. *A Boy in That Situation*, Harper & Row [2]

Hardy, Thomas. *Jude the Obscure*, Airmont, Bantam, Bobbs-Merrill, Houghton Mifflin, New American Library, Norton, St. Martin [7]; *Tess of the D'Urbervilles*, Bantam, Houghton Mifflin, New American Library, Norton, Penguin, St. Martin [4]

Harris, Frank. *My Life and Loves*, Grove Press [4, 6]

Hawthorne, Nathaniel. *The Scarlet Letter*, Bantam; Dell; Dodd, Mead; Holt, Rinehart & Winston; Houghton Mifflin; Modern Library; New American Library; Norton [2, 4, 10]

Head, Ann. *Mr. and Mrs. Bo Jo Jones*, New American Library [2]

Heller, Joseph. *Catch-22*, Modern Library, Simon & Schuster [2, 4]

Hemingway, Ernest. *Across the River and into the Trees*, Scribners [4]; *A Farewell to Arms*, Scribners [2]; *For Whom the Bell Tolls*, Scribners [4]; *The Old Man and the Sea*, Scribners [2]; *The Sun Also Rises*, Scribners [2, 4]; *To Have and Have Not*, Scribners [4]

Henry, Marguerite. *The Little Fellow*, Rand McNally [2]

Hentoff, Nat. *This School Is Driving Me Crazy*, Delacorte, Dell [2]

Heyman, Abigail. *Growing Up Female in America*, Holt, Rinehart & Winston

Hinton, S.E. *The Outsiders*, Dell, Viking [2]

Hirson, Roger O. and Schwartz, Stephen. *Pippin*, Avon

Hitler, Adolf. *Mein Kampe*, Houghton Mifflin [5]

Hoenig, Gary. *Reaper: The Inside Story of a Gang Leader,* Bobbs-Merrill [2]

Hoffman, Elizabeth. *This House Is Haunted*, Raintree [2]

Holland, Isabelle. *The Man without a Face*, Harper & Row

Holt Data Bank Fourth Grade Text. *Inquiring into Culture*, Holt, Rinehart & Winston [2]

Homer. *The Odyssey*, Airmont, Doubleday, Harper & Row, Macmillan, New American Library, Oxford University Press, Penguin [2, 5]

Hooks, William H. *The Seventeen Gerbils of Class 4-A*, Coward [2]

Hughes, Langston. *The Best Short Stories by Negro Writers*, Little, Brown [1, 2, 4, 7, 10, 11]

Hugo, Victor. *Hernani*, French & European, Larousse [7, 9]; *Les Miserables*, Dodd, Mead; Fawcett; Penguin [7]; *Notre Dame de Paris*, Penguin [7]

Hunter, Evan. *The Chisholms,* Harper & Row; *Sons* [2]

Hus, Jan. *De Ecclesia*, Greenwood [1]

Huxley, Aldous. *Antic Hay* [4]; *Brave New World*, Harper & Row [2, 5, 6, 7]; *Eyeless in Gaza*, Harper & Row [4]; *Point Counter Point*, Harper & Row [4]

Ibsen, Henrik. *An Enemy of the People,* Penguin; *Ghosts*, Beekman, Dutton [4, 9, 10]

Ipcar, Dahlov. *Cat Come Back*, Knopf [2]

Jackson, Jesse. *Call Me Charley*, Harper & Row [1]

Jackson, Shirley. *The Lottery*, Encyclopedia Brittanica Educational Corp.; Farrar, Straus & Giroux; Popular Library [2, 10]

Johnson, Eric W. *Love and Sex in Plain Language*, Lippincott/Harper, Bantam; *Sex: Telling It Straight* [2]

Jones, James. *From Here to Eternity*, Dell, Dial [4]

Jonson, Ben. *Eastward Ho*, AMS Press [1]

Jordan, June. *His Own Where*, Crowell, Harper & Row

Joyce, James. *Dubliners*, Modern Library, Penguin [4]; *Ulysses*, Farrar, Straus & Giroux; Modern Library; Random House/Vintage [4]

Kantor, MacKinlay. *Andersonville*, New American Library [5]; *Valley Forge*, M. Evans [2, 5]

Kazan, Elia. *Acts of Love*, Knopf, Warner [2, 6]

Kazantzakis, Nikos. *The Last Temptation of Christ*, Simon & Schuster

Kennedy, Richard. *Inside My Feet: A Story of a Giant*, Harper & Row [2]; *The Mouse God*, Little, Brown [2]

Kerr, M.E. *Dinky Hocker Shoots Smack*, Dell, Harper & Row [2, 3, 7]

Kesey, Ken. *One Flew over the Cuckoo's Nest*, New American Library, Penguin, Viking [2, 11]

Keyes, Daniel. *Flowers for Algernon*, Bantam, Harcourt Brace Jovanovich [2, 6]

King, Stephen. *Carrie*, Doubleday [2]; *Salem's Lot*, Doubleday [2]

Kingston, Jeremy. *Witches and Witchcraft* [2]

Kinsey, Alfred. *Sexual Behavior in the Human Female*, Saunders [6]; *Sexual Behavior in the Human Male*, Saunders [6]

Klein, Norma. *It's Not What You Expect*, Avon [2]; *It's OK if You Don't Love Me*, Dial, Fawcett [2, 3, 4]; *Mom, the Wolf Man and Me*, Avon, Pantheon [2]; *Naomi in the Middle*, Dial, Pocket/Archway [2, 10, 11]; *Sunshine*, Avon; Holt, Rinehart & Winston; *Tomboy*, Archway, Four Winds/Scholastic [2]

Knight, David C. *Poltergeists: Hauntings and the Haunted* [2]

Knowles, John. *A Separate Peace*, Bantam, Dell, Macmillan

Korman, Avery. *Kramer vs. Kramer*, New American Library, Random House

Kosinski, Jerzy. *The Painted Bird*, Bantam, Houghton Mifflin

Kotzwinkle, William. *Nightbook*, Avon

LaFarge, Oliver. *Laughing Boy*, Houghton Mifflin, New American Library

La Place, John. *Health*, Prentice-Hall [2, 3, 4, 7]

Larrick, Nancy and Merriam, Eve. *Male and Female under 18*, Prentice-Hall [2]

Lawrence, D.H. *Collected Paintings* [4]; *Lady Chatterley's Lover*, Bantam, Grove Press, New American Library, Random House [4]; *Paintings of D.H. Lawrence* [4]; *The Rainbow*, Penguin [4]; *Sons and*

*Lovers*, Penguin, Modern Library/Random House, Viking [4]; *Women in Love*, Penguin/Viking [4]

Lee, Harper. *To Kill a Mockingbird*, Lippincott/Harper & Row, Popular Library

Leek, Sybil. *Complete Art of Witchcraft*, New American Library

LeGuin, Ursula K. *The Left Hand of Darkness*, Ace, Harper & Row [2]

Lenin. *Declaration of Independence* [5]; *United States Constitution* [5]; *The State and Revolution*, China Books, International Publishing [5]

Levin, Ira. *Rosemary's Baby*, Dell, Random House [2, 4, 11]; *Stepford Wives*, Random House

Levine, Joan Goldman. *The Santa Claus Mystery*, Dutton [2]

Levitin, Sonia. *The Mark of Conte*, Atheneum [2]

Levoy, Myron. *Alan and Naomi*, Dell, Harper & Row

Lewis, Elby. *There Are Two Lives: Poems by Children of Japan* [2]

Lewis, Sinclair. *Cass Timerlane*, Woodhill; *Elmer Gantry*, New American Library; *Kingsblood Royal*, New American Library

Lexau, Joan M. *Benjie on His Own*, Dial [2]

Locke, John. *An Essay Concerning Human Understanding*, Dover, Oxford University Press, New American Library

Loewen, James and Sallis, Charles, eds. *Mississippi: Conflict and Change*, Pantheon [1]

Lofting, Hugh. *The Voyages of Dr. Dolittle*, Lippincott/Harper & Row

London, Jack. *The Call of the Wild*, Ace, Bantam, Grosset & Dunlap, Macmillan, New American Library, Penguin, Pocket Books, Raintree, Tempo [5]

Louys, Pierre. *Aphrodite* [4]; *The Songs of Bilitis* [4]; *The Twilight of the Nymphs* [4]

Lowry, Lois. *Find a Stranger, Say Goodbye*, Houghton Mifflin, Pocket Books [2]

Luther, Martin. *Address to the German Nobility*, Concordia, Doubleday [7]; *Works*, Concordia, Doubleday [7]

Maas, Peter. *The Valachi Papers* [5]

MacDongell. *The Cheerleader* [2]

Machiavelli, Niccolo. *Discourses*, Bantam, Penguin, Routledge [5]; *The Prince*, Bantam, New American Library, Penguin [5]

MacLean, Alistair. *Goodbye, California*, Doubleday, Fawcett [2]

Mailer, Norman. *The Naked and the Dead*, Holt, Rinehart & Winston; New American Library [3, 4]

Malamud, Bernard. *The Fixer*, Dell; Farrar, Straus & Giroux; Pocket Books [2, 4, 7, 10, 11]

Manchester, William. *The Death of a President*, Harper & Row [8]

Manley, Seon and Lewis, Gogo. *Sister of Sorcery* [2]

Mann, Patrick. *Dog Day Afternoon*, Delacorte

Marchetti, Victor and Marks, John D. *The CIA and the Cult of Intelligence*, Dell, Knopf [5]

Marx, Karl. *Das Kapital*, Imported Publishers, Random House, Regnery-Gateway [5]; *Manifesto of the Communist Party* [5]

Mayle, Peter. *Where Did I Come From?*, Lyle Stuart [2]

Mazer, Norma Fox. *Saturday, the Twelfth of October*, Delacorte, Dell, Dial [2, 4]; *Solid Gold Kid*, Dell, Dial [2]

McBride, Will and Fleischauer-Hardt, Helga. *Show Me!*, St. Martin's [2, 6]

McCullough, Colleen. *The Thorn Birds*, Avon, Harper & Row [2]

McNally, Terrence. *Bringing It All Back Home* [2]

Means, Florence Crannell. *The Moved-Outers*, Houghton Mifflin [2]

Meriwether, Louise. *Daddy Was a Numbers Runner*, Pyramid [2]

Merriam, Eve. *Growing up Female in America: Ten Lives*, Dell [2, 6]; *The Inner City Mother Goose*, Simon & Schuster/Touchstone [9, 10]

Metalious, Grace. *Peyton Place*, Simon & Schuster [4]

Mill, John Stuart. *Social Philosophy* [7, 9, 10]; *System of Logic* [7, 9, 10]

Miller, Arthur. *Death of a Salesman*, Penguin, Viking [2, 3]; *A View from the Bridge*, Bantam, Penguin [4]

Miller, Henry. *Sexus*, Grove [4]; *Tropic of Cancer*, Grove [4, 6]; *Tropic of Capricorn*, Grove [4, 6]

Millhiser, Marlys. *The Mirror*, Fawcett [2]

Milton, John. *Paradise Lost*, Airmont; Holt, Rinehart & Winston; Modern Library/Random House; New American Library; Norton [2, 7]

Minear, Richard. *Through Japanese Eyes*, Cite [1, 2]

Mitchell, Margaret. *Gone with the Wind*, Avon, Macmillan [2]

Moliere. *Le Tartuffe*, Harcourt, Brace Jovanovich [7]

Montaigne, Michel de. *Les Essaies*, French & European, Stanford University Press [10]

Morris, Desmond. *The Naked Ape*, Dell, McGraw-Hill [7, 10, 11]

Morrison, Lillian. *Best Wishes, Amen: A New Collection of Autograph Verses*, Harper & Row [2]

Myers, Walter D. *Fast Sam, Cool Clyde, and Stuff*, Viking [2]

Nabokov, Vladimir. *Lolita*, Berkley, McGraw Hill, Putnam [4, 9, 10]

Neufield, John. *For All the Wrong Reasons*, New American Library [2]; *Freddy's Book*, Ballantine, Random House [2]

Nilsson, Lennart. *How Was I Born?*, Delacorte, Dial [2]

Noel, Janet. *The Human Body* [2]

Oakley, Graham, *The Church Mice at Bay*, Atheneum

O'Dell, Scott. *Kathleen, Please Come Home*, Dell, Houghton Mifflin
O'Hara, Frank. *Lunch Poems*, City Lights [2, 4]
O'Hara, John. *Appointment in Samarra* [4]; *Ten North Frederick*, Random
House [4]
O'Neill, Eugene. *Desire Under the Elms* from *Three Plays*, Random
House, Vintage [4]
Orgel, Doris. *The Devil in Vienna*, Dell, Dial [2]
Orwell, George. *Animal Farm*, Harcourt, Brace Jovanovich; New Ameri-
can Library [2]; *1984*, Harcourt, Brace Jovanovich; New American
Library [2, 5]
Ovid. *ARS Amatoria*, Oxford University Press [2, 4, 6, 10]; *Elegies*
Paine, Thomas. *The Age of Reason*, Bobbs Merrill, Citadel [7]; *The Rights
of Man*, Citadel, Penguin [5]
Parks, Gordon. *The Learning Tree*, Fawcett, Harper & Row [1, 2, 3, 4, 7]
Partridge, Eric. *Dictionary of Slang*, Macmillan [2]
Pascal, Blaise. *Pensees*, Penguin [7]
Pasternak, Boris. *Doctor Zhivago*, Ballantine, New American Library,
Pantheon [5]; *My Sister Life; Themes and Variations*
Paterson, A.B. *The Man from Ironbark* [2]
Paterson, Katherine. *Bridge to Terabithia*, Avon, Crown, Harper & Row [2]
Peck, Richard. *Are You in the House Alone*, Dell, Viking [2]
Peck, Robert Newton. *A Day No Pigs Would Die*, Dell, Knopf [2]; *Soup*,
Dell [2]
Perkins, Al. *Don and Donna Go to Bat* [2]
Perry, Marvin. *Unfinished Journey*, Houghton Mifflin
Petronius, Gaius. *Satyricon*, New American Library, Penguin [4, 6, 9]
Pevsner, Stella. *Footsteps on the Stairs* [2]; *Keep Stompin' Till the Music
Stops*, Houghton Mifflin, Scholastic [2]
Plath, Sylvia. *The Bell Jar*, Bantam, Harper & Row [2]
Platt, Charles. *Twilight of the City*, Berkeley [2]
Pomeroy, Wardell. *Boys and Sex*, Delacorte, Dell, Dial [2]
Portal, Colette. *The Beauty of Birth*, Knopf [2]
Prelutsky, Jack. *Nightmares: Poems to Trouble Your Sleep*, Greenwillow [2]
Price, Richard. *The Wanderers*, Houghton Mifflin [2]
Pronzini, Bill. *Snowbound* [2]
Puzo, Mario. *The Godfather*, New American Library, Putnam [2]
Rabelais, Francois. *Gargantua*, Penguin [3, 4, 5]; *Pantagruel*, Penguin
[3, 4, 5]
Raucher, Herman. *Summer of '42*, Dell [2, 3, 6]
Rayner, Mary. *Mr. and Mrs. Pig's Evening Out*, Atheneum [2]

Reich, Wilhelm. *Character Analysis*, Farrar, Straus & Giroux [10]; *Function of the Orgasm*, Simon & Schuster [10]; *The Mass Psychology of Facism*, Simon & Schuster; Farrar, Straus & Giroux [10]; *The Sexual Revolution*, Simon & Schuster; Farrar, Straus & Giroux [10]

Reiff, Stephanie Ann. *Visions of the Future: Magic Numbers and Cards*, Raintree [2]

Reiss, Johanna. *The Upstairs Room*, Crowell, Harper & Row

Remarque, Erich Maria. *All Quiet on the Western Front*, Fawcett, Little [4, 5]; *The Road Back* [4,5]

Rhine, J.B., and Pratt, J.G. *Parapsychology: Frontier Science of The Mind*, C. C. Thomas [2]

Riker, Andrew. *Finding My Way*, Bennett

Riker, Andrew, et al. *Married Life*, Bennett

Robbins, Harold. *The Carpetbaggers*, Trident, Pocket Books [4]; *The Lonely Lady*, Pocket Books, Simon & Schuster [4, 6]

Roberts, Nancy. *Appalachian Ghosts*, Doubleday [2]

Roberts, Willo D. *Don't Hurt Laurie*, Atheneum [2]; *View from the Cherry Tree*, Atheneum [2]

Robinson, David. *Herbert Armstrong's Tangled Web*, Interstate Book Manufacturers

Rockwell, Thomas. *How to Eat Fried Worms*, Dell, Dial, Watts [2]

Roden, Cuban. *Promise of America* [1, 2]

Rose, Reginald. *Twelve Angry Men*, Irvington

Roth, Philip. *Goodbye, Columbus*, Bantam, Houghton Mifflin [6]; *Portnoy's Complaint*, Bantam, Random House [2, 4]

Roughsey, Dick. *The Giant Devil-Dingo* [2]

Rousseau, Jean Jacques. *Confessions*, Penguin [4, 10]

Royko, Mike. *Boss: Richard J. Daley of Chicago*, New American Library

Russell, Bertrand. *What I Believe* [7]

Sachs, Marilyn. *Bears' House*, Doubleday [2]

Sade, Marquis de. *Julliette*, Grove Press [4, 5, 6, 7]; *Justine or the Misfortunes of Virtue*, Grove Press [4, 5, 6, 7]

Salinger, J.D. *Catcher in the Rye*, Bantam; Little, Brown [2, 3, 4, 5, 7, 10]

Samuels, Gertrude. *Run, Shelly, Run*, Harper & Row/Crowell, New American Library [2, 3, 4]

Savonarola, Girolamo. *Writings* [7]

Schnitzler, Arthur. *Casanova's Homecoming*, AMS Press [4]; *Reigen* [4]

Schul, Bill, and Petit, Ed. *Secret Power of Pyramids*, Fawcett [2]

Scoppetone, Sandra. *Happy Endings Are All Alike*, Dell, Harper & Row [2]; *Trying Hard to Hear You*, Bantam, Harper & Row [2]

Sebestyen, Ouida. *Words by Heart*, Bantam; Little, Brown

Segal, Eric. *Love Story*, Avon, Harper & Row [2]

Selby, Hubert, Jr. *Last Exit to Brooklyn*, Grove Press [4, 6]

Selden, George. *The Genie of Sutton Place*, Dell; Farrar, Straus & Giroux [2]

Sendak, Maurice. *In the Night Kitchen*, Harper & Row [2, 4]; *Where the Wild Things Are*, Harper [2]

Shakespeare, William. *King Lear*, Airmont, Metheun, New American Library, Penguin, Pocket Books [3, 5]; *The Merchant of Venice*, Airmont, Cambridge University Press, Methuen, New American Library, Penguin, Pocket Books, Washington Square Press, Wiley [1, 2, 7]; *Tragedy of King Richard II*, Airmont, Methuen, New American Library, Penguin, Pocket Books, Washington Square Press [5]

Shaw, George Bernard. *Man and Superman*, Airmont, Penguin [4]; *Mrs. Warren's Profession*, Garland [4]

Shearer, John. *I Wish I Had an Afro* [1, 2]

Sheehy, Gail. *Passages*, Bantam, Morrow [2]

Sheffield and Bewley. *Where Do Babies Come from?*, Knopf, Lyle Stuart

Sheldon, Sidney. *Bloodline*, Morrow, Warner [6]; *Rage of Angels*, Morrow, Warner [6]

Shelley, Percy Bysshe. *Prometheus Unbound* [5, 7, 10]

Shepard, Ray A. *Sneakers* [2]

Shulman, Alix K. *Memoirs of an Ex-Prom Queen*, Knopf [2]

Shulman, Irving. *The Amboy Dukes* [4]

Silverstein, Charles and White, Edmund. *The Joy of Gay Sex,* Crown, Simon & Schuster/Fireside

Silverstein, Shel. *Where the Sidewalk Ends*, Harper & Row [2]

Simon, Sidney. *Values Clarification*, Hart Publishing [2, 10]

Sinclair, Upton. *The Jungle*, Airmont, Bantam, Bentley, New American Library, Penguin [4, 5]; *Oil!* [5]; *Wide Is the Gate* [5]

Smith, Lillian. *Strange Fruit* [2, 4]

Snepp, Frank. *A Decent Interval*, Random, Vintage [5]

Snyder, Anne. *Ny Name is Davy: I'm an Alcoholic*, New American Library [2]

Snyder, Zilpha K. *The Witches of Worm*, Atheneum [2]

Solzhenitsyn, Aleksandr. *August 1914*, Bantam; Farrar, Straus & Giroux [5]; *Cancer Ward*, Bantam; Farrar, Straus & Giroux [5]; *Candle in The Wind*, University of Minnesota Press [5]; *The First Circle*, Bantam [5]; *The Gulag Archipelago*, Harper & Row [5]; *The Love Girl and the Innocent*, Farrar, Straus & Giroux [5]; *One Day in the Life of Ivan Denisovich*, Dutton; Farrar, Straus & Giroux; New American Library [2, 3, 5]; *Stories and Prose Poems*, Farrar, Straus & Giroux [5]

Spencer, Scott. *Endless Love,* Avon, Knopf

Stanley, Michael. *The Swiss Conspiracy*, Avon [2]

Steig, William. *Sylvester and The Magic Pebble*, Simon & Schuster [5]

Stein, Sol. *The Magician*, Delacorte, Dell

Steinbeck, John. *In Dubious Battle*, Penguin; *Of Mice and Men*, Bantam, Penguin, Viking [2, 3, 4, 7, 10]; *Grapes of Wrath*, Penguin, Viking [2, 3, 4, 5, 7]; *The Wayward Bus*, Penguin [4]

Swift, Jonathan. *Drapier Letters* [4, 5]; *Gulliver's Travels*, Airmont, Bantam, Bobbs Merrill, Dell, Grosset & Dunlap, Houghton Mifflin, New American Library, Norton, Oxford University Press, Pocket Books [4, 5]

Taves, Isabella. *Not Bad for a Girl*, M. Evans [2]

Taylor, Theodore. *The Cay*, Avon, Doubleday

Terkel, Studs. *Working*, Avon, Pantheon, Random House [2, 3]

Thomas, Marlo. *Free to Be—You and Me*, McGraw Hill [2]

Thomas, Piri. *Down These Mean Streets*, Knopf, Random House [2, 4]

Thompson, Thomas. *Richie*, Dell [2]

Tibbits, Albert B. *Let's Dance* [2]

Tolstoy, Leo. *The Kreutzer Sonata* (from *Complete Works*), AMS Press [4, 10]

Travers, P.L. *Mary Poppins*, Harcourt, Brace Jovanovich [2]

Tunis, John. *All-American*, Harcourt, Brace Jovanovich [2]; *Yea! Wildcats*, Harcourt, Brace Jovanovich [2]

Twain, Mark. *The Adventures of Huckleberry Finn*, Bantam; Bobbs-Merrill; Grosset & Dunlap; Harper & Row; Holt, Rinehart & Winston; Houghton Mifflin; Longman; Macmillan; New American Library; Norton; Penguin; Pocket Books [1, 2, 3, 10, 11]; *The Adventures of Tom Sawyer*, Airmont, And/Or Press, Bantam, Grosset & Dunlap, Longman, New American Library, Pocket Books [2]

Ungerer, Tomi. *Zeralda's Ogre*, Harper & Row [2]

Vandermeer, Ron and Atie. *Oh Lord!*, Crown [2]

Vasiliu, Mircea. *Once Upon a Pirate Ship* [2]

Voltaire. *Candide*, Bantam; Holt, Rinehart & Winston [4]

Vonnegut, Kurt, Jr. *Breakfast of Champions*, Delacorte/Seymour Lawrence, Dell, Dial [2]; *Cat's Cradle*, Delcorte, Dell [2]; *God Bless You, Mr. Rosewater*, Delcorte, Dell [2, 3]; *Slaughterhouse-Five*, Dell, Dial [2, 3, 4]; *Welcome to the Monkey House*, Delacorte, Dell [2, 3, 4]

Wagner, Jane. *J.T.*, Dell

Wahl, Jan. *Crabapple Night* [2]

Wallace, Irving. *The Fan Club*, Bantam [4]

Waugh, Alec. *The Loom of Youth* [4]

Waxman, Stephanie. *Growing up Feeling Good: A Child's Introduction to Sexuality*, Panjandrum [2]

Weissberger, Bernard A. *The Impact of Our Past: A History of the U.S.*, McGraw Hill

Wentworth, Harold and Berg, Stuart. *Dictionary of American Slang*, Crowell [2, 3, 4]

White, E.B. *Charlotte's Web*, Harper & Row [2]; *Stuart Little*, Harper & Row [2]

Whitman, Walt. *Leaves of Grass*, Adler; Doubleday; Holt, Rinehart & Winston; Norton; Penguin [3]

Wilde, Oscar. *Salome* (from *Complete Works*), Collins [4, 7]

Wilder, Laura I. *Little House in the Big Woods*, Harper & Row [2]

Willingham, Calder. *End as a Man*, Vanguard [4]

Wilson, Colin. *The Sex Diary of Gerard Orme* [4]

Wilson, Edmund. *Memoirs of Hecate County*, Godine, Octagon [4]

Winsor, Kathleen. *Forever Amber*, New American Library [4]

Wojciechowska, Maja. *Tuned out*, Dell, Harper & Row [2]

Wolcott, Patty. *Super Sam and the Salad Garden*, Addison-Wesley [2]

Wolfe, Tom. *Electric Kool-Aid Acid Test*, Bantam; Farrar, Straus & Giroux [2]

Woods, George A. *Catch a Killer* [2]

Wright, Richard. *Black Boy*, Harper & Row [1, 2, 4, 7, 10]; *Native Son*, Harper & Row

Zindel, Paul. *My Darling, My Hamburger*, Bantam, Harper & Row [2, 4, 6]; *The Pigman*, Bantam, Harper & Row [2]

Zola, Emile. *J'Accuse*, French & European [5]; *Nana*, Airmont, French & European, Penguin [4]

# Appendix 4
# Where to Go for Help

## A SELECTED LISTING OF ORGANIZATIONS ACTIVE IN INTELLECTUAL FREEDOM

State and local library and education associations, state departments of education or public instruction, and local chapters of the American Civil Liberties Union are all excellent sources for advice and support.

The following national organizations can also provide assistance.

American Association of School
    Librarians
50 E. Huron St.
Chicago, IL 60611
(312) 944-6780

American Booksellers Association
122 E. 42nd St.
New York, NY 10168

American Civil Liberties Union
22 E. 40th St.
New York, NY 10016
(212) 925-1222

American Federation of Teachers
11 Dupont Circle N.W.
Washington, DC 20036
(202) 797-4400

American Library Association
Office for Intellectual Freedom
50 E. Huron St.
Chicago, IL 60611
(312) 944-6780

Association of American
    Publishers
1 Park Ave.
New York, NY 10016
(212) 689-8920

First Amendment Lawyer's
    Association
Suite 1200
1737 Chestnut St.
Philadelphia, PA 19103
(215) 665-1600

Freedom to Read Foundation
50 E. Huron St.
Chicago, IL 60611
(312) 944-6780

Media Coalition, Inc.
342 Madison Ave
New York, NY 10017
(212) 687-2288

National Ad Hoc Committee
 Against Censorship
22 E. 40th St.
New York, NY 10016
(212) 686-7098

National Council for the Social
 Studies
Suite 406
2030 M St. N.W.
Washington, DC 20036
(202) 296-0760

National Council of Teachers of
 English
1111 Kenyon Rd
Urbana, IL 61801
(217) 328-3870

National Education Association
1201 16th St. N.W.
Washington, DC 20036
(202) 833-4000

National Science Teachers
 Association
1742 Connecticut Ave. N.W.
Washington, DC 20009
(202) 265-4150

P.E.N. American Center
156 Fifth Ave.
New York, NY 10010
(212) 255-1977

Writer's Guild of America East,
 Inc.
22 W. 48th St.
New York, NY 10036
(212) 575-5060

Writer's Guild of America West,
 Inc.
8955 Beverly Blvd.
Los Angeles, CA 90048
(213) 550-1000

# Appendix 5
# Inservice Training in
# Intellectual Freedom

## AN OUTLINE FOR A WORKSHOP ON THE LIBRARY BILL OF RIGHTS AND SELECTION/ACQUISITION POLICIES

### Purpose

The workshop outlined below has been presented for public and school library clerical, paraprofessional, and professional staff. Its objectives are:

1. To introduce or review the Library Bill of Rights and several of its "Interpretations."*
2. To relate them to the selection/acquisition policy of the sponsoring school or public library.
3. To provide practical examples and promote discussion of common censorship difficulties encountered in public or school libraries.

The workshop outline provides a framework for discussion. Evaluations received from more than 300 participants have indicated the workshop's chief strengths are:

1. The usefulness of the discussion of the statements of professional belief contained in the "Library Bill of Rights" and its "Interpretations."
2. The inclusion of practical, "real-life" examples of citizen questions, complaints, or objections to library materials as a major part of the discussion.
3. The opportunity provided to participants to raise issues relating to intellectual freedom and censorship and to receive feedback from the facilitator and other participants.

---

*The Library Bill of Rights and its "Interpretations" are found in Appendix 2 of this book.

## Role of the Facilitator

The facilitator is responsible for the presentation of the material listed below, for promoting discussion, and for keeping the workshop on schedule. To promote discussion the facilitator should be prepared to provide 3–5 practical examples of censorship problems relating to the statements under discussion. It is recommended that examples be drawn from accounts in the library or local and national press. Participants may (and in the author's experience most often do) provide their own examples.

## Materials

The workshop relies on the *Intellectual Freedom Manual* (Chicago: American Library Association, 1974; in revision). Extra copies of the Library Bill of Rights and its "Interpretations" may also be obtained from the Office for Intellectual Freedom, American Library Association, 50 E. Huron St., Chicago, IL 60611. Throughout the workshop, transparencies are used with an overhead projector in order to focus audience attention on the statements under discussion.

## Suggested Schedule

(Note: Times are approximate and may vary according to the number of questions and the amount of discussion.)

| | |
|---|---|
| 10 minutes | Introduction: Introduce the facilitator, mentioning his/her professional credentials and interest in intellectual freedom and censorship. Review the workshop's objectives and schedule. |
| 10 minutes | The First Amendment and the Library Bill of Rights: review them briefly, providing a short history of the Library Bill of Rights. Discussion of the roles of the Office for Intellectual Freedom and the American Library Association can also be useful here, as is an overview of the contents of the *Intellectual Freedom Manual*. |
| 5–10 minutes | Discuss public and school libraries as tax-supported institutions, their responsibility to taxpayers and elected officials, their responsibility for appropriate materials selection. |

30 minutes        Discuss "Free Access to Libraries for Minors." Note common restrictions on access, including borrowers' cards limited to adult use, restrictions on interlibrary loan, etc. Note the advantages and disadvantages of requiring parental permission for use of certain materials. Discuss known examples of specific titles or types of materials restricted to adult use only.

10–15 minutes     Discuss "Statement on Labeling" and "Expurgation of Library Materials." Review definitions of labeling and expurgation. Provide examples of each for discussion.

Break

20 minutes        "Diversity in Collection Development": present the statement. Using known examples (e.g., *Little Black Sambo*), discuss censorship that occurs for the reasons outlined in the statement.

15 minutes        Review the sponsoring library's selection/acquisition policy. Note especially where the principles expressed in the Library Bill of Rights can be used in support of library policy.

30 minutes        "Challenged Materials" and "Dealing with Complaints About Resources": in addition to presenting the two statements, discuss procedures or practices in use in the sponsoring library. Participants may wish and should be encouraged to share their experiences in dealing with censorship.

5–10 minutes      The facilitator should conclude by giving a very brief review or summary of the material covered and by highlighting the results of discussion.

# Recommended Reading

## THE FIRST AMENDMENT, INTELLECTUAL FREEDOM, AND CENSORSHIP

Berninghausen, David K. *The Flight from Reason*. Chicago: American Library Association, 1975.

De Grazia, Edward. *Censorship Landmarks*. New York: R.R. Bowker, 1969.

Downs, Robert B., ed. *The First Freedom*. Chicago: American Library Association, 1960.

Emerson, Thomas I. *The System of Freedom of Expression*. New York: Random House, 1970.

Haight, Anne Lyon, and Chandler, Grannis B. *Banned Books; 387 B.C. to 1978 A.D.* New York: R.R. Bowker, 1978.

McCormick, John, and MacInnes, Mairi, eds. *Versions of Censorship*. Chicago: Aldine Publishing Company, 1962.

*Newsletter on Intellectual Freedom*. Chicago: American Library Association. Published 6 times a year.

Oboler, Eli M. *Fear of the Word: Censorship and Sex*. Metuchen, NJ: Scarecrow Press, 1974.

U.S. President's Commission on Obscenity and Pornography. *The Report of the Commission on Obscenity and Pornography*. Washington, DC: U.S. Government Printing Office, 1970.

## SCHOOLS, SCHOOL BOOKS, AND CENSORSHIP

Arons, Stephen. "The Crusade to Ban Books." *Saturday Review* (June 1981): 17–19.

Burger, Robert H. "The Kanawha County Textbook Controversy: A Study of Communication and Power." *Library Quarterly* 49 (2) (1978): 143–62.

Donnelson, Ken. "These I Believe: Some Statements About Censorship." *Minnesota English Journal* 12 (1) (1976): 15–19.

Eick, Charles F. "Constitutional Law—First Amendment—Right to Receive Information—Board of Education's Removal of Selected Books from Public High School Library Violates Students' First Amendment Right to Receive Information, *Minarcini v. Strongsville City School District*, 541 F. 2d 577 (6th Cir. 1976)." *Texas Law Review* 55 (1977): 511–23.

Estreicher, Aleta G. "Schoolbooks, School Boards, and the Constitution." *Columbia Law Review* 80 (1982): 1092–1123.

Fisher, Louis, and Sorenson, Gail Paulus. "Censorship, Schooling and the Law." *High School Journal* (March 1979): 320–25.

Harpaz, Leora. "A Paradigm of First Amendment Dilemmas: Resolving Public School Library Censorship Disputes." *Western New England Law Review* 4 (1) (1981): 1–103.

Jenkinson, Edward B. *Censors in the Classroom: The Mind Benders*. Carbondale, IL: Southern Illinois University Press, 1979.

Koletsky, Joe. "Case Note: First Amendment—Free Speech: Right to Know—Limit of School Board's Discretion in Curricular Choice—Public School Library as Marketplace of Ideas." *Case Western Reserve Law Review* 27 (1977): 1034–55.

Massie, Dorothy C. "Censorship in the Schools: Something Old and Something New." *Today's Education* (November–December 1980): 56GE–60GE.

Melnick, Robert Russell. "Commentary: Secularism in the Law: The Religion of Secular Humanism." *Ohio Northern University Law Review* 8 (1981): 329–57.

Niccolai, Frances R. "The Right to Read and School Library Censorship." *Journal of Law and Education* 10 (1) (1981): 23–36.

O'Neill, Robert M. *Classrooms in the Crossfire: The Rights and Interests of Students, Parents, Teachers, Administrators, Librarians, and the Community*. Bloomington, IN: Indiana University Press, 1981.

Orleans, Jeffrey H. "What Johnny Can't Read: 'First Amendment Rights' in the Classroom." *Journal of Law and Education* 10 (1) (1981): 1–15.

Ricci, Richard. "Public School Library Book Removals: Community Values v. First Amendment Freedoms." *Notre Dame Lawyer* 57 (1981): 166–88.

Smith, Richard P. "First Amendment Limitations on the Power of School Boards to Select and Remove High School Text and Library Books." *St. John's Law Review* (52) (1978): 457–84.

Stanek, Lou Willett. *Censorship: A Guide for Teachers, Librarians, and Others Concerned with Intellectual Freedom*. New York: Dell Publishing Co., 1976.

Taylor, Kenneth I. "Are School Censorship Cases Really Increasing?" *School Library Media Quarterly* 11 (1) (1982): 26–33.

Tuill, Phyllis. "Little Black Sambo: The Continuing Controversy." *School Library Journal* 22 (7) (March 1976): 71–75.

Yesner, Seymour. "Our Changing Censorship." *Minnesota English Journal* 12 (1) (1976): 9–13.

## LIBRARIES, LIBRARIANS, AND CENSORSHIP

Allain, Alex P. "The First and Fourteenth Amendment as They Support Libraries, Librarians, Library Systems and Library Development." *Women Lawyers Journal* 60 (Spring 1974): 55–73.

American Library Association. Office for Intellectual Freedom. *Intellectual Freedom Manual*. Chicago: American Library Association, 1974. (New edition forthcoming.)

Anderson, A.J. *Problems in Intellectual Freedom and Censorship*. New York: R.R. Bowker, 1974.

Busha, Charles H. *Freedom versus Suppression and Censorship*. Littleton, CO: Libraries Unlimited, Inc., 1972.

―――. *An Intellectual Freedom Primer*. Littleton, CO: Libraries Unlimited, Inc., 1977.

Darling, Richard L. "Access, Intellectual Freedom, and Libraries." *Library Trends* 27 (3) (Winter 1979): 315–26.

Gerson, Lani. "Librarians and Freedom of the Mind." *Bay State Librarian* 70 (2) (Fall/Winter 1981): 7–13.

McShean, Gordon. *Running a Message Parlor: A Librarian's Medium-Rare Memoir about Censorship*. Palo Alto, CA: Ramparts Press, 1977.

Manley, Will. "Facing The Public." *Wilson Library Bulletin* 56 (7) (March 1982): 524–25.

Nocera, Joseph. "The Big Book-Banning Brawl." *New Republic* 187 (11) (September 13, 1982): 20–25.

O'Neill, Robert M. "Libraries, Liberties and the First Amendment." *University of Cincinnati Law Review* 42 (2) (1973): 209–51.

Serebnick, Judith. "A Review of Research Related to Censorship in Libraries." *Library Research* 1 (1979): 95–118.

Shields, Gerald R. "Intellectual Freedom: Justification for Librarianship." *Library Journal* 102 (6) (September 15, 1977): 1823–25.

Shuman, Bruce A. "Intellectual Freedom Courses in Graduate Library Schools." *Journal of Educational Librarianship* 18 (2) (Fall 1977): 99–109.

Watson, Jerry J. and Snider, Bill C. "Book Selection Pressure on School Library Media Specialists and Teachers." *School Media Quarterly* (Winter 1981): 95–108.

White, Howard D. "Library Censorship and the Permissive Minority." *Library Quarterly* 51 (2) (1981): 192–207.

Woods, L.B. "For Sex: See Librarian." *Library Journal* 103 (15) (September 1, 1978): 1561–66.

## SELECTION AND CENSORSHIP

Bartlett, Larry D., and others. *Selection of Instructional Materials; A Model Policy and Rules*. Des Moines, IA: Iowa State Department of Public Instruction, 1980.

Bonk, Wallace J. and Magrill, Rose. *Building Library Collections*. Metuchen, NJ: Scarecrow Press, 1979.

Boyle, Deirdre. "Censorship vs. Selection—A Round Table Discussion." *Sightlines* 13 (1) (Fall 1979): 8–14.

Fiske, Marjorie. *Book Selection and Censorship; A Study of School and Public Libraries in California*. Berkeley and Los Angeles: University of California Press, 1968.

Futas, Elizabeth, ed. *Library Acquisition Policies and Procedures*. Phoenix, AZ: Oryx Press, 1977.

Gellatly, Peter, ed. *Sex Magazines in the Library Collection; A Scholarly Study of Sex in Serials and Periodicals*. New York: Haworth Press, 1981.

Katz, William A. *Collection Development: The Selection of Materials for Libraries*. New York: Holt, Rinehart and Winston, 1980.

Merritt, LeRoy Charles. *Book Selection and Intellectual Freedom*. New York: H.W. Wilson, 1970.

Moon, Eric, ed. *Book Selection and Censorship in the Sixties*. New York: R.R. Bowker, 1969.

Roberts, Don. *Report on Past and Present Censorship of Non-Book Media in Public Libraries*. Washington, DC: Council on Library Resources, Inc., 1976.

Rom, Cristine. "Little Magazines: Do We Really Need Them?" *Wilson Library Bulletin* 56 (7) (March 1982): 516–19.

Swan, John C. "Librarianship Is Censorship." *Library Journal* 104 (17) (October 1, 1979): 2040–43.

Taylor, Mary M. *School Library and Media Center Acquisitions Policies and Procedures*. Phoenix, AZ: Oryx Press, 1981.

Woods, L. B. and Perry-Holmes, Claudia. "The Flak if We Had *The Joy of Sex* Here." *Library Journal* 107 (16) (September 15, 1982): 1711–15.

# Index

## Compiled by Linda Schexnaydre